ECOLOGY and the QUALITY of LIFE

ECOLOGY and the QUALITY of LIFE

Edited by

SYLVAN J. KAPLAN, Ph.D.

Consulting Psychologist
Chevy Chase, Maryland

and

EVELYN KIVY-ROSENBERG, Ph.D.

Professor of Biology
Jersey City State College
Jersey City, New Jersey

CHARLES C THOMAS • PUBLISHER
Springfield • Illinois • U.S.A.

Published and Distributed Throughout the World by

CHARLES C THOMAS · PUBLISHER

Bannerstone House

301-327 East Lawrence Avenue, Springfield, Illinois, U.S.A.

© *1973, by* CHARLES C THOMAS · PUBLISHER

ISBN 0–398–02828–1

Library of Congress Catalog Card Number: 73-1496

With THOMAS BOOKS *careful attention is given to all details of
manufacturing and design. It is the Publisher's desire to present books
that are satisfactory as to their physical qualities and artistic possibilities
and appropriate for their particular use.* THOMAS BOOKS *will be true
to those laws of quality that assure a good name and good will.*

Printed in the United States of America

Y–1

CONTRIBUTORS

James P. Archibald
Senior Pastor
Capitol Hill United Methodist Church
Washington, D. C.

Elise Boulding
Associate Professor of Sociology
University of Colorado
Boulder, Colorado

B. Bruce-Briggs
Professional Staff Member
Hudson Institute
Croton-on-Hudson, New York

Earl Cook
Dean of the College of Geosciences;
Professor of Geography and Geology
Texas A&M University
College Station, Texas

Robert C. Cook
Retired Director and President
Population Reference Bureau
Washington, D. C.

William J. Gold
Minister
First Unitarian Church
Richmond, Virginia

Thomas Green
Co-Director
Educational Policy Research Center
Syracuse University Research
  Corporation
Syracuse, New York

Willis W. Harman
Director of the Center for the Study of
  Social Policy
Stanford Research Institute;
Professor of Engineering-Economic
  Systems
Stanford University
Stanford, California

Paul S. Henshaw
Visiting Professor
Department of Government
University of Arizona
Tucson, Arizona

Sylvan J. Kaplan
Psychologist in Private Practice
Chevy Chase, Maryland

Peter Kivy
Chairman, Department of Philosophy
Newark College of Arts and Sciences
Rutgers University
Newark, New Jersey

Evelyn Kivy-Rosenberg
Professor of Biology
Jersey City State College
Jersey City, New Jersey

Donald S. Kline
Assistant Professor of Business and
  Economics
School of Business
Alfred University
Alfred, New York

Marya Mannes
Journalist
New York City

Robert J. Matthews
Graduate Student
Cornell University
Ithaca, New York

George H. Miller
Rear Admiral, USN (Ret.)
Washington, D. C.

Ronald Munson
Associate Professor
Department of Philosophy
University of Missouri
St. Louis, Missouri;
Post-Doctoral Fellow
Department of Biology
Harvard University
Cambridge, Massachusetts

Raymond L. Nelson
Retired Supervisor
Eastern National Park Services Training
* Center*
Friendship, Maine

Hubert E. Risser
Assistant Chief and Principal Mineral
* Economist for the Illinois State*
* Geological Survey*
Urbana, Illinois

Russell F. Rhyne
President
Patterns and Systems
San Carlos, California

Sheldon J. Segal
Director
Biomedical Division;
Vice-President
Population Council
New York City

Gilven M. Slonim
Vice-President and Executive Director
Oceanic Educational Foundation
Washington, D. C.

Lee M. Talbot
Senior Scientist
President's Council on Environmental
* Quality*
Washington, D. C.

Harland W. Westermann
Dean
School of Community Services
Virginia Commonwealth University
Richmond, Virginia

Paul Wilcox
Psychiatrist in Private Practice
Traverse City, Michigan

Charles Williams
Deputy Director
SRI Center for the Study of Social
* Policy*
Stanford Research Institute
Washington, D. C.

PREFACE

ON APRIL 23, 1971 a group of interested human ecologists met at Jersey City State College to present various points of view on the meaning of *Quality of Life* on this planet. Ideas were presented and exchanged from different vantage points. Among those involved were a naturalist, an expert in population problems, one interested in work and leisure, a planner, geographer, an educator, and a psychologist. The audience which was made up of faculty members, students, and invited guests, all were very much involved in questioning presented ideas and offering some of their own.

This approach was very much enlarged when the World Future Society met in Washington, D.C., May 14, 1971 and added still other ideas concerning this concept which has been essentially taken for granted without having been effectively understood or questioned.

In addition, several people who had not been participants at either conference but who, we knew, have been thinking about the subject and who had something of interest to say about it, were invited to add their thoughts.

We hope this book is as thought provoking for its readers as it was interesting for its contributors and editors.

EVELYN KIVY-ROSENBERG

CONTENTS

ECOLOGY and the QUALITY of LIFE

SECTION ONE
INTRODUCTION

The three chapters which follow present the reader with a sense of some of the issues and questions surrounding the matter of quality of life. Sylvan Kaplan calls attention to the need for accommodating to diversity of thought and feeling. Paul Henshaw defines and elaborates upon the questions requiring discussion. Ronald Munson introduces some roadblocks to reason and concludes that their employment are necessary to insuring that the future will not be tragic.

[CHAPTER ONE]

THE CHALLENGE

Sylvan J. Kaplan

A s the issues for America to consider are being presented to its citizenry in order that they, the populace, might decide upon how they would care to be governed for the years immediately ahead, one must raise a challenge—are the issues being debated those of prime consequence? Are we, citizens of the human race, worrying about the appropriate questions? The matter of ending a war in Southeast Asia; the significance of insisting that our children mingle with each other, no matter what their skin colors, in seats on a school bus so that they will have equal educational opportunity; distribution of wealth—are these the critical issues which will determine the ultimate fate of our species? If these are not primary, why are they the campaign issues for the election of the leadership of the world's most sophisticated country? How can we justify expenditure of time, money, and emotion upon these questions unless they (a) are a matter of human survival, (b) pertain vitally and indispensably to the future of the human race, (c) provide us with diversion and entertainment, or (d) are matters to be discussed, since *something* must be debated in a campaign for self governance?

The fact is that what most of the thoughtful scholars will identify as the most serious issues facing the human race today are beknown to very few people. In the Club of Rome Report, Meadows and his associates[1] show rather dramatically that most Americans are concerned principally and essentially with those matters which affect their immediate lives. Few are worried about cosmic issues and even fewer are able to seriously contemplate that there is likely to be upon this planet within the next five decades a state of human affairs which is calculated to crush the present way of life. Those who would pronounce such prophesy are seen as prophets of doom to be ignored, derided, or at most to be given polite but constrained hearing. To the mass of humanity apple pie and motherhood, nation and flag, and tradition retain much currency. And certainly, to those dying and hungry, living in rodent infested homes and discriminated against by their contemporaries, the issues of immediacy and expediency by far dominate their reason and their emotions.

The questions to be considered by the reader throughout his tour of the pages which follow should be: do these issues discussed with such thoughtfulness seem to be interrelated? Are the authors of these chapters addressing themselves to the same topics? Is there a common core to the issues which seem to be under consideration? And, above all, when all is said and done in the reading of this Compendium, is there a generalization to be made? Is the human race in trouble; has it passed a point wherein it is too far gone to *turn* back? Need there be such a point?

The editors of this book have not deliberately sought to obtain diversity of viewpoints, as they asked the proponents of the various subjects which follow to address themselves to their specialties. No specific end points were asked of the authors other than their views.

Obviously, some material presented is relatively incontestable, and the reader may find these hardened facts somewhat reassuring. But once the *givens* of population and natural resources are assessed, what then? It will be in the minds of humanity that the responses to these factual data must be integrated and acted upon. And the authors of the chapters who address *attitudes* will be those who reflect this book's purpose. What is man's relationship to his environment? What is the Quality of Life?

Can the human animal think in terms of macro-issues? Is it within the human capability to behave reasonably? Can the human species act with unanimity?

These are some of the questions which should be apparent as the reader proceeds. If he or she is not asking them, the authors of each chapter are. The reader should endeavor to assess whether the authors are asking the questions and answering them in the same or similar ways.

While the authors overlap in their treatment of their subjects, for convenience of the reader the book is divided into *Givens, Attitudes,* and *Methods and Answers.* Population and Resources givens will follow the Issues, Factors, and Questions raised by Paul Henshaw and Ronald Munson. The views of a variety of specialists are sought to examine how the human race may view such things as its cities, its oceans, its works, its play, its concepts of how to live with God, man, and the institutions, and ideas adopted by the human being partaking of these *Commons.*[2]

In order to set the stage for what follows, I would like to introduce the contributors to what I find to be four concepts which characterize the societal status of today and the next decade or two. It is clear that on every front there is:

1. an ever-increasing rate of change.
2. greater diversity of opinion, action, and human need.
3. interdependence or mutual influence of everything upon everything else.
4. an urgent requirement for flexibility and resiliency regarding the personal and social drives of all human beings.

But the direction in which the society is moving is not clear. It may move in a manner to make freedoms restricted. It may move to provide for greater individual expression. The direction of this move may closely resemble the pathway of the present, which is very ambiguous and filled with conflict, or it may be vastly different in character from today, leading to greater oppression of individual desires, or greater release of individual expressions for personal and social gratification.

This ambiguity will place heavy demands on all institutional forms. The need for responsive organization and the ability to deal with uncertainty is and will continue to be extreme.

From the trends[3] one may assume that the next decade or two will provide for a continuation of life much as we know it—with the principal exception of greater speed of change for everything. There will be new technology, more people with many new and differing needs, desires, and demands. It must be repeated that it will be required for all to anticipate the necessity for new organization of societal institutional structure and function, as opposed to merely altering societal institutional structure and function.

The coming decades will bring more social breakdown. In the future, comparisons between past and present will reveal more divorce, more crime, more delinquency, more drop outs, more family alterations than we have always known. There will be more business starts and failures, more human experimentation with environment, more institutional failure, more of everything.

The many more people will have depleted more of our natural resources during the next twenty years. Before the year 2000, part of the world will have experienced famines. Many organic and inorganic resources will have been exhausted, and many species of life will have become extinct.

But of all, perhaps the most significant change to be anticipated is the multiplicity of attitudes. So many people experiencing differing things, all with different backgrounds, are going to respond differently. They will be better educated and more informed. Some will have come out of a period where their immediate forebears were impoverished and ignorant. The young and the old, in general, will be enlightened, have more resources, be less fearful of their survival, and expect much more of the environment.

Some people will realize more of what is happening to their world and will try to assist their fellow man. But some will try to do this by one means; others will try to do this by other means. Frictions between human beings will continue at an increasing tempo. The probability of violence will increase. The differences between people will tend to become greater rather than lesser.

This difference between attitudes will see some still living with self-centeredness because they must fight for survival. The ghettos will be filled with these types, although even in this group of ghetto residents, those fighting for survival will be the minority. These, striving to survive, will exploit others to do so, causing their inner city neighbors anxiety and stress. This survival type, incidentally, will respond principally to power—an organization which gives them power, or which controls them through power, will be understood. And organization which is permissive will be viewed by such persons as weak and as one to be exploited.

There will still be those who strive for security and peace. These persons will seek salvation through sacrifice and profess some form of religiosity to support their need for security. Such persons may reside in central cities, in suburbia, and in the countryside. They will regard institutions with a widely assorted set of views and usually will be critical of those who profess a religion or creed different from their own. But basically, they will ascribe to orderliness and nonviolent behavior. They prefer security and peace.

There will be those who feel that independence and self expression can best be achieved by conquering the universe to overcome want. Conquest, to them, will imply constructive work rather than destructive, violent behavior. There may be those among this type who might accept a violent approach as necessary to problem solving. Most of this type will condone scientific work for learning how to control and manipulate the environment, and they will understand a societal organization which invests economically for this practical purpose.

There are, and there will be, those who are concerned with others. These types generally will be sincerely altruistic people. They will have shifted the thrust of their personality dynamics from a position of egocentricity to one of sociocentricity. They will be community, societal, and world conscious people, concerned with bringing people closer in views and deeds. This type of person will strive to affiliate with fellow human beings. They will be more tolerant of differences between people. They will require less of institutions because they ask less organization of society to meet their needs. Generally, these types will be less aggressive, even gentle people.

There will be the types who prefer one or more of these views; there will be those who hold to views unlike any of these. As Toffler[4] has suggested some will find living in the future unacceptably torturous; others will find that to live in the past is untenable.

In short, the human animal is thinly a rational being; his and her feelings are diverse in kind and in degree. So are his and her intellectual views. Such a conclusion on the part of this behavioral scientist leads him to conclude that the future charges the best of us with the responsibility for accommodating to diversity of opinion, need, thought, and action.

The relationship of humankind to its environment—ecology and the quality of life—depends upon an effective comprehension and adjustment to this human condition.

[CHAPTER TWO]

THE ISSUES, FACTORS, AND QUESTIONS

Paul S. Henshaw

THE ACCEPTED ASSIGNMENT is identification and characterization of the trends and conditions associated with the interrelated elements of ecology and the quality of life.

Ecology is defined as the dynamic interaction of an entity with its environment. Usually the reference is to living things as the entities, and here the concern will be with human beings as the entities. With respect to environment, it is important to have in mind also that one human being comprises part of the environment of another and must be so evaluated.

Quality of life is not as easily defined—mainly because of the subjectivity involved. An approach can be made, nevertheless, by saying it consists of the experiences that cause a person from time to time to express happiness, or late in life to say, "I am glad I have lived." The conditions of happiness and satisfaction, however, are clearly dependent first, on ability to survive, second, on a reasonable state of health, and third, on a multiplicity of things that permit or cause the achievement of desires or aspirations. In last analysis it can be said that quality of life equates to flexibility of options, to freedom of responsible action, and to the level of interpersonal relations. Options and actions, in addition, depend so directly on life support and operational systems that it is meaningful to evaluate quality of life in terms of elements such as per capita income, per capita caloric intake, mortality rates, literacy, schools, libraries, automobiles, television sets, newspapers, people per physician, etc., accepting fully that quality of life involves substantially more than that represented by comforts and the amenities.

Man's Position in Nature's Ongoing Scheme

Man arose on planet earth, and its biosphere is his home. The occurrence of human beings, however, was very late in the sequence of events that comprise the earth's overall cosmology.

Indications are that the earth and other parts of our planetary system came into existence some five to six billion years ago, that the earth's hard crust and the oceans had formed as early as four and a half billion years in the past, and that primitive life came into being as far back as two to four billion years ago. Man, emerging as he did from other living things, was not distinguishable as a species until one to two *million* years ago, a more precise time depending on the definitions of *Homo sapiens* used. Man as a species is endowed with intellect as well as life, and for the purposes here, it is important to recognize the nature of the emergence of intellect and the particular significance this facet of development has had.

From the beginning of planet earth to occurrence of the human species in its most advanced form, there has been a continuous feature. It is growing complexity—the tendency to elaborate and use increasingly elaborate systems. Evidence indicates that as cooling of the original gasses and particles occurred, atoms united to form molecules—simpler ones at first, like water, ammonia and methane, and then more complex ones. The chlorophyll molecule, as commonly known, enabled the use of sunlight in the formation of carbohydrates, and the nucleoproteins, the elaboration of the replicating molecule deoxyribonucleic acid, DNA. On the basis of generalized thoughts, it can be said that nature's *discovery* of DNA constituted one of the most noteworthy events in the history of planet earth, inasmuch as the replicating molecule appears to have provided the basis for both life and intellect as we know them—and indeed for the human species as we know it.

The DNA molecule not only enabled the passage of properties *as a kind of information* from one molecule to another, but also, by *mutational potential*, the acquisition and storage of information, thereby adapting for its continued survival. Because of the tendency of this molecular entity to resist dispersal, to accumulate and use materials for its surroundings, and thus to display preservative as well as adaptive capabilities, early DNA can be regarded as having indications of consciousness—some awareness of *self* as distinguished from all else. Then with acquisition of a cell membrane enclosing itself and some amount of surrounding medium as *functional protoplasm*, an operative metabolizing unit was established, life existed, and there was adaptive use of signals from the environment—the latter being a condition for both consciousness and intellect.

Central to the functional operation of consciousness and intellect, of course, is *information* as the chief ingredient and commodity. By transfer and logical use of information, rationalization, objectivity, and coordinative management are achieved on a continuing basis. Randomness is thus transformed into order; disorganization is transformed into organization; and purposeful work is accomplished for survival and functional behavior.

Action in primitive organisms is mainly reflexive. Genetic information is programmed into such organisms by natural means, and incoming information from the environment interacts with stored information—genetic and other—culminating in cause and effect type reactions. With development of nervous systems and logic circuits of increasing complexity, discriminative capabilities were acquired and elaborated, thus increasingly enabling the ability of living things to comprehend and control the conditions and forces of nature. The human species, as evident in such a multiplicity of ways, is far advanced in these respects and is in a class by itself.

Several things are thus evident at the same time: the first is that the human species, as a product of the earth and descendent from primitive forms, stands intellectually preeminent in the world of living things; the second is that because of its ability to acquire, process, and use information logically and rationally—that is, to perform intellectually—the human species is coming to perform a new and different role in the operation of earth cosmology which is to augment the course of evolution; and a third is that by its choices of what is *right* and *best* for itself, the human species is providing a kind of *willful guidance* for the processes of change. Man, it can be said, has been nature's way of changing from the more randomized progression (aided, of course, by natural selection) to one with elements of objectivity. Although accomplished inadvertently more than deliberately, man is coming to provide a kind of *conscience for evolution*—to say what is *desirable* and *good* with respect to directions to be taken, and according to criteria of his own choices and making. Because of man's ability to augment and alter, it can be said also that evolving the human species—the species with advanced intellect—has been nature's way of achieving change more rapidly. Clearly the mind of man has been a most remarkable product of evolution, and clearly also the means not only of creating new problems of great magnitude, but also for producing the intelligence that must be relied upon in the resolution of them. In addition, it is providing a fateful alternative: the means by which the human species will either emerge triumphantly with a vast new potential into the next stage of evolution for man, or fail miserably and fade into oblivion.

Successes Leading to Predicaments and Frustrations

Primitive people, like other organisms, competed for the usable resources of the earth; and like other animals, human beings used freely, discarding and polluting without reservation or concern. At this earlier time, with the human skills much less developed and the human numbers low in relation to the vastness of the land and the oceans, such behavior made little difference in the environment.

By means of his growing intellect, man learned to save lives and thus to increase his numbers more rapidly. Likewise, he learned to use the earth's resources at an accelerating rate. Not only did the rate of resources consumption increase, but also the rate of increase became faster. Growth in numbers of people and growth in resources utilization were *exponential*—that is, according to the Compound Interest Law. During the pioneer period of colonization and land development, growth was considered good and in the general societal interest. During the pioneer period, there came into being systems of land ownership, wages, investment, and manufacturing, all of which contributed additionally to the accelerating rates of resources consumption and waste accumulation. At the earlier time such developments had the appearance of being reasonable and rational, and there was an attitude of optimism about the future.

With industrialization, the human attitude somehow seemed to harden—to become Faustian—to become that of wanting to extract the last vestige of wealth from the earth as fast as possible, letting the consequences be what they would. There seemed a growing willingness to sell one's soul for riches and power.

No complex mathematics is required to reveal that with increasing consumption rates and a finite earth, the human species is operating in a *growth-overshoot-and-collapse* mode, this characterization having been used recently in "The Limits to Growth."[1] As in case of a culture tube, it is a matter of when the growth curve turns back and the growth process itself ceases. As now apparent, existence of the present generation of human beings coincides with the time when the growth curve begins to turn—the beginning of very noteworthy change. It is a time when human attitudes and goals must be reexamined or risk collapse. But, this is only the resources and waste side of the ecology story.

Economics, governance, warfare, and foreign policy are also features of the human environment and are strong determiners of the quality of life. They, of course, are man-made rather than naturally occurring, but must be taken into account along with population, resources, and waste, as attention is given to the question of whether human survival influences are to have particular significance in the period ahead.

Stemming from needs to overcome disorder, governments have been formed, with designated or assumed powers to tax and manage as considered desirable and necessary. Along with increasing opportunities to manage and control there is increasing opportunity for, and a tendency toward, arrogance, graft, and corruption; and along with the growing powers of governments, there is amplifying complexity, greater remoteness, and multiplying restraints, all of which cause the people—the constituency for which governments were formed to serve—to lose control over the factors that affect their lives.

Similarly, stemming from primitive animalistic competition required for survival and from assumed jungle rights to kill as necessary to protect or sustain the individual, there has been an increase in the efficiency and the *art* of killing—indeed, an enormous increase. At present the killing potential held in readiness on the earth is considered sufficient to destroy all human life several times over—and by different means. In the progression of *civilization* armies were formed and warfare ritualized, not for the purpose of sustaining life, as in earlier times, but for purposes of adventurism, affairs of state, and defense—real or imagined. Now we speak of *just* and *unjust* wars, and we have rules for killing and for the humane treatment of captured combatants, who only a few moments earlier were mass killers and the destroyers of whole ways of life. Now we have *civilized* wars in which women, children, and the elderly are *supposed* to be spared, while homes, cities, and entire life support systems are obliterated. Somehow our sensitivity to big atrocities seems to have disappeared. With respect to affairs of state we seem to tolerate anything, irrespective of how inhumane or how barbaric, whereas for small engagements or personal encounters our indignation and our revulsion shoot up.

Our concepts of patriotism and defense—let us say in the United States, although it would be true of other countries as well—have become so *advanced* that we have highly developed surveillance systems to determine whether dissenters are *loyal* to the *regime in power*; and we accept that it is morally right for us to resort to espionage in other countries, bribing, corrupting, and subverting as necessary to achieve ends conceived as being in *our* interests. Under chauvinistic nationalism, we have come to accept that it is right and proper to traffic in human lives and human misery in support of the affairs of state, of the economy, and of employment as part of the economy. Resort to force of arms, it is necessary to conclude, is strange behavior for *civilized* people who have had experience with the settlement of conflicts by courts of law.

Tragically, the economic systems that have been developed are also shot through with inconsistencies and dangers, fully as pressing and as immediate as those of growth, governance, and *defense*; and of course they are closely interrelated. Accepting that economics is the means for creating and distributing wealth, the human species has followed a peculiar and obviously threatening course in dealing with the things we regard as wealth. When the human species was more primitive, its number fewer, and it was as much like animals as like what we now regard as human, it lived on the land in a more relaxed manner, using the earth's resources freely and as needed. Since then, human beings have invented or resorted to money, ownership of property, interest, investments, and wages; and they have accepted, or caused, profits and earnings to become the main driving force to keep the economic system operative. This has been especially true for the United States and the European countries that contributed so much to formation of the United States. There are other countries, of course, that have employed and utilized various forms of common sharing. In the more capitalistic countries, in particular, success and status have come to be recognized especially in terms of wealth accumulation, and the welfare of societies and social groups have been seen as directly related to wealth. Industrialization, growth, and expansion became the watchwords and the symbols of affluence. Exploitation, extravagant use of materials, and even waste were accepted. During the period of the frontier, growth and exploitation procedures can by certain criteria be said to have worked well; but it is already obvious that for the period of growth complexity and concentration such procedures will not only be a hindrance to progress but in all probability, would stop it.

Societal Precepts and their Growing Obsolescence

Laws are intended as guidelines for behavior, but they sometimes have provided sanction for wrong-doing. In a strictly legalistic society any action within the law or not covered by it is considered legal, irrespective of basic morality or of rightness or wrongness in the eyes of society as a whole. By accepting legality exclusively as the standard to live by, individuals move away from ethical standards and personal integrity to acceptance of the idea that any prevarication, cheating, or thieving they can get away with under the law is legitimate and acceptable. As is generally evident, growing loss of morality in business, government, and throughout society is worsening.

Stemming from primitive animalistic competition and primitive barter functions, human societies in different parts of the world have developed and fostered the *free enterprise system* as the main means of creating and distributing wealth. Moreover, this system has been defended vigorously by insisting that competition is the right and best way to deal with those who are indolent and to provide the incentive required to make economies operate successfully in time. With the rights of ownership, inheritance, machine use, investment, usury, and of special tax shelters available to those not required to use all of their income for family support, there has emerged an operative system that causes the rich to become richer and the poor to remain poor, thus creating a widening separation between the *haves* and *have nots*.

When the human species was young, its number much smaller, and the resources vast, growth and increases in rates of growth were logical and rational—that is, in the sense that there was no conflict with the availability of resources at the time. Now, with deteriorating regard for fairness in the operation of various of the economic and social systems and with a change in motivation being pressed upon us by natural processes as we change from the pioneer period of expansion to the modern era of concentration, a fundamental question is whether our concepts of liberty and freedom as key elements in our views about quality of life can remain the same. There is question, for example, of how much the growth and profit motivations can be employed with benefit in the future. Going farther, there is question whether the democratic process of majority vote can be relied upon to give satisfactory decisions when any positive action leads to spreading and probable irreversible barrenness.

In the United States, and of course in other countries as well, with high value placed on the importance of material things, with an economic system involving practices increasingly incompatible with environmental quality, and with a tendency in the competitive process to tolerate some amount of hypocrisy, dishonesty, and favoritism, an atmosphere conducive to corrupt behavior is being maintained. With ethical standards being what they are, increasing numbers of people find it impossible to resist the temptations to clip a little (or a lot), as money and other forms of wealth pass through their hands. The problem, it is plain to see, goes beyond the question of *law and order* to the ethical integrity of leaders and of the social and economic systems under which we operate.

As *civilized* human beings acting as societies, we are doing astonishing and outrageous things. In athletics we have developed competitive games and made winning almost a life or death matter, and in business we have employed much the same attitudes, philosophy, and approaches. High value has thus been placed on superiority and ability to excel. Amazingly, we have developed labor unions and in effect given sanction for legalized extortion; we have tolerated organized crime; we have permitted banks to extract interest fees for doing no more than loaning money, and we have allowed governments to manipulate gold standards, credit, interest rates, inflation, and taxation when the expressed intent is to operate in accord with the principles of free enterprise. We also have required small agriculture, small business, and small industry to make their way in strict accord with principles of the free enterprise system, while we have provided large subsidies, tariffs, and tax shelters for big agriculture, big business, and big industry.

In government we have created unwieldy bodies of legislators considered to be representatives of the people who very often— seemingly more often than not—are the pawns of special interests. We have permitted important social policy to be handled by people acting as politicians more than as statesmen serving in behalf of all the people. At the level of government, we have looked at problems of limits without raising question about the number of people making demands for goods or about the growing rates of resources utilization in military, industrial, and other kinds of establishments. The emphasis, instead, continues to be on *bigger* and *faster*. With respect to the Presidency, we have placed the power of life or death over many of the people of the world in the hands of one person—one whose mind is necessarily as limited and as biased as the minds of other men. We have made the Presidency a symbol of power, and we have made it possible, if not necessary, for the President to place the affairs of state above the affairs of people ("Ask not what your country can do for you, but what you can do for your country").

With respect to wars, we have the rules to keep them manly, *clean*, and *respectable*, yet in times of combat *anything goes*—pillaging, corrupting, subverting, torturing, murdering, hybridizing, and raping. We have fostered war crimes trials and have tried, condemned, and hanged men of other nations for *crimes against humanity*, yet in recent years have shown ourselves to be guilty of similar crimes.

Human beings, while intellectually strong, reveal themselves to be morally weak. One needs only to look about in any large community and take note of the dishonest, deceptive, and heinous acts that take place constantly at all levels of society to be convinced of this generalization. Sadly, there appear to be few among us who do not have their price in terms of money, protection, or freedom from torture, and continuously it seems there are many among us who are willing, if not impelled, to take advantage of these weaknesses by resort to the barbarous and inhuman acts of kidnapping, blackmail, and extortion. Perhaps worse than the cruelty and criminality involved is the utter contempt shown for humanitarian precepts. The human species, of course, has a history of slavery, piracy, cruelty, and oppression, and it might be asked whether human behavior is any worse now than formerly, but we are compelled to ask at the same time whether the processes of civilization are in reality making headway.

Features in addition to growth, exploitation, pollution, governance, economics, espionage, warfare, foreign affairs, and social behavior could of course be considered, but what has been said seems sufficient justification for making the generalized points that need to be made. There are two. The first is that with continuing acceleration of growth and exploitation at present rates, an economic and social collapse seems imminent in the fairly near future, and the second is that with continuation of the present economic and social practices, which are so shot through with hypocrisy, dishonesty, and favoritism, growing disillusionment and fear is to be expected which will combine with that resulting from the degradative consequences of over-rapid growth and exploitation to make the generalized breakdown more precipitous. The first development, which in some degree is in progress already, is, or would be, the consequence of natural limitations, and the second, which in some degree also exists already, is the consequence of man-made arrangements. Both, however, can be affected and redirected by the human will.

Quality of the Human Character and of the Societal System

When we look directly at the substance of human personality, we seem impelled to accept: first, that human beings, despite the tendencies to be considerate and compassionate, remain fully as bestial as their animal counterparts—in certain respects much more so—and second, that the moral stamina and the ethical standards of society are deteriorating rather than advancing.

So very often we see efficient, high minded, and public spirited people go into big business, big labor, or big government only to become subject to the pressures of growth, exploitation, winning, and excelling and thus to become arrogant, greedy, dishonest, deceptive, and domineering—sometimes within the law and sometimes beyond it. *Swashbuckling* may have been tolerable in earlier times, and in some degree, economic progress may have been achieved because of it; but in a period of growing concentration, complexity, distrust, and doubt it is necessary to ask whether such bravado can be tolerated at all.

Being committed, as we are in our present form of government, to an electoral process that provides representatives of factions of people rather than of people generally, we have an operative situation with which it is difficult to cope from the stand-point of fairness simply because factions without the voting strength get passed over. Seniority systems and filibustering, likewise, stand in the way of efficiency at the level of operation, and at the expense of the system.

The operation of governments is representative of the operation of societies, and the operation of societies is like the operation of individuals. Action very often is initiated by deeply embedded primitive instincts—instincts which are having expression also in the Faustian drive for riches and power. The need to deal with this problem is not new, but it is becoming increasingly critical.

Threats of Catastrophy and Elements of Time

From points made, it is evident that human society at the present stage of its history is threatened with three types of disaster. The first is nuclear holocaust. This could occur at any moment, be short lived, and essentially fatal to the human species. The second is ecologic and economic collapse. This problem, as seen, is understood and anticipated in terms of living room, food, energy, pollution, and nonrenewable resources. All of these factors involve limits with times of exhaustion or accumulation sufficient to turn back industrialization and growth by harsh and disruptive means estimated on the basis of careful projections to occur in decades and less than a century. The third type of impending disaster is continuing demoralization, disillusionment, frustration, and fear, resulting in a people's rebellion. In recent years some rebellion has been seen already, and depending on growing hardships and unfairnesses, this could intensify and spread rapidly.

As consideration is given to today's cultural problems, there may be those who would call attention to the fact that new and awesome weapons, man's unfairness to man, and people's insurrections have been faced before and that the human species not only survived, but progressed and advanced. If there are such, they face the necessity of answering with respect to (a) the probable finality of nuclear war, (b) the inexorableness and the inevitability of collapse of late exponential growth processes, and (c) the erosiveness of hypocrisy and deceptiveness in business and government during a period of rapid and efficient communications.

Assuming that there is willingness to make some moral and ethical adjustments, it is possible that proper attention to one of the problem areas just considered would prove to be a key to the other two. Although it would probably be impossible to accomplish, it is suggested that if the false pretenses and the unfairnesses could be removed from business and government, the likelihood of war and of a people's rebellion would greatly diminish.

Options and the Probability of Constructive Action

Any turn away from the exploitive growth mode would be a turn away from the existing brinkmanship and flamboyancy. It would be a situation in which birth rates would become more nearly equal to death rates and capital investment would become more nearly equal to depreciation. This would be a kind of *equilibrium state,* as suggested in "The Limits to Growth."[1] Ideas of such a turnabout, according to one line of thinking, would have an immediate appeal; but it would be obvious at the same time that because of worldwide commitments to the pressurized growth system, such an orientation would be exceedingly traumatic, perhaps second only to the trauma expected from continuation of the present growth and exploitation approach.

As in case of much decision making, the problem will necessarily be one of *trade-offs—*of *relative risks,* choices, and options. Ignoring the knowledge of compound interest processes and hedging the bets in favor of continued growth, assuming that somehow technology will provide, would be taking great chances. Similarly, any sudden and superficially considered steps to eliminate competition, growth, profits, and winning could prove equally hazardous.

Already useful bookkeeping is being done on the world's resources, and improvements on the methodologies are being made continuously. Likewise, communications systems are nearing a point of development at which the people of the world could express their views about the policies employed in making decisions about how the resources are to be utilized. In addition, much is known about requirements for efficient operation of large complex systems. Potential for resolution of some of the underlying problems of this period are in sight. There is question, however, whether such potential will be further developed and utilized. In the past, human societies have responded more to crises than to needs. Now that we are confronted with a situation in which as a people we are impelled to react, by default, if not by design, it will make a great deal of difference as to how we hedge our bets. Primarily, the question is whether human beings are yet ready to behave rationally; that is, like human beings rather than animalistically.

The Future

Two questions now stand out. They are (a) whether an equilibrium state necessarily means a reduction in quality of life, and (b) whether, as seems necessary, there are approaches for dealing holistically with the overall situation.

The equilibrium state question exists in terms of the Law of Demand and Supply. Man in this case is the user and makes the demand, and man plus his environment makes the supply. The demand varies directly with number of users, and the supply, with man's skills plus the earth's carrying capacity.

With respect to the demand side of the demand and supply equation, the human species, so far as is known, is under no mandate to produce the maximum number of souls on the earth. It is true that the Bible, which many use as a guide on cultural matters, says *be fruitful and multiply, subdue the earth and have dominion over it;* but it does not say how much to multiply, how much to subdue, nor how much to have dominion. Certainly it does not ask for fruitfulness to the point of lasting jeopardy to the family or the society, and certainly it does not ask for subjugation to the point of *doing the earth in* as a life support system. Population policies are man-made, and whereas in earlier periods they appear to have related to protection, in more recent times they appear to have been associated with ideas about growth and expansion. Stable population levels, in themselves, would not be expected to have an adverse effect on quality of life.

With respect to the supply side of the equation, it is clear that the human species is under no obligation to consume the resources of the earth as fast as possible; that is, apart from satisfying a set of values that is coming to appear irrational and unsound with respect to the future. M. King Hubbert[5] has said, "It now appears that the period of rapid population and industrial growth that has prevailed during the past few centuries, instead of being the normal order of things and capable of continuance into the indefinite future, is actually one of the most *abnormal* phases of human history." Equitable and prudent use of resources makes sense, and it is a way of providing the greatest amount for the greatest number. The earth's resources are still vast, providing they are used and conserved well. The recycling potential is great, and in addition, large amounts of radiant energy come to the earth daily from the sun. Although a wealth and distribution system different from the one now widely employed would be required, there appears to be no reason at this stage for saying that even with an equilibrium state economy there should not be an expanding quality of life for a long time to come.

Now, as to whether human society will find it possible to deal holistically with its ecologic problems is much less evident, simply because they are global in character. In recent centuries the whole thrust of human life has been country oriented, and issues between nations have been settled by show of force or use of force—an approach which has essentially no meaning in dealing with the underlying environmental problems. Thus far the experience in dealing with transnational problems by rational rather than savage, animalistic means has been limited and faltering, and the question now is whether there is yet a way. Being steeped in a tradition of nationalism, as we have been, any direct move to transnational action may seem beyond reasonable expectations. However, because of emerging developments in the fields of communication and information use—that is, in the fields of information and cybernation—there may be important new potential.

The present worldwide communication system, in addition to use for bookkeeping on the world's resources, could, with modest adaptations for voice check identification and tallying, be used to enable people of the world to set standards and establish goals—for example, standards for air, water, land, and sound pollutions, and general guide lines for resources development and wealth distribution. By such action a realistic participatory democracy would be created, thereby permitting people to regain some control over the factors that control their lives.

Let us suppose that the people of the world would by means of a worldwide cybernated voice vote facility adopt a *Declaration of Interdependence* to give guidance, inspiration, and confidence much as the Declaration of Independence did for the people of the United States during their pioneer period. Such a simple step by itself would go a long way toward changing the direction of things. It would open the way for cooperation on goals and standards-setting so much needed in establishing a period of *benign* growth as characterized by Krafft Ehricke[6] in his forthcoming book—a kind of growth based strongly on recycling of materials and on carefully considered use of new materials. This kind of step, besides giving prospects of better and more fair use of resources, would be expected to reduce the needs for wars, and mitigate strongly against the practices of pretense and deception which pervade the societal behavior and which stand so very much in the way of mutual respect among people and in the way of confidence about the future.

Thoughts such as those just expressed may seem visionary, over-idealistic, and like impossible dreams, but let it be remembered that we are at a stage in human history when completely new concepts are called for—and required.

Fateful Challenge

A straightforward look at the ecology and quality of life of our period brings a command—indeed, a real mandate to leaders and analysts, particularly scientists. In a period of great affluence the imminence of social and economic collapse is difficult for the average person to see except in terms of localized problems resolvable with the expenditure of more funds. This then causes a frightful responsibility to rest on the shoulders of analysts.

Traditionally, scientists have narrowed their fields and become authorities in small domains. Narrowing allows for precision testing, careful documentation, a feeling of certainty and security—and a feeling of satisfaction. The rules of rational analysis, nevertheless, apply as much to complex problems as to those more easily defined. Scientists, like others, it seems necessary to accept, have become corrupted by the smug and mercenary attitudes of our period—a condition revealed by two illustrations. At a hearing on problems of ecology recently the writer listened to testimony by two physicians, one speaking for industrialists and the other for the environmentalists. Both paraded a long list of credentials to establish credibility, and then proceeded to give conclusions that were diametrically opposed. In another instance *credible* scientists, people who in their own domains remain rigidly objective, on entering into the recent polemics on *Limits to Growth* have come forth with emotional outbursts rather than reasoned opinions as the analysis began to raise question about exploitiveness touching their own fields of interest. In connection with the same polemics, it has been amazing to see so much evidence of ambivalence on the part of supposedly hardheaded scientists; that is, a tendency to accept the validity of evidence pointing toward the necessity of an equilibrium state and then offering solutions that ignore the evidence and which, if implemented, would contribute to intensification of the problems.

The disciplines of science are rigorous, and those who flout them, not only damage themselves, but corrupt the institution of science itself. Moreover, dishonesty in science, including unwillingness to face the hearts of problems simply because they lie beyond the limits of one's own selected ken, when offering advice to the public on matters as critical and as vital as the environment must be regarded as equivalent to the shirking of responsibility and to betrayal and treason in times of war.

The effort here has been to characterize the problems of ecology in relation to quality of life, to indicate scope, and to lift sights. A Declaration of Interdependence as an approach to resources conservation, to greater fairness among people, and to the circumvention of war is not out of order at the present time, irrespective of how visionary and how different. It makes sense, and quite obviously, this or something equivalent will be a requirement for human fulfillment in the period ahead. Scientists have major responsibilities, and they go beyond the call of duty in the laboratory. More than ever before scientists are being called upon to accept their role as citizens as well as that of analysts and specialists.

[CHAPTER THREE]

THE CLOCKWORK FUTURE: DYSTOPIA, SOCIAL PLANNING, AND FREEDOM

RONALD MUNSON

THE WRITING OF UTOPIAS, like the sewing of samplers, has almost become a lost art. Plato's *Republic*,[7] Bacon's *New Atlantis*,[8] and More's *Utopia*[9] are not merely outstanding examples of the genre, but they have had few contemporary rivals. Utopias are still written occasionally—B. F. Skinner's *Walden Two*[10] is perhaps the one currently best known. But the predominate mode of this kind of imaginative literature is undoubtedly the *dystopia*. A dystopia is a utopia stood on its head; whereas a utopia imagines a social and political system that the reader is encouraged to approve of, a dystopia presents one that prompts his disapproval.

Why the dystopia is today a more favored form than the utopia is something of a puzzle. Certainly it is not because it is a new literary type that is just now being exploited. One need only recall *Gulliver's Travels*[11] to recognize that as a form the dystopia has not just appeared on the scene. Nor could it be that we have no need of utopias. The times are troubled and our courses of action unclear. It would be undeniably useful to have available representations of life in imagined ideal societies to serve as a focus for discussion of

26

the alternatives open to us. Perhaps, of course, dystopias predominate for reasons no weightier than those that prompt us to read mystery novels rather than the lives of Methodist ministers—evil is more interesting than good.

I think, however, that there is a weightier reason. Writers of dystopias, so it seems to me, are disturbed by trends or tendencies they believe they detect in our current society. These they extrapolate and (often) magnify to create an imagined society which they offer as a possible future for our own. Thus in dystopias we are not simply being presented with a social and political system that invites our disapproval; we are being warned that such a system is nascent in our own. Unless we take steps to check the trends, we might well find ourselves citizens in the abhorrent society depicted.

Modern dystopias deal with many themes, but one predominates in frequency and importance. It can be put quite generally in this way: extrapolating from the present, the society of the future will be one in which massive social planning by a few will eliminate individuality and freedom and impose conformity.

Eugene Zamiatin's *We*[12] was probably the first dystopian novel in this century to stress the theme of loss of identity and freedom through organization. Though the work was written in Russian, it was originally published in English translation in 1924, and for several decades it has had both a direct and indirect effect on other dystopian works.

We is the story of life in a united state that is planned and organized in every detail. It is a society in which "nobody is *one*, but *one of*," for "we are all so much alike."[13] All activities in the State are regulated by a Table of Hours, and no one is permitted to act on his own initiative:

> Every morning, with six-wheeled precision, at the same hour, at the same minute, we wake up, millions of us at once. At the very same hour, millions like one, we begin our work, and millions like one, we finish it. United into a single body with a million hands, at the very same second, designated by the Tables, we carry the spoons to our mouths; at the same second we all go out to walk, go to the auditorium, to the halls for the Taylor exercises, and then to bed.

No one has a name but only a number, and all live in identical rooms with transparent walls, for this "makes the difficult and exalted tasks of the Guardians much easier." Sexual life is controlled, eugenics is practiced, and one is obliged to stay healthy. The "glorious task" of the society is to go into space and "subjugate to the grateful yoke of reason the unknown beings who live on other planets, and who are perhaps still in the primitive state of freedom." If they fail to understand they are being offered a "mathematically faultless happiness," then "our duty will be to force them to be happy."[15] In sum, personal freedom is to be replaced by physical well-being obtained through detailed planning and regulation.

A better-known example of a dystopian work which uses the same theme of loss of freedom and individual identity because of centralized social planning is Aldous Huxley's *Brave New World*.[16] Huxley published the novel in 1932 as a parody of H. G. Wells' *Men Like Gods*,[17] but he later came to believe that the society he depicted was not as improbable as he had initially thought. The continued popularity of the book is some indication that a great many people are similarly convinced and share Huxley's fear that our own society may be moving in the direction of the unpleasant world he portrayed.

The society of Huxley's novel is a world state in which war has been eliminated, and the prime aim of the rulers is to keep everything functioning smoothly. The World State's motto, "Community, Identity, Stability," expresses its ideals, and to achieve them, it relies upon both biological and social controls. Eugenics and dysgenics are systematically practiced; superior gametes are selected to produce Alpha Plus, Alpha, and Beta progeny. Inferior gametes are chemically tampered with, and by cloning, groups of ninety-six identical twins with almost subhuman traits are created. These give the society its unskilled workers. Behavior is controlled by reinforcing approved behavior patterns with sex and entertainment as rewards and by using a euphoric drug, soma.

Huxley's brave new world differs in a marked way from the brutal tyranny of George Orwell's *Nineteen Eighty-Four*.[18] In Orwell's society individuals are forced to conform to the roles planned for them. They are punished if they do not. Huxley's citizens conform because they want to, and they want to because they have been conditioned that way. By rewards their behavior has been shaped so that they desire what the society wishes them to desire. (Strangely enough, the principles of social organization underlying Huxley's dystopian work are quite similar to those of the society in Skinner's utopian *Walden Two*.)

The two works I have discussed are representative of a large class of dystopian novels. Indeed, a major portion of recent science fiction contains the same theme of the dangers of the planned society. Writers who project such fears about the present into an imagined future find a large and sympathetic audience, and the popularity of this theme with both writers and readers is indicative, I suggest, of a deep distrust of all social planning. It is an expression of the basic fear that freedom and individuality are even now threatened and with an increase in planning, will eventually be destroyed wholly.

Distrust of planning is especially prevalent in this country. As Athelstan Spilhaus recently observed:

> In the United States, planning is suspect. The reactions of some "liberals" to long-range, far-reaching plans is to label them dema-gogic or autocratic. On the other hand, the reaction of some "con-servatives" to the same plans is to label them wild-eyed, idealistic, or socialistic.[19]

The reasons for this distrust are no doubt partly historical, bound up with the attitudes and virtues of an individualistic frontier so-ciety. Partly, too, they may be the result of political opinions about the countries most associated with large-scale planning, the Com-munist ones. Unquestionably, however, many people have principled or philosophical objections to social planning. They believe, that is, that there are features of a planned society that are either objection-able in themselves or objectionable because they violate our funda-mental commitments as a democratic society.

I now want to turn to an examination of what seems to me the most important and most frequently entertained doubt about the legitimacy of social planning. It is the doubt that, as I said earlier, appears as a frequent and significant theme in dystopian works—namely, that planning destroys individuality and freedom.

I should say first, though, something about what I shall take *social planning* to mean. Social planning, in its most general sense, is the rational and deliberate preparation for meeting the needs of the citizens of a society. It is not crisis management; rather, it is the considered attempt to anticipate and avert crises and to prepare for those that cannot be averted. Though most planning today is still limited in time and scope, long-range and large-scale preparation is also a legitimate and even necessary part of social planning. In economic terms social planning involves the production and distribution of goods and services, but this phrase must be construed broadly to cover physical resources, education, science, and recreation, as well as food, housing, and consumer products.

That a planned society requires the loss of freedom and individuality and the institution of total control and conformity is, if correct, a serious objection to the idea of social planning. Walter Lippman might well have been summing up recent dystopian literature when he put the point this way: "If a society is to be planned, its population must conform to the plan: if it is to have an official purpose, there must be no private purposes that conflict with it."[20]

This doubt is worth our careful attention, for it expresses an anxiety about a matter most people take to be central to the character of their lives. In considering it, however, we must avoid the trap of regarding freedom as something that dwells in some empyrean realm far above the course of human events. Freedom is really very practical and down to earth. It must be in what we do or say, in how we act or live, or it is nowhere. When this point is accepted, it becomes clear that planning in some degree or other is requisite for being free and that the extension of freedom may require a great deal of planning.

Freedom is incompatible with necessity, including the necessity of responding to immediate physical and biological needs. Thus the person who is under the control of present circumstances cannot be free. In a situation characterized, for example, by severe food shortage, lack of shelter, hazardous surroundings, and threats to life and safety, an individual can only devote his attention and energies to staying alive. Life under such conditions does not permit the projection of desires and plans beyond the immediate, and all actions are directed toward the single goal of survival. A society such as our present one does much to generate freedom for individuals by freeing them from the onerous press of necessity. Such *freedom from* circumstance can result only from the operation of a relatively highly-organized society that is to a great extent planned.

Perhaps even critics of social planning would be willing to admit that a society must be planned at least to the extent that a matrix for supporting individuals against necessities is provided. But in truth more than such immediate support is required. Present crises of population, pollution, food, power, and the like are enough to put us on notice. If we expect to enjoy in future years anything like the freedom from the pressures of natural necessities that we have possessed in this century, then we must do a great deal of planning that is broad in scope and range. Particularly we must not rely solely upon the sort of short-term or nonce planning that serves us well enough from week to week and from season to season, but is progressively becoming more and more inadequate. Those who champion social freedom not just for those of us who are alive now, but for future generations, should also be championing the long-range planning required to make it possible.

Social freedom must, of course, involve more than the mere removal of conditions that restrict actions to securing the basics of life. In particular, freedom must include the capacity to act in accordance with one's own desires and intentions. We cannot consider even the well-cared for slave a free man, because he does not act out of his own interest and initiative; rather he acts to execute the desires and intentions of another.

This is the aspect of freedom that the constructors of dystopian societies regard as most important and see threatened by a planned society. In both *We* and *Brave New World*, to recur to our examples, the citizens are adequately fed, housed, and cared for; they are free from material worries. They are not however, free to plan courses of action and carry them out.

The lack of initiating prerogative in the dystopian social systems is regarded as connected with uniformity and the loss of individuality. In Zamiatin's World State all citizens perform the same tasks at the same time in a minutely regulated way. The motto of Huxley's World State ("Community, Identity, Stability") contains the expression of a goal to make all like one. In his essay *Brave New World Revisited*, Huxley explicitly expressed his disapproval of this goal:

> Physically and mentally, each one of us is unique. Any culture which, in the interests of efficiency or in the name of some political or religious dogma, seeks to standardize the human individual, commits an outrage against man's biological nature.[21]

There is, however, no necessary connection between uniformity or the destruction of individuality and *every* planned society. Such a connection is to be found only in the type of society portrayed in the novels—the *overplanned* society. The implicit criticism of planning rests on the mistaken assumption that planning and regimentation are the same. But regimentation involves the formation of uniform groups and their subjugation to strict controls. One of the aims of planning in a democratic society, on the other hand, is to avoid just such states of affairs. How much planning is too much planning is a legitimate question, but it cannot be answered in the abstract. It can only be tested in an experimental way by examining the outcomes of programs to determine whether or not the gains in general well-being outweigh the losses caused by restrictions on individuals. In any event, regimentation is not a necessary feature of planning.

The individuality which the dystopians see threatened is developed by such actions as making choices, carrying out intentions, altering plans, giving way to fancies, and taking risks. Circumstances in which such behavior is possible are not necessarily *natural* ones, ones that exist without being intentionally constructed. Indeed, in any society of any size and complexity a real and constant danger is that such circumstances will disappear or become highly restricted for a large number of citizens. Private interest groups, economic organizations, government bureaucracies, and various sorts of social institutions are among the factors that change circumstances so as to pose a threat to a private citizen's freedom to act—just as the dystopians suggest. In threatening such freedom, they likewise threaten individuality that is dependent on it. Individuality requires the possibility of constructing different life styles by making choices that others do not make, by acting in ways that others do not act, by taking risks that others will not take. What the dystopians fail to recognize, however, is that the continuation of a society in which the exercise of such options is possible requires the careful coordination of economic, environmental, and social factors. Without planning and the policies based upon it, circumstances in which individual initiative can exist would disappear, and with them would go individuality. That the circumstances are with us now does not, of course, mean that they will be forever.

It is, to be sure, undeniable that an individual in society is not completely free from restraint in the way he exercises his choices and expresses his desires. A society cannot afford to tolerate the actions of those who threaten the well-being of others. The philosophical theory of a *social contract* as the basis of a political state is intended to capture the notion that individuals must give up some of their *natural* freedom to enjoy freedom from the threats posed by others—to secure civil liberties. Social organization, then, protects the individual and provides a context within which he can carry out his plans and purposes. Planning in general is thus an ingredient in the circumstances under which what we regard as individuality can flourish.

Planning is not all of the same character, of course. Repressive, stifling, autocratic, or totalitarian societies can be planned. But planning can also be carried out in accordance with the democratic aim of protecting and extending individual liberties. Spilhaus, whom I quoted earlier, can serve as an example of a careful thinker who advocates continuous long-range planning as a means to realizing the democratic objective. In his opinion, such planning needs to be very broad in scope; it should cover not only people's physical needs, but also their wants, the often "ill-defined psychological needs in mobility, communications, recreation, culture, and beauty which keeps us intellectually well and humanly alive." The aim of such planning he takes to be to increase the kinds and number of choices an individual may make, for:

> To increase choices is to increase freedom. Increasing choices is democratic. Increasing choices allows individuals to make combinations for themselves which most closely fit their own views of "quality of life." Increasing choices, therefore, preserves individuality.[22]

It is hard to imagine that anyone who accepts the ideals of freedom and individuality and who is familiar with the conditions of modern life could find anything to object to in this passage.

I have tried to show that social planning is not in principle inimicable to freedom and individuality. Indeed, I have gone further and suggested that, despite the deep distrust of planning characteristic of our society and evidenced by dystopian literature, planning is an aid and adjunct to the very realization of the democratic state it is so often seen as threatening.

Just so I will not appear a blind proponent of planning, however, I should like to conclude by offering three criticisms of planning as it is currently being practiced and developed in this country. I shall be brief because of space, not because I think the criticisms unimportant.

(1) *Quis Custodiet Custodes?*

The ancient question of who will watch the guardians raises a serious doubt about present practices. Planners are in many ways cut off from the people they profess to serve, hovering over society but not controlled by it. The arrangements they propose often appear as edicts handed down from high, usually via a government agency. What ordinary citizen, for example, has a voice in the policies of a planning (as well as regulatory) group like the Federal Reserve Board? Who, for that matter, had a say in the appointment of members to the Council for Environmental Quality? It seems more than reasonable to believe that if a planning group with even broader responsibilities than those of existing agencies were established, then it would be an important instrument in the regulation of our lives. Yet we would have no more control over it than we have over present groups of more restricted scope.

Another way of expressing this criticism is that current social planning comes close to violating a basic democratic principle. It is fundamental to a democracy that citizens have control over the policies that shape their lives. The control may be exercised only indirectly through elected representatives, yet the ultimate control must rest with the people. It is not allowed that representatives should divest themselves of part of the power entrusted to them. Often, however, when they rely upon the programs developed by appointed planners and adopt those programs as policies, this appears (in effect) to be what is happening. The planner is thus given powers he is not entitled to have, and he is exercising a prerogative that citizens in a democracy have reserved for themselves.

If something like a permanent national planning board is to be developed, something needs to be done about this state of affairs. The more influence planners acquire over the life of the society, the more they must be brought under the control of society. The direct election of planners is perhaps the most obvious possibility of instituting accountability; in any event, more attention needs to be devoted to working out some means to keep planners responsible and responsive to the will of the citizens of the society. This is a challenge from the dystopians that has not been met.

(2) *Soft Planning*

Futurists and planners of every stripe have concentrated their attention almost fully upon technological issues. Material resource projections, population predictions, and social forecasts are typical of the sorts of areas that have received the lion's share of attention. With some justice we can say that the focus has been on planning that would give us freedom *from* coercive circumstance. It is perhaps only natural that this should be so, for not only have most of those committed to the development of long-range planning been scientifically and technologically oriented, but the condition of our natural and social resources has seemed to demand immediate action.

We must recognize, however, that planning for a democratic society must go beyond planning merely for a society of material adequacy. The states of both *We* and *Brave New World* satisfy their citizen's physical necessities. Democratic planning has to include planning for such *soft* commodities as freedom, individuality, and justice. This requires, for one, that we rid ourselves of the habit of regarding such notions as ethereal abstractions and recognize that they are bound up with the way people live and with the circumstances under which they live. Such notions are philosophical ones, but they are not *empty* philosophical ones. Such planning requires, for another, that we investigate alternative forms of organizations and procedures to determine which ones best enable the realization of freedom, individuality, and justice throughout the society. Such matters, as John Dewey stressed, cannot be settled by abstract philosophical theory alone but only by taking an experimental approach in planning and execution.[23]

(3) *Control Technology*

The last point I want to raise is a problem for future planning and not criticism of present. I have talked of freedom as involving making plans and choices, of initiating actions, but I have shirked one matter that needs to be discussed in this connection. I have done so because I do not know how to give a clear and direct answer to the problem it involves. In *Brave New World* citizens act without hindrance in the pursuit of their desires, and in this sense they are free. But the hitch is they desire only what they have been programmed to desire by biological and social techniques. How legitimate is such a procedure?

Traditionally we have assumed that making arrangements for a society meant finding out the needs and desires of its members and attempting to secure them. Recently it has been suggested, notably by B. F. Skinner, that we employ techniques of *behavior control* to induce members of our culture to work for its survival.[24] Presumably this would involve not discovering what individuals desire, but getting them to desire the society's goals by shaping their behavior through reinforcement.

Psychological conditioning is just one of several possible technologies that have been put forward for consideration as instruments of social control. Biological techniques such as cloning, positive and negative eugenics, and (far more distantly) some limited form of genetic engineering are others.

If by using such techniques we are able to rehabilitate criminals, put an end to racial conflict, stabilize society, eliminate heritable diseases, increase the level of health and intelligence, and replace an individual whose qualities we admire with a genetic twin, can we afford to ignore these control techniques? For the moment the answer seems to be that we can and should. One reason for waiting —perhaps forever—seems to me completely persuasive. I mentioned in my first point above that as society is now organized social planners are wholly free from accountability. The same is so for the control technologists who are in positions to put these techniques into operation. But the deliberate use of any of these techniques on a large scale could have the consequence of destroying the entire character of our society. A world like the one Huxley imagined would not necessarily come about, but there is a risk that it would. We simply cannot allow this risk to be taken for the whole society by a handful of people. If the *society*, in accordance with its principles, should choose to change its own character by approving the use of the techniques, then planning and technology can carry out this decision. But no elite group in a democratic society has the legitimate power to make this decision on its own.

The problem of control technology is one of *dangerous knowl-*

edge, of knowledge with the potential of totally altering the nature of the society that produced it. The problem was faced before in the case of the development of the atomic bomb, and it was faced in secrecy by a small group of scientists and politicians. Whether their decision was correct or not, or whether they had any alternative to making it, is still debatable. What does not seem to me debatable, however, is that we should not let the same situation recur. Such momentous decisions as those about the use of control technology must be made by the society as a whole and not by a minute self-selected portion of it.

What worries me most about current discussions of the topic of control technology is the frequent failure to recognize that decisions about it must be made in just this way in a democratic society. Indeed, this point is sometimes ignored in such a fashion as to be tantamount to a tacit rejection of it. Skinner,[24] for example, speaks of "the designer of a culture," yet he nowhere explains how the planner is to receive his legitimacy. Even Van Rensselaer Potter, who shows great awareness of issues of principle, often seems to speak as if dangerous knowledge presents problems that specialists alone must handle. He suggest, for example, that by a "consensus of interdisciplinary groups" we can seek "wisdom," or "the knowledge of how to use knowledge to better the human condition."[25] Further, he argues that "Existing mechanisms for arriving at complex decisions involving facts and values must be supplemented by a fourth arm of government instructed to consider the consequences of major research programs and to recommend legislation."[26] This comes very close to being a recommendation that we have experts solve our moral problems, though it is in nowise intended to be.

Control technology is a case in which practice ought not proceed until theoretical questions are answered and values are settled. Experts in a variety of disciplines can contribute to the development of understanding of the multiplicity of problems it involves, but they ought not regard themselves as the decision makers. In fact, again, one of the problems they should be considering is how planners in this area can be made responsible to the people and how the people can be brought into the decision-making process. If we are to avoid a society in which Skinner's *designer* and Potter's *interdisciplinary groups* become our guardians, then we must take this problem seriously.

"There are two attitudes we can take with reference to the future," Ernst Mayr wrote in *Biological Man in the Year 2000*. We can assume the attitude of watchers of a Greek tragedy. Without raising a finger they let the play drift inexorably toward its blood-stained conclusion. Or we can behave like utopians, to a greater or lesser degree, and propose measures that will better the fate of mankind and hopefully better mankind itself."[27] The future is not a play, and there can be no doubt about which course should be preferred. Planning, good or bad is a necessity, and it is the duty of us all to keep it from being bad, if we cannot make it perfect. With planning there is a chance that the future will also not be a tragedy.

SECTION TWO

GIVENS

In this section Robert Cook and Sheldon Segal deal with population, its changes, threats, and effects. Remarkably, Mr. Cook wrote his paper over a decade ago, and we find it startlingly timely. Hubert Risser, Donald Kline, and Earl Cook build their cases upon the population's parasitical employment of the resources our planet affords. Thus the relationship of the human being to the environment—ecology—reveals its grim projections for all to ponder.

[CHAPTER FOUR]

POPULATION: SOME PITFALLS OF PROGRESS*

Robert C. Cook

Can man live in space? One answer is simple; man does. How long can he survive in space? The obvious answer is: only as long as his consumption matches the supplies in his environment.

When the Russians sent Gargarin and Titov orbiting around the earth, and when we fired our astronauts one hundred miles beyond the earth's surface, a temporary but complete ecology was provided for each man. Scientists had, in fact, designed genuine worlds, tiny but complete. Technology had produced environments, adequate to meet the demands of consumption, in which man felt no great discomfort.

When we think of space, we ordinarily think of astronauts, but the fact is that all of us are surviving in space. We live upon a relatively small space-capsule, orbiting around the sun. Aboard this space-craft we have essentially all the resources we will ever have.

How long can we live without discomfort? The answer: most of the human race has never lived without it. Only in our time has it even appeared possible that all of the human race could ever have enough food and shelter to be comfortable.

How long can man survive in this orbit at this speed of consump-

*Reprinted by permission of Publishers of *The Nation*. Originally published January 13, 1962, entitled "Pitfalls of Progress."

tion? This is the real question. All, or a large part, of the human race could die from a shortage of survival necessities. We are already suffering from major miscalculations of the vital elements of human ecology.

Mankind has a history of waste more costly than its history of hostility. It is long past the time that we understand the ecology of man—to grasp the true measure of our resources—and of ourselves. The study of ecology, or what is called *the balance of nature*, yields flashing signals like those which warn the astronaut in flight, but which we ignore at our peril.

The study of the interrelationships of living things with one another and with the basic natural resources of earth, air, water, and food is called ecology, after the Greek *oikos* for house. Surely it is apparent that we face critical survival problems in the House of Man. What may not be so apparent is that we live in a closed environment, with a finite amount of resources. Today we have dangerously upset —even without fallout—the balances which have been built up through ages of growth. There are even some nature lovers who say that man is the greatest contaminant, and they have an impressive array of evidence for their version of *only man is vile*.

People can readily see the peril of unbalancing the resources of a ship going to the moon. Why is it so difficult for them to see that human life depends upon the ability of plants to *fix* solar energy? Or, the air one breathes nourishes one's life only because it has the right proportion of oxygen—which is again dependent upon plants and the photosynthetic cycle? In our rivers the germs are invisible, but the dirt is not. Any citizen—or senator—can see what man has done to the Potomac. Each year a thousand American cities and towns have water shortages. They are not secret. You do not need a Geiger counter to see that our resources have not matched our technology on even a short-term, sustained-yield basis. One can only suppose that it does require imagination to see how truly ominous it is when one turns a faucet, and for reasons of human waste, no water comes out.

People's ability to destroy, coupled with their inability to understand their relation with their environment, has created waterless deserts in China and the Near East. These deserts are as man-made as the Appian Way or the aqueducts of Los Angeles.

Where are the grassy valleys of the Southwest which Coronado noted in the sixteenth century? Is there any hope for man to learn from the Carolina hills, so foolishly allowed to erode, and which have had their plant cover built back only since the soil-conservation movement began forty years ago? Who remembers the Kansas dust storms of the thirties, or the water problem in Los Angeles ten years ago?

Time is running out. Man's technology and his population are both exploding. Ever since man first chipped a flint in a cave, he has been introducing new means of attempting to control his environment. Looking back, it is suprising how much one hand-tool like the axe can do to upset the balance of nature. Probably one has to forgive the ignorant pioneers who swung their axes—one at a time—and changed the conservation pattern of a continent. But their heroic story also includes heroic waste on a heroic scale. The waste of topsoil in the Mississippi Valley probably still remains the largest single effect man has made on earth. Fallout has affected the air of at least an entire hemisphere, but not yet has it had such effects upon man's resources as the axe that leveled forests and the plough that broke the plains. No doubt, in time, it will.

It matters not to the ultimate balance-sheet whether the earth's vital materials are depleted by swords or by ploughshares. The point of this essay is that technology is advancing at such an accelerating rate that crises which experts had predicted for two centuries from now will soon be breathing down our necks. The manner in which we are wasting resources, increasing our population, and bringing in technological changes without any forethought as to the biological or social ecology of invention and change is creating one small crisis after another—usually to the aggravation of the other crises of our time.

There is abundant evidence that the great upsurge of nationalism and the haste for technological advance which are now so apparent and understandable in the developing countries will further accentuate our basic ecological problems. Social movement increases social dislocation. Industrial development inevitably means more air and water pollution and more wasteful use of water and other vital elements. *Vital* here means essential to the maintenance of life.

But because progress is our most important unofficial religion, we devoutly believe *science will come up with something.* Our grand-fathers mumbled, *Necessity is the mother of invention.* If we continue to waste as much as our grandparents and parents, our grand-children may find themselves living in primitive, pioneer conditions.

The sad fact is that man cannot always hope to solve a problem with an invention.

Perhaps the greatest technical and cultural progress in history has been the medical advance which has lowered the death rate. But since the birth rate has not been lowered at the same time and at the same rate, death control has caused a biological revolution which has upset man's relation to his earth.

For the first time in history we could, theoretically, properly feed all of humanity. To do so would require a massive mobilization of technology and presupposes great social changes. The tragic fact is that we are not now doing it. While massive, outright famine has been averted in the face of rapid population growth, two thirds of the earth's people are to some extent hungry—some of them very hungry.

Even if we were to apply scientific methods to world food production, the growth of population and the increased industrial uses of our resources might mean we could not properly feed all of the next generation. For the first time we are facing the problem posed before the planners of Project Apollo, the *moon-shot.* The question: You need more than one person to establish a camp on the moon. It would be fatal to have too many. What is the optimum?

We face this question here on earth: What is the optimum population, the largest population for the greatest good?

Man's reaction to the lowering of the death rate has been to say *marvelous!* One considers this a great good, or one rightly should. But the effects of altering the pattern of dying are many and complicated. They are not fully understood, and even where the experts in genetics and demography believe they know certain answers, the political and social leaders of our day still prefer to ignore the facts.

Consider: Where formerly less than a half of all children grew to maturity, today, in the advanced countries, nine-tenths reach voting age. But the rate of population growth, which in the past only under very exceptional circumstances ever rose to 2 percent a year (on rare occasions, 3 percent for short periods), has now reached

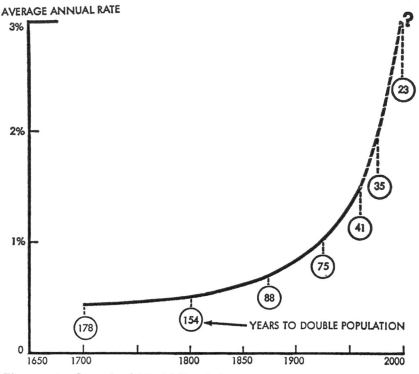

Figure 4-1   Growth of World Population

the point where these percentages have become the norm for entire continents.

At these rates of increase in such regions as tropical Latin America, i.e. at three percent a year or better, we could create enough human protoplasm to cover the surface of the earth in no more than three centuries.

It may very well be that in terms of the resources available to us—this in spite of our ability to produce substitutes for many substances already being exhausted—the three billion people who now inhabit the earth are about as many as the planet can really adequately maintain.

A few years ago it was calculated that if the entire U.S. food surplus were distributed fairly to the world's 1.8 billion hungry people, each person would get the equivalent of about two cupsful of rice every nineteen days. Our own production can help people and nations, but it is still only a minute part of the food needed to feed the growing number of people in the world.

Today, with the world population at three billion, the annual rate of increase is about 1.7 percent, and the doubling time is just forty years. If the rate continues unchanged, the earth's people will number six billion by the year two thousand. In many of the economically underdeveloped lands the annual rate of natural increase is far higher than 1.7 percent: 2 percent in India and China; 3 percent in tropical Latin America; 3.5 percent in Taiwan and Singapore; and 4 percent in Venezuela. A 3 percent annual increase doubles the population in twenty-three years; 4 percent, in less than eighteen.

Thus a generation hence, the number of people in most of the underdeveloped countries that will have to be fed will be nearly doubled. If no progress is made during the crucial years just ahead in improving the per capita welfare in these countries, what prospect is there that it will be possible a generation hence?

Whether we are now close to *our best demographic weight*, no-

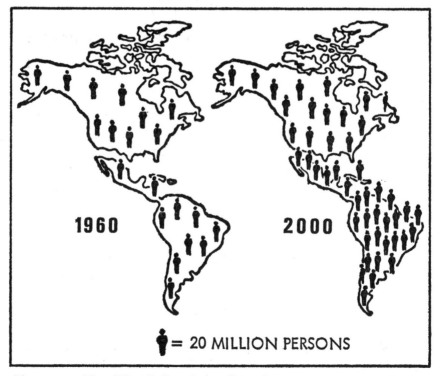

Figure 4-2 New World's Population Growth

body knows. Perhaps we shall never arrive at precise figures. How can you calculate human values? Yet it is clear that we should not bring more than one hundred million children into the world each year if half of them are destined to starve—rapidly or slowly.

What means can be found to provide for the three billion inhabitants of the earth today? How can we give our children the basic essentials for a good life? Again, no one now has a scientifically respectable answer.

Tonight two thirds of the human race will go to bed hungry. We cannot stop the gnawing pain in any half-starved belly by saying that our human technology is theoretically capable of feeding everybody abundantly. The point is that our technology is not doing this.

We must get over our mystical belief that if a thing is technically possible, it is socially possible. Technology is not really magic. There is a price for progress. There are limits to science; there are limits to the earth's resources. There are limits to man's social skills which we must not accept as final. Yet we must not pretend they do not exist. Detroit gives an eighteen-year-old a one hundred mph projectile. Physicists give the new colonels megatons for massacre. Massive technology in a new country has its real dangers, and it has dangers for this country.

If the current rate of population increase is maintained, there is virtually no likelihood that *miracles* of technology will assure the people who are hungry today that their children will be less hungry tomorrow. This country may help some countries to be better off five years from now and far worse off twenty years from now. Let us not dream, nor lie to others, or to ourselves, about human survival. Foreign-aid programs are needed, but let us not fool ourselves that they can ever suffice to meet the rising needs of greatly expanded populations.

Problems of survival and the consumption of irreplaceable resources on a global scale cannot always be solved by gadgets—nor even by basic new discoveries. We are running out of water, energy resources, arable land, and certain vital minerals. If even a very modest harmony of ecology is in prospect for our children, it is crucial that we recognize our stewardship over the earth. The human race may indeed be the culmination of the evolutionary process; but the nuclear bomb and these problems of ecology raise the question of whether we are socially intelligent enough to survive. For survival, social invention must parallel scientific, technical, and mechanical invention; and in this area we are still chipping flints.

For research in ecology, planning, and population control we spend less than a hundredth of what we lay out for our technically exquisite creation of ecologies for one, two, three, or twenty astronauts. We spend freely—nay, extravagantly—upon space, upon bombs to kill, and upon medical research to defer death. But when it comes to spending to learn how to live, we are misers.

As man approaches the moon, we will find that here on earth the human race will also be rationing its supplies. We have time now to choose whether we will do this by the inhumane methods which have so often prevailed in the past, or whether we shall do it with forethought and wisdom in the interest of the greatest number. The House of Man is a marvelous house. Let us be sure we do not defile it beyond some ecological point of no return.

[CHAPTER FIVE]

POPULATION AND BIOLOGICAL MAN*

SHELDON J. SEGAL

I SHOULD LIKE to discuss the population factors that contribute to the equation that we all hope will add up to the quality of life. Although you have all heard the numbers game played over and over again, I should like to tell you a little about the population problem. More importantly, I should like to tell you what is being done about the problem and what the prospects are for the future.

First, what is the problem? The rate of population growth is now unprecendented. In some countries the population is doubling in thirty-eight or forty years. Indefinite population growth, on a finite planet with finite resources, is obviously a situation that cannot be sustained for a long period of time. There is little agreement on a hypothetical number of people which the earth with its resources can support. At present, there are about 3.5 billion people on the earth. There are some who say that even this is beyond the carrying capacity of the earth. There are others who say that the leveling off figure must come at about 6 billion—a figure that we shall certainly reach at or near the end of this century—while others predict that the world's population could go as high as 16 billion. These are numbers that do not carry us, by anyone's calculations, into the very

*Presented at a conference on Human Ecology at Jersey City State College, Jersey City, N.J., April 23, 1971.

49

distant future. These are figures that our children and grandchildren may have to contend with. Regardless of the absolute figure, none of us would condemn the people on earth, at some future time, to live under a condition of maximum-number supportability. This issue is terribly current and perhaps overdue for our consideration.

What is being done about the problem of population growth? In the last ten years a revolution in the public health field has occurred. Several governments have come to the realization that they have a responsibility for birth control as well as their traditionally accepted responsibility for death control. It is, to a large extent, the progress made in death control that has brought about the current imbalance leading to the unprecedented population growth rate. Birth rates have not increased in the last twenty or thirty years; rather, a dramatic decrease in death rates has been the case. It is this difference between birth rates and death rates which leads to the present rate of population growth.

There are now official national family planning programs in over thirty countries, whose peoples account for two thirds of the world's population. All of the population giants of the world, including the People's Republic of China, India, Pakistan, Indonesia, Brazil, and almost all of Southeast Asia, have national family planning education and service programs which are provided for by actual line items in the annual budgets of the health ministries or departments of these countries.

In the case of Brazil, although the government does not itself expend funds directly for family planning, it subsidizes private agencies which provide the services. The list of other countries that provide national family planning programs is long and cuts across all of the usual divisions—East and West, Communist and non-Communist, Catholic and non-Catholic.

Perhaps the most vigorous program in terms of numbers of people and sums of money involved is that of India with its more than 0.5 billion people. The Indian family planning program employs more people (over 180 thousand) than any other governmental service, excluding the postal service and the railway. An evaluation of their level of success depends somewhat on what one's expectations have been. In my judgment the program is rather badly maligned in discussion, when, in fact, it has been making some important strides toward success. This success can be estimated in terms of the percentage of the population now using effective contraception, although this may be somewhat less impressive than the absolute numbers. In India there are approximately 100 million couples in the reproductive age group, so that when 6 million of them are using effective contraception, the program has reached (as is now the case) 6 percent of the target population. Certainly, there remains a long way to go; but the 5, 6, and 7 percent figures must be attained before, and I am confident this will occur, the 10 and 15 percent figures can be reached.

It is difficult in a country like India to bring about change in so personal a matter of behavior as human reproduction. It is a country in which the literacy rate is less than ten percent and in which over eighty percent of the population lives in rural areas. In general, those in rural areas live in small population units representing over a half million villages throughout the countryside, with electrification not having reached most of them. All of this makes it very difficult to launch a countrywide educational program: it means house-to-house visits and face-to-face confrontations. It is a terribly difficult task, and I think that the level of success is itself a credit to the program so far.

India, like other countries that have gone ahead with national family planning programs, has obviously had to use those methods of contraception already developed. Unfortunately, the birth control methods in man's armamentarium have, in general, been developed by Western man for Western man. The oral contraceptive is a nonsense method for an Indian village woman who has never had anything as pretty as a little dial pack of pills; who has no bedstand or medicine chest to keep her pill package in. Similarly, a diaphragm is inappropriate for life in a village without plumbing. Thus, the countries that have proceeded with a family planning program have had to do so with the limitations of the existing contraceptive methodology, and these limitations have been severe, indeed.

We then have to ask, when looking to the future, what are the chances of improvement in contraceptive technology, and are there possibilities of new contraceptive modalities better suited for the needs of a developing world? I think that there are good prospects in this area of scientific technology, and I would like to tell you about where these issues now stand. First, however, I would like to emphasize that I am not presenting a case for new contraceptive technology as being a panacea and cure-all for the population problem. We will still require a tremendous effort to bring about social change, such as new roles for women and social security for the aged. Many aspects of life and problems that exist in our social structure influence fertility patterns; progress must certainly be made in these areas. But in addition, the task of national family planning programs will be made simpler, and greater success would be possible, if new methods of fertility regulation can be provided.

The experience of the past has shown that the one feature of contraceptive methodology that is perhaps more important than any other in the developing countries, where health services are strained to begin with, is the feature of a one-time-only method. That is to say, a method that has to be repeated time after time, and therefore requires the sustaining of motivational levels over and over again, is very difficult to implement. This means that methods like the daily oral contraceptive or a vaginal method that has to be used at the time of each coital exposure taxes the program both in the educational and logistical aspects. For this reason, the intrauterine device has been particularly attractive to many countries, and because of its availability in the early 1960's, this one-time-only method had a great deal to do with influencing government leaders to initiate family planning programs. In spite of the fact that this method has a serious limitation, that is, the requirement for medical participation or the training of specialized personnel to actually do the insertion in place of a physician, it has played a very important role and continues to do so. In India, for example, the annual rate of insertion of IUDs continues to be around 250 thousand, which has plateaued from a peak level of a million insertions annually a few years ago.

There is a very important line of research progressing toward the development of a subdermal implant that can be placed by paramedical personnel. This implant is made of a material known as Silastic, a synthetic rubber elastomer that has two important properties. The first is that it is nonreactive when placed under the skin. The second is that it allows many hormones or molecules of various types to pass through at a slow and constant rate. This implant will contain a reservoir of antifertility drug or hormone released constantly and gradually over a long period of time which can then give an antifertility effect for the duration of its life span, perhaps three to five years. Thus, a single visit by a worker or a visit by the woman to a clinic for the insertion procedure can replace a year or longer of pill-taking. Studies with this method are ongoing in several countries including the United States, Brazil, Chile, Italy, and India; and a system now exists that would provide one-time-only contraception for a full year following a single subdermal implant of Silastic capsule containing a synthetic progestin. Work is continuing, however, in the effort to develop other methods, or a particular form of this method, that will last much longer than one year.

There is a considerable amount of effort toward improving an existing one-time-only method that is now widely used, the sterilization procedure. Both male and female sterilizations have been adopted in national family planning programs, but the necessity to improve this method has been made very apparent. Less than two years ago, as part of Pakistan's national family planning program, an effort was made to increase the level of acceptance, particularly in East Pakistan, of the male sterilization operation. When the great tidal wave occurred in 1970, many children were lost, and couples found themselves childless and unable to have the operation reversed and fertility restored. This was not only a great personal tragedy, but it was also a blow to the concept of permanent sterilization as a method of fertility limitation. Although no effort was ever made in the past to deceive people into thinking that this method could be used for temporary sterilization, the assurances of restoration of tubal or vas patency cannot be great. Thus, even before the disaster, and certainly now, considerable effort was under way to improve the chances of reversibility in the sterilization operation for the male and female. In the case of male vasectomy, studies are being done with plugs that could be removed at some later time, clips that would be applied to the external surface of the vas and later removed, and even a microvalve that could be turned on and off at will. Here again, these efforts are being made to improve the prospects of reversibility because the important one-time-only aspect of this method is realized.

It might be mentioned that there is frequent misunderstanding about the extent to which research in fertility regulation is directed toward methods to be used by the female. It is occasionally commented, perhaps facetiously or cynically, that the reason for this direction is that men, in general, do the research. This is not quite true. There is a great deal of work being done on contraceptive methods applicable to the male. However, there will always be more research done on the female, because the female system is more amenable to controlled interference. There are links in the reproductive chain of events subject to controlled interference on the female side which simply do not exist on the male side. The male and female reproductive systems are analogous up to the point of producing the gamete, the egg in the case of the female and the sperm in the case of the male. At that point, the male drops out of the system and the rest of the steps in the reproductive chain-of-events are the responsibility of the female system. The fertilization process itself, early zygote development, passage of the newly fertilized egg through the fallopian tube, preparation of the lining of the uterus for implantation, the implantation process itself—all of these steps are additional steps in the female system for which there is no analogy on the male side. Thus, it may appear an expression of male chauvinism that there is quite a bit of work going on for control of female reproductive processes and less in the male, but more, it is a reality of the biology and physiology of reproduction that is expressed.

While it is true that there are several exciting possibilities for new methods or improvements in existing methods applicable to the female, which may have great significance for the developing countries, these new possibilities may not become important realities for some time. I think what is important now is that the means used to bring the existing methods to people who need them be improved. We can do a great deal with what is now available, but there is a need to upgrade the health care delivery systems. I think that we must concentrate on this in the near future.

Finally, after touching on the subject of family planning services, I would return to the more general issue of population growth and why it is so important that these programs are successful. The issue, very bluntly, is whether we can solve our problems by voluntary methods or whether we will have to look toward involuntary methods in the future. This issue is very real in terms of the population problem. I, for one, believe that the loss of voluntarism in connection with human reproduction will be a tremendous step backward for civilized people, and we should do all we can to prevent that from happening. The planners of involuntary procedures to restrict human reproductive capacity are already at the drawing boards. If we do not make voluntary systems work now, our future chances of retaining this right, this human dignity, may be very slim, indeed.

[CHAPTER SIX]

SOME PROBLEMS OF FUTURE MINERAL SUPPLY AND USE*

Hubert E. Risser

As we enter the last thirty years of the twentieth century there is, among those who have a regard for the future, a growing concern about problems of future mineral supply and utilization. This concern is related primarily to two aspects of the situation. One deals with the adequacy of mineral resources to meet future needs and provide a continuity of mineral supplies for growing national and world requirements. The other deals with the impact of mineral production, processing, and use on the environment.

In modern industrial nations, and perhaps to only a slightly smaller degree in most less-developed nations, minerals serve three basic purposes. First, mineral fuels are a source that provides warmth for mankind, heat for industrial processes, and perhaps most important of all to human progress, inanimate energy for the performance of work that would be impossible to accomplish with the meager power of human and animal muscle. Second, minerals provide people with strong and durable materials that are available from no other source. Earth materials are the basis for all major construction and building projects. In addition, it is the metal minerals that make possible the machines and devices with which the energy of fuels can be harnessed and applied to the accomplishment of useful work. Third,

*Presented before the World Future Society, Washington, D.C., May 14, 1971.

minerals provide nourishment for agricultural crops to feed an expanding world population.

Like most other forms of human activity, the production and use of minerals has been growing steadily. Annual expansion in use has ranged from less than 1 percent per year for some specific minerals to 6 percent or more for others. Among the fastest growing uses has been the consumption of mineral fuels for generating electric power. The production of electricity in the United States has been doubling about every ten years, and by far the greatest portion has come from mineral fuels. Projections indicate that as much power will be generated by electric utilities in the 1970's as was generated in the last sixty-nine years.

Rapid though it has been, the growth in the use of many of the mineral commodities in the United States has been outpaced by growth in other parts of the world. For example, from 1960 to 1970 the annual United States consumption of iron ore grew by 26.9 percent. Use of iron ore by the rest of the world increased by 52.1 percent, or almost twice as much. This greater growth in other parts of the world can be expected to continue as the peoples of other nations press their efforts to gain larger quantities of material goods and shift burdens of labor to inanimate machines. And as the efforts of other nations succeed, the pressure on supplies of mineral resources will increase at an ever-expanding rate.

In 1968 the reported world consumption of steel was 583 million tons, or about 334 pounds per person for the entire world population. But while the world average is 334 pounds per person, the average consumption in the five major steel consuming nations was 1169 pounds, and that of all other nations was 142 pounds. In India, which has more than 500 million persons, per capita consumption averaged only 24 pounds. This is less than ten percent of the per capita consumption of 316 pounds in the United States in 1894.

The growing demand for mineral commodities, coupled with declining availability in many areas and the greater effort required to find new deposits, poses national and international problems of future mineral supply. Few, if any, industrial nations are completely self-sufficient in mineral supplies. As these nations use up their own best reserves of minerals, they become increasingly dependent on outside sources, and the competition for these sources is becoming more acute with the passage of time.

The United States today imports all of its chromite, 99 percent of its manganese and a major part of its asbestos, nickel, and tin supplies (Fig. 6-1). The only domestic source of tin and of most of our nickel is waste scrap metal. Important percentages of the copper, lead, and zinc consumed in the United States also come from imports and scrap recovery (Fig. 6-2). To a lesser extent this also is true of other metals.

Always accompanying any production of mineral materials are financial costs and a combination of environmental effects (Fig. 6-3). These environmental effects may range in severity from completely innocuous, or even beneficial, to highly detrimental. But some effects will always be present, even if they consist only of the void left by the removal of the mineral. The effects, in general, are proportional to the quantities of minerals involved. The magnitude of such effects can be demonstrated to some extent by certain examples.

In 1970 a total of 1,740,000 tons of sand, gravel, and stone were consumed in the United States, mostly for construction purposes. If this material had all been obtained from one square mile of area, it would have resulted in a hole about 850 feet deep. Extracting the quantities of these materials projected for the period 1970 to 2000 would result in a hole 808 feet deep that would take up an area equal to that of the entire District of Columbia (sixty-seven square

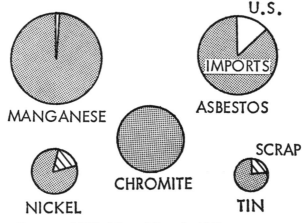

Figure 6-1   Sources of U.S. Mineral Supply 1969

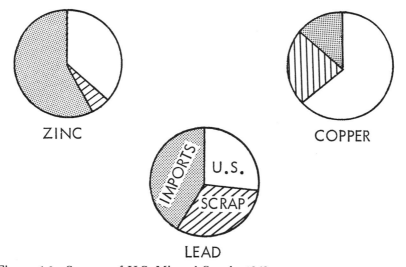

Figure 6-2   Sources of U.S. Mineral Supply 1969

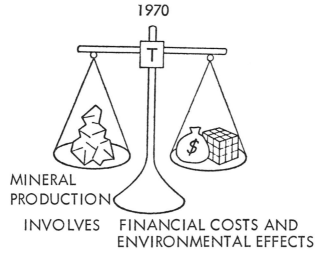

Figure 6-3

miles). The depth would be almost one and one half times the height of the Washington Monument. Fortunately, the production of the needed materials will actually occur at much shallower depths and in widely scattered locations, but in each location some environmental effects will occur that must be dealt with.

There are three principal ways in which the environmental effects

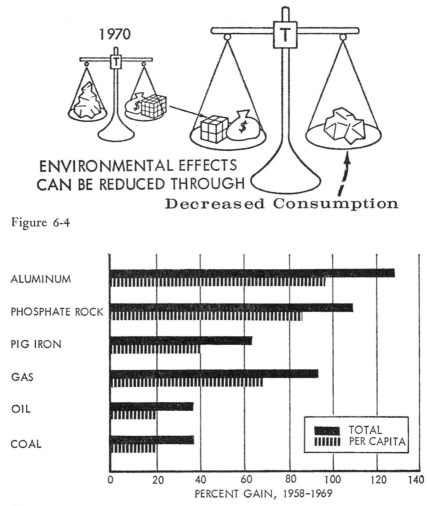

ENVIRONMENTAL EFFECTS
CAN BE REDUCED THROUGH
Decreased Consumption

Figure 6-4

Figure 6-5 Mineral Consumption Growth

of mineral production and consumption can be reduced. One is through a reduction in the consumption of mineral materials (Fig. 6-4). There appears, however, to be little likelihood of this occurring, for instead of declining, the use of minerals is increasing on both total and per capita bases (Fig. 6-5).

A second way of reducing environmental effects is by greater expenditures, either for more expensive methods of production and consumption or on corrective measures (Fig. 6-6). Such expendi-

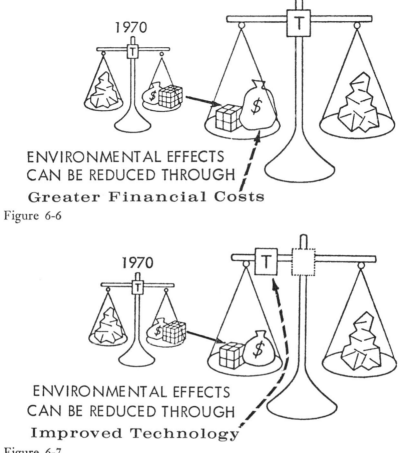

ENVIRONMENTAL EFFECTS
CAN BE REDUCED THROUGH
Greater Financial Costs

Figure 6-6

ENVIRONMENTAL EFFECTS
CAN BE REDUCED THROUGH
Improved Technology

Figure 6-7

tures, of course, will add to the cost and will ultimately be paid by the consumer.

A third way in which a more favorable balance between production and use of minerals and their environmental effects may possibly be achieved is through improved technology (Fig. 6-7). Technological changes may result in cost increase, cost reductions, or in some cases, no cost change at all.

In the past we have grown accustomed to abundant quantities of low-cost fuel energy and mineral materials. In the face of rapidly growing worldwide demands upon the decreasing resources of mineral materials, the supplying of these needs, with a minimum of detriment to the environment, will be one of the greatest challenges of the coming decades.

Progress will require new attitudes and much new research. The quantities demanded will depend on the number of people and the amounts required to satisfy their wants. The ability or inability to satisfy these wants will be dependent on the success of research along the following lines:

1. Finding better means of exploration for discovery of hidden deposits.
2. Finding more efficient means of recovering deposits that are known.
3. Developing processes for upgrading and utilizing lower grades of material than are used now.
4. Extending the substitution of plentiful materials for those that are scarce.
5. Improving and increasing the procedures for reclaiming and recycling materials that are now lost as scrap.

All these and still other approaches will be required to supply our future needs for mineral materials.

[CHAPTER SEVEN]

GLOBAL FOOD PRODUCTION, THE GREEN REVOLUTION, AND NUCLEAR ENERGY CENTERS*

DONALD S. KLINE

IF A BOTTLE is filled halfway to the top, a pessimist will say it is half empty and an optimist will argue that it is half full. The on-going global discussion of population growth and food production —the race between the *stork* and the *plow*—may be viewed in this manner.

In the 1960's the pessimists seemed to have held sway. The Paddocks[28] and Borgstrom[29] predicted mass famine in Asia first, then Africa and Latin America starting in the mid 1970's. More recently, spokesmen for the *green revolution* such as Brown[30a, b] and Borlaug[31] are viewing the *bottle* as half full. The use of hybrid, high-yield, lodging-resistant rice and wheat, especially in Asia, may buy Spaceship Earth perhaps two decades of time—time to slow down the stork.

If these pessimistic-optimistic observations are viewed as polar positions on a *people-food* continuum, where would a *massive technological fix*[32] be placed with regard to the probabilities of famine

*Presented before the World Future Society, Washington, D.C., May 14, 1971.

or no famine? More specifically, how can a nuclear powered, agro-industrial complex (NUPLEX) help nations of Asia, Africa, and Latin America both to avert famine and to stimulate reasonably stable socioeconomic development?

This paper has three objectives. First, it *traces* the global, temporal patterns of population and cereal grain production and trade. Second, it *examines* the nature and some implications of the *green revolution*. Third, it *describes* the dimensions of the nuclear energy center from the viewpoint of providing the two key inputs, water and fertilizer, for the continuation of the *green revolution*.

The Stork and the Plow: The Stork

The journalistic label *population explosion* is well known. Let us review the trend in Table I.

Two observations are generally made about these data. First, the

TABLE I

THE STORK

A. Millions	N.A.	L.A.	W.E.	E.E.	AFR	ASIA	OCE	TOTAL	DC'S	LDC'S
1940	146	131	279	297	172	1,176	11	2,212	733	1,479
1950	168	163	278	296	199	1,380	13	2,497	755	1,742
1960	197	206	300	339	235	1,620	16	2,913	852	2,061
1970	225	265	321	390	278	1,980	19	3,478	955	2,523
1980	254	348	352	440	333	2,470	22	4,219	1,068	3,151
1990	283	455	388	483	410	3,090	26	5,135	1,180	3,955
2000	312	592	421	526	517	3,870	29	6,267	1,288	4,979
B. % Change										
1930's	8.1	20.2	8.1	8.8	11.0	12.3	10.0	11.3	8.4	12.8
1940's	15.1	24.4	−.3	−.3	15.7	17.3	18.2	12.9	3.0	17.8
1950's	17.3	26.4	7.9	14.5	18.1	17.4	23.1	16.8	12.8	18.3
1960's	14.2	28.6	7.0	15.0	18.3	22.2	18.8	19.4	12.1	22.4
1970's	12.9	31.3	9.7	12.8	19.8	24.7	15.8	21.3	11.8	24.9
1980's	11.4	30.7	10.2	9.8	23.1	25.1	18.2	21.7	10.5	25.5
1990's	10.2	30.1	8.5	8.9	26.1	25.2	11.5	22.0	9.2	25.9

N.A.—Canada and United States
L.A.—rest of Western Hemisphere
W.E.—Western Europe, excluding U.S.S.R. and Communist East Europe
E.E.—U.S.S.R. and Communist East Europe
AFR—Africa
ASIA—including Japan
OCE—Oceania
DC's—Canada, United States, East Europe, Western Europe, Oceania
LDC's—Asia, Africa, and Latin America

Source: United Nations: *The Future Growth of World Population*, 1958.[33]

rising *level* of global population puts increasing pressure on re-sources, generates increasing outputs of *goods* (houses, medical care, autos) and *bads* (pollution, congestion, anxiety), and requires rapidly increasing inputs (labor, capital, raw materials, knowledge). Second, the pressures are unevenly *distributed*. The LDC's are growing more rapidly than the DC's and within the former, Latin America has the most active *stork*.

Before we move on to the *plow*, one further point should be made. If we view global pressures on resources as a result of the frantic activity of the stork, we should look at *all* animals that that overworked creature, in fable, brings to mothers the world over. In other words, animals other than humans are also users of plant energy and therefore must be counted as human *population equivalents*. Borgstrom[29] has estimated that in 1960 animals equated to an *additional* global population of 15 billion humans.

> Recognizing what modern animal feeding has established as minimum protein requirements of various species of livestock, their total protein consumption has been computed; what the nutritionist has called the *average standard* man (an individual weighing 154 pounds, 70 kilograms, and with a protein requirement of about 2.5 ounces, 70 grams, daily) has been adopted. Using this as a unit, it then becomes feasible to appraise each category of livestock in terms of numbers of standard men they represent as protein consumers, i.e. population equivalents (pp. 7 to 8).

TABLE II

GLOBAL BIOMASS

(by animal type and country, 1960)

Animal	Millions	Country	Millions
Cattle	8,089	India	2,193
Man	3,000	Mainland China	1,528
Pigs	1,942	United States	1,272
Sheep	988	U.S.S.R.	1,125
Buffaloes	940	Brazil	1,100
Horses	653	Argentina	500
Poultry	645	East and West Pakistan	450
Goats	288	Mexico	396
Camels, Mules, Asses	275	Australia	370
Other, including pet dogs,		Other	9,066
cats, wild animals	1,180	Total	18,000
Total	18,000		

Source: George Borgstrom.[29]

That stork, in fable and rhyme, delivers both human and animal babies. The kinds of animals and their population equivalents already on the scene are shown in Table II. Also shown is the revised "biomass" data for the larger nations of Spaceship Earth.

The simplest way to measure population density is, of course, persons per square mile or kilometer. A second method, more meaningful, is to view persons per acre or hectare of tilled or arable land. An even more meaningful technique is derived from the above type of data. The ratio of *total biomass* to the sum of tilled land, pasture *and available water* is even more meaningful.

From the above Table it can be seen that cattle and pigs count for more than three times the number of people. Another *surprise* may be that India becomes the nation with the greatest pressure of living matter on resources. Can India afford, regardless of the sociocultural value structure, to keep such a *biomass*, mainly cattle?

The Stork and the Plow: The Plow

We often hear the statement that a certain percentage of the global population goes to bed hungry at night. Such a statement is

TABLE III

ESTIMATED SOURCES OF GLOBAL CALORIC INTAKE

(percent, 1958)

	N.A.	L.A.	W.E.	E.E.	AFR	ASIA	OCE	TOTAL	DC'S	LDC'S
Rice	.8	.4	1.1	.7	2.7	41.1	.6	21.2	.9	32.4
Wheat	17.7	14.0	30.8	41.7	10.6	13.0	25.5	19.6	13.7	12.8
Corn	1.6	17.3	1.8	1.5	14.1	5.0	.5	5.4	1.6	7.6
Rye, Barley	.4	.6	3.1	8.7	3.2	2.5	—	3.1	4.5	2.4
Sorghum[a]	—	.4	—	.4	14.2	6.1	—	4.1	.2	6.5
Total	20.5	32.7	36.8	53.0	44.8	67.7	26.6	53.4	20.9	61.7
Cassava	—	7.3	—	—	11.6	1.1	—	2.0	—	3.2
Potatoes	3.2	3.2	6.7	9.2	8.6	3.2	3.0	4.9	6.7	3.9
Fruits[b]	9.1	12.3	6.4	3.5	11.5	11.4	5.6	9.6	5.9	11.5
Sugar	15.8	14.0	11.2	8.0	4.1	4.1	16.3	7.3	11.1	5.1
Fats, oils	19.9	8.0	16.8	9.2	7.5	5.3	12.3	8.9	14.5	5.8
Livestock	30.6	14.7	20.8	14.0	6.3	3.8	35.2	10.8	20.7	5.1
Fish	.2	.3	.9	.4	.5	.9	.6	.7	.5	.8
Other[c]	.7	.2	.4	2.7	5.1	2.5	.4	2.4	11.7	3.9

a—includes millet
b—includes nuts and vegetables
c—other grain, roots, tubers

Source: Brown.[30a]

supposed to indicate the magnitude of the world food problem. Such a statement, though, is operationally empty unless we become far more specific as to which kinds of food staples provide which amounts of calories, proteins, and fats in which countries.

CALORIES. If a caloric level were the only relevant dimension of the world food problem, it would be possible to feed Spaceship Earth by growing, in the United States alone, sugar beets in the northern agricultural area and sugar cane in the southern. Such a vision, much like the one that goes "in six hundred years or so, the weight of Terra's human mass will exceed the mass of the planet itself," is interesting but not useful. Table III shows the estimated dietary sources of calories for 1958.

To be noted from the above data are the importance of the grain group, the dependence of Asia on rice, the significance of livestock to North America and Oceania, the importance of corn in Latin America and Africa, of cassava in Africa, and interestingly, the lack of great importance of livestock in the LDC's.

Borgstrom[29] has suggested that the true *hunger gap* is the disparity between the *primary calories* utilized by people in the DC's and LDC's. Primary calories refer not only to the intake of plant calories (wheat, rice), but also to the intake of plant calories by animals which, in turn, survive and produce animal calories for humans. For every one calorie of animal foodstuff utilized by humans five to eight primary (plant) calories are needed by the animal. When adjustments of this type are made, the American takes in some 11,000 primary calories daily, the New Zealander about 13,000, and the Indian or Kenyan about 2,400.

With regard to *calories*, 90 percent of the global consumption comes from plant products and only ten percent from animal foodstuffs. But, with regard to *protein* consumption the ratio shifts to about 67 percent from plants and 33 percent from animals.

PROTEINS. It is thought by nutritionists that protein intake is the best gauge of global nutrition standards and deficiencies. Watt and Merrill[34] have estimated that the following *percentages* of protein are provided by the indicated foodstuffs: lentils, 24.7; chickpeas, 20.5; hard red spring wheat, 14.0; sorghum, 11.0; soft red winter wheat, 10.2; corn, 8.9; rice, 7.5; potatoes, 2.1; sweet potatoes, 1.7; bananas, 1.1; and cassava, 0.6.

It is also thought by experts (biologists and nutritionists) that animal protein is more suitable to human physiology than plant protein. If so, then Table IV indicates the nutrition gap between the areas of the DC's and LDC's.

There are also economic aspects of the utilization of plant and animal protein by humans. Animal protein is more readily available for humans and does not require additional processing such as milling, fermentation, and toasting. Animal protein is also cheaper, as less is needed to provide certain intake levels, and is easier to compose in a diet.

TABLE IV

DAILY AVERAGE PROTEIN CONSUMPTION PER PERSON
(1962-1964, in grams)

Area	Animal	Total
North America	63	
Oceania	62	
Europe	44	
Latin America	27	
ADEQUATE UN LEVEL	22	
Near East	18	
Africa	11	
Far East	8	
Developed Countries		84
Developing Countries		52

Source: President's Advisory Committee: *Report of the Panel on World Food Supply.*[35]

Of course, involved in all this are matters of custom and taste. Sacred cows are not eaten in India. Africans prefer white corn to imported yellow corn. New hybrid rice in Asia is not easily acceptable as to taste, color, texture, and baking qualities. The dimension of attitude links up with those of biology, economics, and agriculture.

GLOBAL FOOD PRODUCTION. Grain accounts for over 50 percent of global caloric intake (see Table III). Seventy percent of the world cropland is used to produce grain. Reasonably comparable data is available for grain production and trade. Therefore, it would be logical to view world food production and trade trends via grain data.

In 1963 Lester Brown[30a] viewed the global food situation in terms of total grain production, both in total tonnage and index of *per capita* production. Table V shows these data.

TABLE V
GLOBAL GRAIN PRODUCTION

Part A

Millions Metric Tons	N.A.	L.A.	W.E.	E.E.	AFR	ASIA	OCE	TOTAL	DC'S	LDC'S
1934-38[a]	109	31	67	153	26	260	5	651	334	317
1948-52[a]	169	31	65	134	32	272	7	710	375	335
1957-60[a]	199	42	84	177	38	348	7	895	467	428
1961	218	44	88	189	40	366	11	956	506	450
1965	215	57	115	169	52	403	10	1,021	509	512
1968	236	62	120	235	59	447	20	1,179	611	568
1980[b]	284	70	130	251	54	538	14	1,341	679	662
2000[b]	375	116	176	325	82	836	21	1,931	897	1,034
1980[c]	284	77	130	251	60	595	14	1,411	679	732
2000[c]	375	140	176	325	100	1,014	21	2,151	897	1,254

Part B

Per Capita Index 1934-1938—100										
1934-38[a]	100	100	100	100	100	100	100	100	100	100
1948-52[a]	131	75	95	85	102	85	118	93	106	86
1957-60[a]	136	84	115	100	106	96	103	103	119	96
1961	144	84	119	105	108	98	151	107	126	97

a—averaged

b—assumption of maintained current per capita consumption in the LDC's.

c—assumption of a 10% increase in per capita consumption in the LDC's by 1980 and a further 10% increase by 2000

Source: United Nations: *FAO Yearbooks.*[36]

The above data in Part A are subject to revision as the attempt to update the Brown study has drawn upon the 1970 FAO yearbook. Two points should be noted; both are not news to those who deal in global statistical comparisons. First, the lag time is discouraging. The 1970 book was published in 1969 and latest data contained in it is for 1968. Second, there are inconsistencies in the way data are reported by region and by country.

GLOBAL GRAIN TRADE. If the protein gap (see Table IV) is somewhat as stated and until the LDC's are more fully able to utilize the *green revolution*, it is reasonable to expect the role of grain exporting nations to remain important.

Over 90 percent of global rice production is consumed in Asia. Corn was heavily exported by Latin America prior to World War II. But, since that war, Latin American exports have significantly decreased, North America has taken a dominant export role, and both Europe and Asia have become large importers. Table VI shows *net* gain by area for selected years.

TABLE VI

GLOBAL NET GRAIN TRADE

(millions metric tons)

	N.A.	L.A.	W.E.	E.E.	AFR	ASIA	OCE
1934-38[a]	*5.3	*9.1	†23.7	*4.7	*.7	*2.2	*2.8
1948-52[a]	*23.4	*.8	†22.0	n.a.	†.3	†5.9	*3.4
1957-60[a]	*31.6	*1.1	†22.4	†.4	†1.2	†10.1	*2.8
1961	*39.4	†.2	†25.3	*.4	†2.2	†16.0	*6.0
1965	*55.0	†1.0	†46.0	†6.0	†3.9	†21.0	*7.0
1968	*48.0	†1.5	†22.0	†.8	†1.5	†31.0	*7.0
1980[b]	*58.0	†2.0	†28.0	†2.0	†3.0	†30.0	*7.0
2000[b]	*94.0	†7.0	†34.0	†4.0	†6.0	†54.0	*12.0

*means net exports
†means net imports
a—averaged
b—assumption of continued trend prevailing over past quarter-century.

Source: United Nations: *FAO Trade Yearbooks*.[36]

It can easily be seen that up to the present North America and, to a far lesser degree, Oceania continue to be the world's *breadbasket*. In 1968 the so-called *green revolution* was just beginning to have an impact on global grain production and trade patterns; such a pattern change had not yet registered in the above available statistics.

The Green Revolution to the Rescue?

In a paper prepared for a symposium on science and foreign policy Harrar[37] stated:

> the "Green Revolution" is the phrase now widely used to describe the dramatic changes that have been taking place in the levels of food grain production in many of the developing nations. These changes have indeed been revolutionary in their effect on traditional agricultural patterns and production figures. The most important aspect of this phenomenon is the hope it offers of the possibility of gradually eliminating chronic hunger, malnutrition and the all-too-frequent famines from regions where they have been long ever present threats to the society.

The testimony of Dr. Harrar and others had been given to the United States Congress in December, 1969. By 1970, the use of the hybrid wheat and rice has spread to an estimated 44 million acres, mainly in South Asia. This phenomenon is seen in Table VII.

TABLE VII
THE SPREAD OF HIGH-YIELD RICE AND WHEAT
(thousands of acres)

1969-70 Crop Year

Crop Year	Wheat	Rice	Total	Wheat		Rice	
1965/66	23	18	41	India	15,100	India	10,800
1966/67	1,542	2,505	4,047	Pakistan	7,000	Philippines	3,346
1967/68	10,173	6,487	16,660	Turkey	1,540	Pakistan	1,891
1968/69	19,699	11,620	31,319	Afghan	361	Indonesia	1,850
1969/70	24,664	19,250	43,914	Iran	222	S. Vietnam	498
				Nepal	186	Burma	356
				Tunisia	131	Malaysia	316
				Morocco	99	Nepal	123
				Algeria	12	Ceylon	65
				Guatemala	7	Laos	5
				Lebanon	4		

Source: United States Agency for International Development: *War on Hunger.* April, 1971.[36]

These are the raw data on plantings—a growing potential for increased food production. What have been the results? Brown[30b] speaks of a *quantum jump in production* and relates yield improvements in wheat in Mexico and to a lesser degree, in India and Pakistan to growing social unrest and possible decreasing use of labor inputs. Hybrid rice yields are also increasing, especially in West Pakistan and Ceylon.

India: A Laboratory for the Green Revolution and the Nuplex

Of the estimated 44 million acres planted with the new varieties of wheat and rice as of the 1969-70 crop year, India accounted for 26 million. Table VIII shows that the gains in production and yield of wheat crop have been rapidly accelerating in the 1968-70 period.

The optimist, then, sees the *green revolution* as almost a panacea for the hunger problems of the LDC's. Borlaug[31] has suggested that if the governments of the LDC's "aggressively employ and exploit agricultural development as a potent instrument of agrarian prosperity and economic advancement" we could eliminate many of the *social ills* in poverty-stricken societies.

On the other hand, the pessimist, although admitting that great strides have been rapidly made in total production, yield, and farm

TABLE VIII

ESTIMATED INDIAN WHEAT PRODUCTION AND YIELD
(1960-1970)

	Production (000 metric tons)	Yield (pounds / acre)
1960	10,322	670
1961	10,977	730
1962	12,072	750
1963	10,829	680
1964	9,853	610
1965	12,290	790
1966	10,424	700
1967	11,393	780
1968	16,568	1,020
1969	18,700	1,070
1970	21,000	n.a.

Source: U.S. Department of Agriculture, Economic Research Dept. As reported in Brown, L.: *The Social Impact of the Green Revolution.* New York, Carnegie Endowment for International Peace, International Conciliation, No. 581, January, 1971, pp. 9, 13.[39]

income, is apprehensive about certain *second generation* problems of the *green revolution.*

The continued performance of the agricultural revolution in these nations will depend on the availability of two key inputs: water and fertilizer. In 1969 an observer of the Indian scene[40] addressed himself to the question of water. Referring to the planning of Indian governmental officials two years ahead (from May, 1969), he noted:

> by then wheat output may have reached a plateau, for the new dwarf varieties have already been sown on about three-fourths of the irrigated acreage available for wheat. It is only on the irrigated tracts —where application of water can be controlled—that great increases in output are assured. . . . Looking ahead, development experts are coming to recognize that the green revolution will proceed by fits and starts and that the amazing new seeds will carry India only a part of the way to a food supply that will remain adequate for a population steadily expanding by more than a million a month. The big challenge, they say, will be the development of water resources.

Governmental planning, whether *good* or *bad,* will also have a significant impact on the dimensions of success of the *green revolution.* In late 1970 another observer of the Indian scene[41] reflected:

> In 1966, a drought year, the new seeds were still relatively scarce, as were the fertilizers necessary to their success. Rather than distributing

them throughout the country, the government sought to concentrate them in 32.5 million acres of the country's best land. This turned out to be the Punjab, where, most agree, farmers are well off and more 'progressive' than in other areas. Blessed with favorable weather as well as the new seeds, the strategy paid off in 1967-68. Wheat was abundant in the Punjab . . . All of this, the skeptics contend, is somewhat misleading. The Indian agriculture ministry had demonstrated that given optimum conditions—and, always, favorable weather—impressive increases in food production were possible. But the success was limited to the 32.5 million acres, only one twelfth of India's 390 million acres under cultivation. To have a major effect on the food supply problem, similar increases would need to be achieved in the vast stretches of poorer, drier farmland, and in the more difficult crops, like rice.

The 1970 symposium on the *green revolution*[42] covers well an examination of such *second generation* problems. Mosher,[43] one of the speakers, suggested that the results of rapid agricultural change have three types of effects: those that are wholly constructive, those that reveal deficiencies, and those that raise important policy issues. Effects in the first category are self-explanatory—increases in total production, yield, and selective improvement of farm income.

Second category effects raise difficult questions of resource use. First, there is a growing shortage of irrigated lands in which to plant the new varieties of wheat and rice. As stated above, the optimal areas of the Punjab were first utilized. A continuation of production and yield gains in India may well depend upon the development of irrigation infrastructure and water management in drier areas such as around the Gulf of Kutch.

Second, there are questions with regard to labor inputs. On the positive side, increased labor will be needed for seedbed preparation, the application of fertilizer and pesticides, weeding, and water management. But, in the longer run, less labor may be needed by the increasingly capital-intensive agricultural operations. The key question may well be whether the *green revolution* will, on balance, require increasingly capital-intensive or continued labor-intensive agricultural systems.

Third, since the agricultural transformation increases farmer dependence on *purchased* inputs, such as seeds, fertilizers, pesticides, and water, greater demands will be placed on the local and national credit structure. Further, these inputs must have time, place, and form utility as far as the farmer is concerned. Double and triple cropping, possible in areas of high annual and diurnal mean temperature, will place greater emphasis on marketing, storage, and transportation networks and facilities and farm extension services.

Fourth, the differential impact of price changes are and will be twofold. With supply now increasing faster than economic (market) demand, unless the Indian government establishes *floor* prices, falling prices will harm the small farmer who has not yet gained from the *green revolution; his* volume will not rise rapidly enough to counteract falling price. During the June-November 1968 period, for example, Indian wholesale wheat prices fell twelve percent below the like year-earlier period. But, for the minority of farmers in on the *ground floor* of this amazing agricultural transformation, yields are pushing volume up faster than prices may be falling. These thoughts are based on the assumption of minimal government intervention in the price mechanism. The curve at which prices *are* set may cause future rise and fall of governments.

Fifth, increased food supply may reduce the incentive of rural peoples to decrease the birth rate. Recent comment by the Population Reference Bureau[44] suggests that this may be a vital longer term negative factor.

The third category of effects of the *green revolution* according to Mosher, those which raise important policy issues, are the tendency toward larger farms, tendency to make farm mechanization more profitable, and changed patterns of international trade (see Table VI).

It may be, further, that the social and political consequences of the revolution will, in the longer run, have greater impact than the agricultural-economic aspects. As the revolution in India spreads out from the wheat acres (Punjab) into the rice areas (Bengal) social and political unrest caused by increasing income differential may intensify. It is entirely possible that, in its social dimension, the *green* revolution may turn *red* as blood flows in the streets and countryside from clashes between the new, rich *wet* (irrigation) farmers, and the old, poverty-stricken *dry* agriculturalists.

If the two crucial inputs into this agricultural transformation are water and fertilizer, there may be a significant role to play for the nuclear powered, agro-industrial complex (NUPLEX).

What Does a Nuplex Do?

The interrelationships between technology and society are growing sources of national and global concern and research. One only need ponder the rising concern with pollution of all forms and the SST controversy of the late sixties and early seventies.

Writing in 1966, Alvin Weinberg[32] suggested:

> In view of the simplicity of technological engineering, to what extent can social problems be circumvented by reducing them to technological problems? Can we identify Quick Technological Fixes for profound and almost infinitely complicated social problems, "fixes" that are within the grasp of modern technology, and which would either eliminate the original social problem without requiring a change in the individual's social attitudes or would so alter the problem as to make its resolution more feasible.

Very broadly stated, the purpose of the Nuplex is to aid in the bringing into food production many of the hundreds of millions of coastal desert acres in the LDC's. As population pressures increase and as increased yields from the *green revolution* possibly begin to dampen, Spaceship Earth will need to expand the amount of arable land. The potential is seen in Table IX.

TABLE IX

PRESENT AND POTENTIAL GLOBAL AGRICULTURAL USE OF LAND

Classification	Billions of Acres
Grain	1.6
Other Major crops	0.7
Minor crops	1.1
Permanent pastures and meadows	6.4
Irrigated	0.3
Arid	12.1
Within 500 miles of the sea	8.0
Within 300 miles of the sea	5.2
Of arid land within 300 miles of the sea	
in Africa	1.8
in Asia	1.5
in Australia	0.9
in South America	0.6
in North America	0.4

Source: Taken and adapted from Moyers, J.C., and Kuhns, Helen: *World Arid-Area Summary*. From Reviews of Research of Arid Zone Hydrology (Geneva, UNESCO, 1953) and Meigs, P.: *Geography of Coastal Deserts*. Geneva, Arid Zone Research Report No. 8, 1966.[45]

The Nuplex is a gigantic piece of technology which utilizes a systemic approach to the food-energy-water problems of certain areas in certain LDC's. Preliminary feasibility studies[46, 47, 48] have suggested sites in Western Australia (Shark's Bay), India (Kutch and Western Uttar Pradesh), Mexico (Baja California), Peru (Sechura desert), and the Middle East (Sinai-Negev) as suitable for Nuplex construction. The authors' research has also explored the Kenya-Somali coast of East Africa as a possible site.

More specifically, the dimensions and objectives of the Nuplex are seen in Table X.

Since India has the largest *biomass* of any nation (see Table II) and is the only LDC at the present time willing to implement, although slowly and with political difficulty, a nuclear energy center, it would be meaningful to briefly examine one plan to feed India's future millions.

TABLE X

ESTIMATED DIMENSIONS OF A NUPLEX

On Site:

Energy generated	minimum 1 million kilowatts (elect)
Desalted Seawater (one crop)	minimum one billion gallons/day
Acreage (irrigated and fertilized)	200,000–300,000
Fertilizer production	ammonia: 2,000 tons/day
	phosphorus: 300 tons/day
Grain produced	1.3 billion pounds/year
People fed	2.4 mililon at 250 kg/year
Cost	$.6–2.5 billion
Number workers and families	250,000–400,000
Aluminum production	514 tons/day
Chlorine production	1,000 tons/day
Caustic Soda	1,130 tons/day
Acreage fertilized (one crop)	10 million
Grain produced	15–45 billion pounds/year
People fed	30–90 million

Source: Mason, E.A.: An analysis of nuclear agro-industrial complexes. In Nader, C., and Zahlan, A.B. (eds.): *Science and Technology in Developing Countries.* Cambridge, University Press, 1969, p. 118; and Oak Ridge National Laboratory (ORNL), 4290, November, 1968.[49]

Noting that the 1965 to 1967 crop failures and threatened famines took place mainly in the state of Uttar Pradesh in India, Hammond[50] envisioned a ten year program (1970 to 1979) to build eight nuclear centers and two *second phase* enlargements of two of them. Of the eight initial centers, two would be on the north shore of the Gulf of Kutch and six would be in the western part of Uttar Pradesh. Each of the eight initial centers would produce enough grain to feed ten to fifteen million people. Thus, a project a year would be able to *keep up with* India's current annual population increment of about fourteen million.

The Nuplex, like its companion phenomenon the *green revolution,* raises many most complex social questions. Meier[51] is concerned about settlements of prior land claims on the Nuplex site and the provision of opportunities for immigrants into a Nuplex area. Such movements to nuclear energy centers might take the pressure off of growing unemployment and dismay in Indian urban areas due to the erroneous perception by rural inhabitants that jobs and a better way of life are to be had in the city.

Additional questions over a wide range of the social and behavioral sciences were raised about the Nuplex by a 1969 Syracuse University Research Corporation paper.[52] The following questions only should serve to stimulate thought as to the complexities involved and indicate the interdisciplinary nature of the research and planning which needs to be done. What is the total political nature of a Nuplex? Is the control to reside in private hands, in state governments, or the national government or a certain combination of the three? What are the legal, moral, and social implications of voluntary or coercive resettlement? How does a Nuplex relate to international economic patterns of input and output flows? What training programs will be necessary for which personnel? What are the problems and costs of converting small-farm, single-family agricultural units into *intensive food-farm* units? How would cooperative farming ventures fit into a Nuplex scheme?

In conclusion, the *green revolution* with or without nuclear centers may aid the *plow* in the race with the *stork.* But, a potential disaster may, at any time, negate the gains won and more. I speak of the danger of plant disease to the genetically more vulnerable hybrids of corn, rice, and wheat being rapidly introduced around the world. The specific situation in mind is the advent of the corn blight in the United States in 1970. In that year it was estimated that 15 percent of the total corn crop would be lost. Forecasts of damage to the crops of subsequent years are expected to range from the same to perhaps as high as 40 percent.

As the number of genetically different varieties of staple grains decrease in the rush to increase yield, the probability of a mutant virus or fungus resistant to present chemicals increases. Are the LDC's courting disaster if they do increase plantings of hybrids and also if they *do not?*

The world *stork-plow* problem is so complex that the range of solutions on the food side read like something from the annals of science fiction. Food may be grown on the surface of petroleum. The oceans may be farmed with robot gardeners. Solar hydroponics may be developed. The controlled fusion process will create food suitable in caloric level and protein content out of water, air, and energy.

It will take hard work, luck, and maybe genius on the part of many individuals to feed the present and future pressing billions on Spaceship Earth at *better* nutritional levels. Perhaps genius is reflected in a young scientist in Bergenfield, New Jersey, who is seeking a way to feed global populations by adding salt-tolerance hormones to seawater in which can be grown enormous amounts of the Western sea-oat.[53] Anyone for a Western sea-oat pancake?

[CHAPTER EIGHT]

ENERGY SOURCES FOR A STEADY-STATE SOCIETY*

Earl Cook

Man cannot continue to expand his numbers indefinitely. At some point in the future his global birth rate and death rate must come into balance. This balance can be either of two kinds. It can be a statistical balance representing wide swings in the death rate by which periods of excess of births over deaths are compensated for by periods, probably shorter and more traumatic, of excess of deaths over births, or it can be an equilibrium balance representing an evolutionary decline in the birth rate to meet an already low and controlled death rate. It is the latter type of balance which is implied by the term *steady-state society*.

Whatever the social shape of the steady-state society, its level of living will depend largely on the energy resources available to it. To put it another way, population and standard of living are interdependent variables dependent on energy. The coin of the steady-state realm will be energy. Consequently, any look into the future, any attempt to discern the quality of a steady-state society, should begin with a discussion of the energy sources available to that society.

A look into the future requires time perspective if it is to have prediction value. Consequently, we need to look first at our past in

*Presented in the University of Minnesota seminar series on the Steady State Earth, March 11, 1971 and also before the World Future Society, Washington, D.C., May 14, 1972.

order to find out where we are and how we got here, before we turn toward the future to consider its constraints and its options.

Energy in the Evolution of Mankind

The history of mankind is the story of his increasing control of energy. By discovery of ways to control energy, to produce and apply power, humans have transformed themselves from puny creatures at the mercy of their environment to creatures with more power than they know how to use well, whose environment now depends upon their grace, and whose very longevity as a species depends upon their own wisdom.

How did this happen?

Sometime several million years ago one of our remote ancestors picked up a stone and threw it, with a purpose directed by his memory and with a trajectory determined by his stereoscopic color vision, his versatile arm, and his semi-erect stance.

That first stone's throw, or something like it, marked the birth of power technology. From it were to flow the use of bola stones and antelope-bone clubs, the design and fabrication of stone tools and weapons, the organization of hunting society, the perfection of the bow and the spear, the development of speech and language; in short, what we call culture.

Perhaps half a million years ago man learned how to **control fire,** the first great natural energy source outside of food to be brought under his control. There followed an abrupt expansion of man's ability to live within hostile environments, to spread out of the warm lands to which he had been confined, and to increase in numbers.

Throughout a long period of exceptional climatic variability and environmental stress highlighted by continental glaciations, when some larger animals with more hair, sharper teeth, and stronger muscles became extinct, mankind flourished. Shortly upon the recession of the latest great ice sheet, about 10,000 years ago, they learned to domesticate certain plants and animals, marking another great step forward in their control of energy.

The invention of agriculture and its spread from the hills of Asia Minor down into the semi-arid floodplains of the Tigris and Euphrates rather quickly led to irrigation and the development of the world's first cities, some five or six thousand years ago, when, for the first time, the power of flowing water was harnessed by man. As man's agriculturally based communities reached the sea-coast, the power of the wind was used to propel sailing craft on voyages of discovery and trade.

Landbased water and windpower technologies, however, were not intensively developed until the late middle ages, when the dim outline of our present technological civilization began to appear in northwest Europe. The great power sources there were the horse, the windmill, and the watermill.[54] Teams of horses drawing heavy plows powered an agricultural revolution in the northern plains.[55] The windmill helped the Dutch reclaim their country from the sea. Water power was applied to all sorts of industrial processes from crushing ore to making mash for beer.

By the thirteenth century the forests of England had become so depleted that people turned to burning coal, despite its noxious smoke. For some four hundred years, however, coal remained just a substitute for wood as fuel.

Then came the steam engine (1698) and the invention of coke (1717). Coke, coal, and the steam engine powered the industrial revolution, which was to make man truly a geologic agent, with power to change the face of the earth and to devour in a few centuries earth resources that had taken hundreds of millions of years to accumulate.

Although steam engines were used to drive trains and ships, to dig canals and mines, and to power a great variety of industrial machines, rapid growth of power production in terms of present rates began less than one hundred years ago. It has been made possible by the invention of electrical means for the generation and distribution of power from central power stations, the first of which was opened in 1881, and by the development and proliferation of internal-combustion engines for use in motor vehicles, ships, locomotives, and airplanes.

Finally, the energy of the atomic nucleus has been successfully tapped. Although the first large nuclear power plant went into operation as recently as 1957, it may not be very long before most power produced at central plants is nuclear.

Energy and Population

In his most primitive stage the capacity of man to use energy was

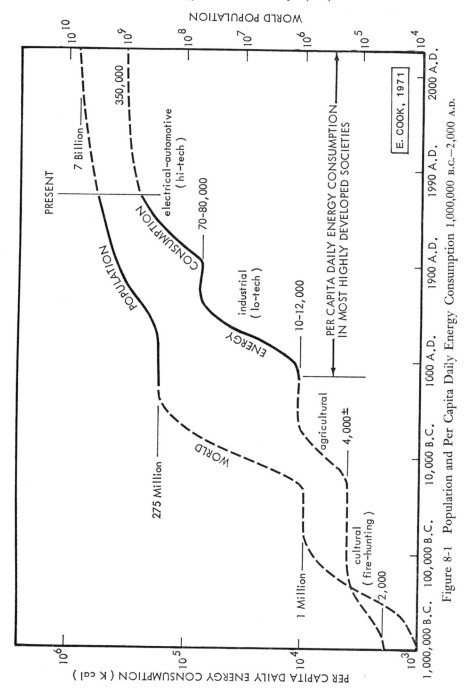

Figure 8-1 Population and Per Capita Daily Energy Consumption 1,000,000 B.C.–2,000 A.D.

limited to the food which he ate, about two thousand kilocalories per capita per day (Fig. 8-1). With his capture of fire his rate of energy utilization may have increased to as much as four thousand kilocalories per capita per day. In a primitive agricultural society the rate rises to about ten thousand kilocalories per capita per day. At the height of the industrial revolution (1850-70), per capita daily energy consumption reached seventy thousand kilocalories in England, the United States, and Germany.[56]

Throughout most of man's history his population has tended to remain in balance with the increase in total energy supply.[57] Human population growth appears to have taken place in three surges, as a result of the cultural (hunting, clothing, and fire), agricultural, and technological revolutions. Each of these surges reflects a great leap in man's control of energy. After each of the first two, population leveled off as resource limits were approached. For example, as the technology of hunting became more sophisticated and efficient, the number of food animals started to decline. Several species became extinct. Later, as primitive agriculture spread throughout the accessible arable world, the older soils became depleted and eroded, and the marginal areas limited expansion. In the first seven hundred years of the Christian Era the total human population may actually have declined.[56] The third surge began about 700 AD, when the first dim outlines of the technological revolution became visible. We are still being swept along in a surge of population nourished by the vast energy resources technological man has been able to develop. Each of these three revolutions brought man to higher levels of per capita use of energy; consequently, man's total energy use has increased even faster than his population.

The relation of energy use to population growth is further illuminated by the fact that for some 1200 years after the beginning of the technologic revolution the rate of population growth in the West European technological society—except for two brief periods of plague—consistently exceeded the rate of population growth anywhere else in the world (Fig. 8-2). Only in recent years, because of the wholesale exportation to nontechnologic societies of the medical and sanitary systems of the technological societies, has this relation started to change.

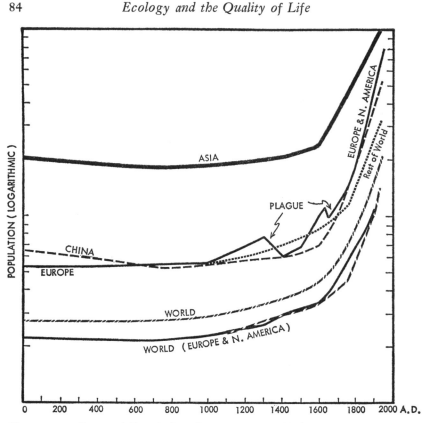

Figure 8-2   Rates of Population Growth in the Christian Era

The intensive use of horse, water, and wind power, and wood and coal for fuel, between 700 and 1800 AD brought the daily per capita energy use to seventy thousand kilocalories in Northwest Europe and North America. It is interesting that the invention and intensive application of the steam engine and the great increase in the use of coal do not appear to have had any great effect on per capita energy consumption. In the United States per capita energy use probably was lower in 1880 than it had been in 1800, and during that century, population grew somewhat faster than total energy consumption (Fig. 8-3), despite the fact that the standard of living materially improved. This seeming contradiction is explained by the great increase in the efficiency of energy use during the nineteenth century, which marked the culmination of the low-technology or industrial revolution.

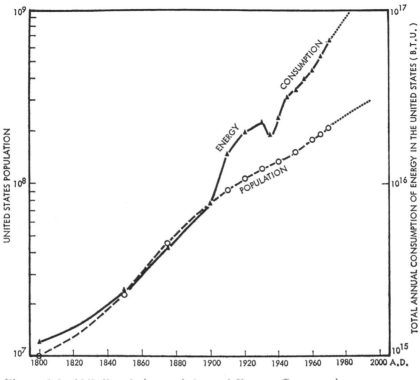

Figure 8-3   U.S. Population and Annual Energy Consumption

The succeeding high-technology revolution was caused by the central power station and the automobile, which gave power true mobility. Now, for the first time, it became possible for the average individual, mass man, to use power in his home and on the road. Beginning shortly before 1900 per capita energy consumption in the United States started a rapid increase from a level of about seventy thousand kilocalories a day, which had persisted throughout most of the nineteenth century, to the present two hundred and twenty thousand; from 1965 to 1970, it increased at a rate of about four percent per year, more than double the rate of population growth.

Not all peoples of the world have participated in the technological revolution; in fact, much less than half of them. About the seventh century AD the world began to divide itself into the *haves* and the *have nots*. At first, the differences would have been hardly perceptible; but by the late Middle Ages, living standards in Northwest Europe probably were appreciably better than those in Asia and Africa, and by the nineteenth century, the contrasts were enormous.

Although the geologic inequities in the distribution of coal and iron may have played some part, the continuing and even widening income gap between the developed and less developed countries (LDC's) seems largely due to (a) a nontechnological culture and tradition in the LDC's, (b) the LDC's lack of the capital necessary for industrialization, and (c) the benefits of modern medicine and sanitation which have dramatically lowered infant mortality rates in the LDC's and increased population beyond supportable limits. Therefore, the per capita energy consumption and income in these countries remains low, while the adult death rate stays high. The industrial regions of the world, with less than 30 percent of the world's population, consume almost 80 percent of the world's energy; and the energy they use is in the capital-intensive forms, the fossil fuels, hydroelectricity, and nuclear power, whereas, in the nonindustrial world the labor-intensive forms still dominate, human and animal energy, fuel wood, and waste.

Some per capita energy consumption figures for 1966[58] are shown in the Table I. It will be noted that there is not a linear relation between per capita energy consumption and standard of living (East Germany, for example); the latter depends on what is done with the energy and with the goods and services produced with it. This Table does not include energy derived from food, wood, and farm wastes, wind, or animal power. Nearly 60 percent of Asia's energy comes from wood and farm wastes; the total shown for India, to be comparable to the curve of per capita consumption in Figure 8-1, should include perhaps 5,100 kilocalories for wood and farm waste and 2,000 kilocalories for food, for a total of 10,500—about the level that has been estimated for primitive agriculture.

Power may be the key to expansion of food produced in the hungry nations, but capital is the key to power, and the hungry nations do not have capital.

Energy-Resource Availability

The great increase in the use of energy by man in the past cen-

TABLE XI

PER CAPITA DAILY ENERGY CONSUMPTION,
SELECTED COUNTRIES, 1966*

		k cal	Comparative Levels
United States		191,300	
Canada		157,000	High
Czechoslovakia		112,700	Technology
East Germany		109,600	
United Kingdom		102,500	
West Germany		85,300	
USSR		75,800	
Poland		72,200	
France		60,300	Low
South Africa		53,100	Technology
Venezuela		49,200	
Romania		41,400	
Japan		39,100	
Mexico	(24,000)†	19,900	Low Technology Advanced Agriculture
Iraq	(19,000)	11,400	
Iran	(14,400)	8,100	Advanced Agriculture
Libya	(13,400)	6,300	
India	(10,500)	3,400	Primitive Agriculture

*Covers only fossil hydrocarbons, hydro and nuclear electricity. Based on figures from Statistical Office of the United Nations, New York.
†Estimated totals, including food, wood, and animal wastes.

tury has come at the expense of the fossil fuels. Oil, coal, and natural gas supply about 85 percent of the world's energy consumption today. Fossil hydrocarbons, as well as uranium, the present *fuel* for nuclear powerplants, are present in finite amounts in the earth's crust. The amount of each that ultimately will be extracted and used for power production will be determined by the amount originally present in the earth's crust, the benefit-cost ratio of extraction and utilization (which must be more than one, expressed in terms of usable energy produced compared to energy expended in production and in environmental protection), and the value of the resource for nonenergy uses.

Technological improvements in extraction, processing, transportation, and utilization can stretch energy-resource reserves measured by quantity, but voracious increases in rates of consumption diminish those same reserves measured in years of availability. The need for environmental protection can also diminish reserves of a particular energy resource measured in availability for a specific use, as for burning in an urban power plant.

Because man has always preferred to increase the efficiency of his consumption rather than moderate his appetite (which requires limiting his numbers or decreasing his material standard of living, or both), he now seeks to prolong his fossil-fuel and nuclear base by discovery of new fields and by application of new technologies (gasification of coal, retorting of oil shale, development of nuclear catalytic burners), and at the same time continues to look longingly at the solar flux for an ultimate solution to his energy-resource problem.

In 1965 L. P. Gaucher of Texaco[59] took a look into the future of U.S. energy consumption (Fig. 8-4). In several ways Gaucher's projections seem overly optimistic today. In the first place, total energy consumption in the U.S. is growing at a considerably greater rate than Gaucher's total energy curve indicates. One can only guess when increasing fuel and environmental-protection costs will start to put a brake on the present rate of increase; one must recognize

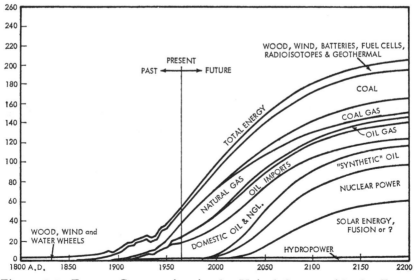

Figure 8-4　Energy Consumption in the United States, with the Future Given in Detail (Gaucher, 1965)

that there are powerful incentives for continued increases built into our commercial power structure.

Next, one must question strongly the inclusion of oil and natural gas as energy resources beyond the year 2050. King Hubbert's[60]

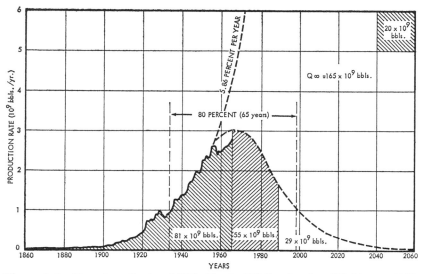

Figure 8-5   Complete Cycle of U.S. Crude-Oil Production (Hubbert, 1970)

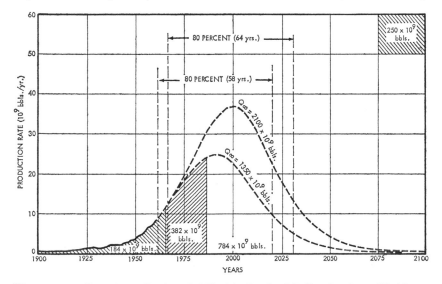

Figure 8-6   Complete Cycle of World Crude-Oil Production (Hubbert, 1970)

calculated cumulative curves of production for crude oil suggest that domestic oil will not be used as fuel beyond the year 2000 (Fig 8-5) when it will be almost 90 percent exhausted and world crude (Fig. 8-6) will not be available beyond 2030, when it will have reached a comparable state of depletion. Natural gas will last no longer than petroleum.

The end of energy use of petroleum and natural gas may come well before the 90 percent depletion stage. Rapid increases in the portion of world oil and gas production used as manufacturing raw materials—to produce petrochemicals and for synthesized protein—foretell the day when these fossil fuels will be too valuable to burn. By the year 2150 (Fig. 8-7), coal will have reached its peak as an energy source and will thenceforward decline.

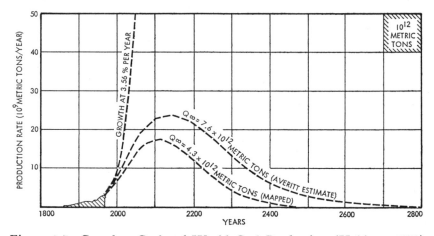

Figure 8-7　Complete Cycle of World Coal Production (Hubbert, 1970)

My own vision of future U.S. energy consumption by sources differs considerably from Gaucher's (Fig. 8-8). Because nuclear power based on the present technology probably will exhaust ^{235}U reserves within a century, and because breeder reactors, even if they start to contribute to U.S. energy requirements by 1990, as now projected by the U.S. Atomic Energy Commission, will come onstream slowly, the enormous gap left by exhaustion of oil and natural gas in the early years of the twenty-first century must be filled by coal, oil shale, and tar sands, or else the energy consumption of the United States will decrease.

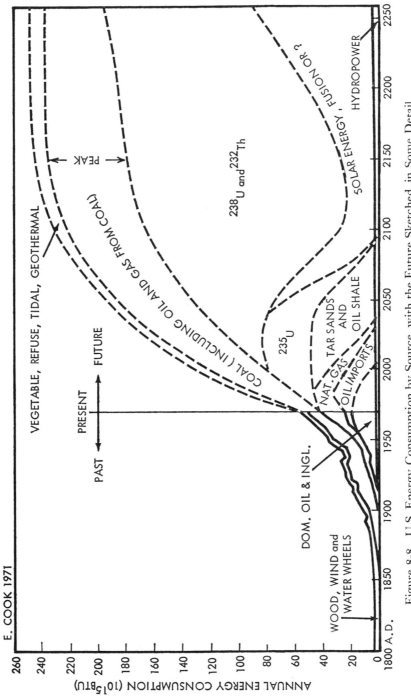

Figure 8-8   U.S. Energy Consumption by Source, with the Future Sketched in Some Detail

The rational ground for disagreement with Dr. Hubbert's[57] cumulative depletion curves for the fossil fuels is limited to the time scale; the ephemeral nature of the resources is apparent. Coal reserves are much greater than those of all the other fossil fuels combined; with advances in technology that appear attainable, coal can provide a major portion of our energy requirements for several hundred years. Although oil shale and tar sand reserves appear small compared to coal, they have not yet been exploited; they lie mostly in North America, and they might be developed to supply a significant portion of U.S. energy needs for a period of fifty years or so. Tidal and geothermal resources, as well as water power, appear clearly inadequate to supply much of the energy needs of the future.[60]

Beyond the year 2100, it seems clear that world energy needs must be met by a combination of coal, nuclear power, and solar energy. Coal will be burned at the mine mouth for power production and will be gasified in the ground or liquified at the mine mouth to produce synthetic gas and oil. Nuclear power, if it is to supply a large part of our energy needs, must be produced by breeder reactors, or nuclear catalytic burners as the Oak Ridge people prefer to call them. In this way all uranium, instead of only ^{235}U (which constitutes only 0.7 percent of natural uranium), can be utilized as well as the immense energy represented by thorium in the earth's crust.

Well before the year 2200, the great problems of heat and radioactive waste disposal from nuclear powerplants (if they are still breeders), as well as the depleted reserves and high cost of coal, will have stimulated much research and development in the concentration and application of solar energy to human needs and to the development of controlled fusion power. The growing of vegetable material for energy uses and the production of power from burning refuse[61] will be greatly expanded but cannot be expected to add much to the world's energy supply. Increases in the efficiency of energy use by direct conversion of solar or chemical energy to electricity will be sought in solar and fuel cells, through magnetohydrodynamic, thermionic, and thermoelectric generation.[62] Considerable increase in efficiency for special applications are expectable, but are not apt to change the gross picture of Figure 8-8.

Income Energy and Fund Energy

The world has been expanding its population and increasing the level of material living, at least in the developed and developing countries, by using up fund energy reserves that cannot be replaced once exhausted. A true steady-state society can be based only on *income* energy resources, those represented by the solar flux and solar energy stored in the hydrologic cycle or in renewable vegetation, or perhaps a quasi-income source, nonrenewable, but which will take thousands of years to deplete at predictable levels of consumption; deuterium in seawater will be a quasi-income resource if a controlled fusion reaction in which only deuterium is required can be achieved. On the other hand, if it turns out that the achievable fusion reaction is the one that requires ^{6}Li (Lithium-6), the quantity of fusion energy ultimately attainable will be about the same as that in all the fossil fuels, enough to last the world a few hundred years at best.[60]

World energy needs at various levels of population and rates of consumption can easily be calculated and compared to the potentially available income sources (Table XII). Seven billion people could be supported at present levels of consumption by the following energy mix (if the first four sources were developed to the maxima that appear practicable):

Plant (agricultural) conversion	37%
Water power	26%
Tidal power	2%
Solar space heating	22%
Nuclear and solar power	13%
	100%

Seven billion people at 2.5 times the present world average consumption (maintaining substantial differentials between the developed and underdeveloped countries) would require:

Plant (agricultural) conversion	15%
Water power	10%
Tidal power	1%
Solar space heating	22%
Nuclear and solar power	52%
	100%

To maintain seven billion people at the present U.S. level of energy consumption would require that 90 percent of the total energy, equivalent to almost ten times the present total world consumption,

TABLE XII
WORLD ENERGY NEEDS AT VARIOUS LEVELS OF POPULATION
AND RATES OF CONSUMPTION

Population (10⁶)	Daily per Capita Consumption (kilocalories)	Totals (10¹⁵ k cal/yr.)	Potential Income Deficits* (10¹⁵ k cal/yr.)
3,600	35,000	46	—
7,000	35,000	89	11
7,000	400,000 U.S. and Canada / 200,000 Other Developed Countries / 40,000 Less-Developed Countries	225	117
7,000	181,000	462 (Brown 1954)	301
7,000	220,000	561	378
15,000	35,000	192	91
15,000	400,000 U.S. and Canada / 200,000 Other Developed Countries / 40,000 Less-Developed Countries	483	318
15,000	220,000	1203	876

INCOME ENERGY RESOURCES POTENTIALLY AVAILABLE†

Water Power (Hubbert, 1970)	23
Tidal Power (Hubbert, 1970)	2
Wood and Conversion of Agricultural Products (Brown, 1954)	33
Solar Heat Could Meet Perhaps 22% of Total Requirements (Brown, 1954)	
Nuclear Breeder or Fusion Power	?
Solar Power	?
	TOTAL

*Based on income resources potentially available; represent amounts to be made up by nuclear and solar power.

†Counting efficient breeders and fusion reactors as income generators.

come from some combination of solar heat, solar power, and fertile or fusion nuclear power.

The Question of Solar Power

There is a wide difference of opinion on the future availability of solar power. Hubbert,[60] for example, states:

Despite the magnitude of solar power [the power of solar radiation intercepted by the earth is about a million times the power capacity of all electric utilities in the United States in 1960] . . . its low areal density makes the direct use of solar power impractical and prohibitive in cost for other than small-scale, special-purpose use.

. . . There is no question that it would be physically possible to cover [the necessary] area with energy-collecting devices, and to transmit, store, and ultimately transform the energy collected into conventional electric power. However, the complexity of such a process, and its costs in terms of metals and of chemical and electrical equipment, as well as of maintenance, in comparison with those for thermoelectric and hydroelectric plants of the same capacity, render such an undertaking to be of questionable practicality.

Therefore, the large-scale uses of solar energy appear to be limited principally to the biological channel of photosynthesis, and to the natural mechanical concentrations of wind and water power.

Hubbert concludes that only nuclear energy with the use of breeder reactors offers the world hope of meeting its power requirements at present or higher levels for centuries to come.

Glaser,[63] on the other hand, believes that solar-power-generating satellites offer enough hope of providing large amounts of power that our recent and present space effort might profitably be redirected to the design, development, and testing of such satellites. Farrington Daniels[64] has long pointed to the advantages of solar energy for special uses and special environments. Harrison Brown[65] held that that in a properly designed world, perhaps two thirds of all space heating (or 20 to 25 percent of all energy requirements) could be done with solar heat.

The problems in the use of solar radiation are its intermittent nature, its low density, and difficulties of storage and conversion. Solar-energy technology, however, has made much progress. Various radiation concentration devices have already been used for heating, cooking, and cooling. The solar cell, which converts sunlight directly into electrical energy, has made the collection of much space data possible and may, in the near future, power the entire satellite global telecommunication system.[66] Weinberg and Hammond,*[67] on the other hand—along with Hubbert—believe that the world's hope lies in the development of nuclear power, for "the energy available in nuclear sources is essentially inexhaustible."

Limits to the Use of Nuclear Power

There are three sorts of constraints, however, on the use of nuclear power. First is the constraint of available technology. Breeder reactors are technologically feasible. Fusion reactors are not, and may

---

*Weinberg and Hammond[67] estimate that 15 million tons of granite would need to be mined and processed each day, if the world's energy economy of the future is based on breeder reactors.

never be. Second is the constraint of the economic cost of the power produced. The present commercial reactors are economically feasible because of low fuel costs, and because of development and insurance subsidies. Breeder reactors have yet to be proved economically feasible, but they probably will be; they will have the advantage of extremely low fuel cost. Third is the constraint of social costs. Reactors which have a high load of radioactivity are inherently dangerous, and care must be taken in design and siting; Dr. Edward Teller[68] insists that reactors should be placed underground, which, if we can judge by Swiss, Belgian, and Swedish experience, would add 4 to 8 percent to the initial capital cost of a powerplant. Radioactive wastes from the present reactor generation need to be managed with more care than they have been, but they pose no great technical or economic problems of safe handling and storage. As the quantity of long-lived radioactive wastes requiring almost perpetual isolation from the biological environment builds up, more care will need to be exercised to construct fail-safe management systems. Thermal effluent from present reactors is a problem, and thermal waste from breeder clusters and from fusion reactors will cause great concern in their siting and operation. Fusion reactors, incidentally, will probably not be as clean as touted,[69] but adequate management of anticipated tritium losses can probably be achieved. Social costs include depletion of nonrenewable resources; in this regard, present reactors are bad, breeders will be relatively good, and fusion reactors very good (if lithium-6 is not required). Social costs also include land and other resources degraded by mining. Present reactors require not too much land disturbance because of mining,[70] breeder reactors a very great deal,[73] fusion reactors using lithium about the same as present reactors, and D-D reactors would require no land disturbance by mining.

Summation

The thermodynamic trend of the universe is toward maximum entropy, or zero available energy. The flow of energy in the world ecosystem is directional and degradational. We can recycle matter and conserve it, but we cannot recycle energy and we can conserve it only in the sense of storage and efficient utilization.

In the sun atomic nuclei are continually trending toward more probable nuclear arrangements and the energy liberated in such

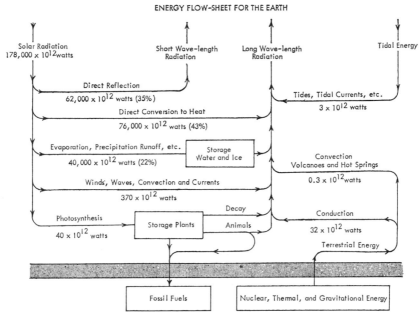

Figure 8-9 World Energy Flowsheet (Hubbert, 1970)

movements is radiated out into space. Some of the radiated energy reaches our own planet (Fig. 8-9); most of that which reaches Earth is either reflected back into space directly (35 percent) or converted into heat and radiated back (43 percent). Almost all of the remaining 22 percent of the solar radiation reaching Earth is used to power the hydrologic cycle. About 0.2 of one percent is used in atmospheric and hydrosperic currents, and about 0.02 of one percent is stored in plants by photosynthesis, and it is from this latter, minute portion of the solar flux that comes all the food necessary to sustain the life of animals, including man.

Over hundreds of millions of years, a further minute fraction of the chemical energy trapped or stored in plants (and some small animals) has been buried under favorable (nonoxidizing) circumstances, preserved, and concentrated to form what we know as fossil fuels—coal and the other solid hydrocarbons or petroleum and the other fluid hydrocarbons. It is this reservoir on which the world now depends for most of its energy supply.

Another kind of energy reservoir is represented by the nuclear, thermal, and gravitational energy within the earth. It has been said that this energy is *frozen* into the earth; by natural processes it slowly *melts* and trickles to the surface as heat flow or geothermal energy. People only recently have begun to learn how to quick-thaw for their own use the nuclear transformations frozen into certain elements of the earth's crust, and they have just started to make use of certain pockets or traps of geothermal energy.

A very small amount of incoming gravitational energy produces the tides of the earth's hydrosphere, which locally can be used as sources of energy.

For purposes of perspective, it is useful to divide the energy sources of our planet into income sources and capital, or fund, sources. Income sources are those of steady direct supply or which represent readily replenishable reservoirs. Fund sources are those which represent energy traps or reservoirs not replenishable on any practical human time scale.

INCOME SOURCES ARE THUS:

    Solar radiation
    Water power

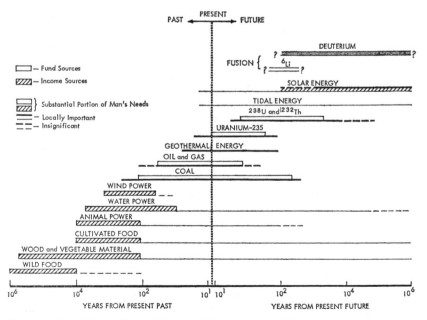

Figure 8-10   Man's Use of Energy Through the Millennia

Wind power
Tidal energy
Photomechanical energy in plants and animals
    Food
    Wood
    Vegetable refuse
Animal (including human) power
Geothermal energy (heat flow)

FUND SOURCES ARE THUS:

Fossil hydrocarbons
    Coal, lignite, peat
    Petroleum
    Natural gas and natural gas liquids
    Oil shale and tar sands
Frozen nuclear transformations:
    Fission
        Uranium-235 (fissile)
        Uranium-238 and thorium-232 (fertile)
    Fusion
        Deuterium (^2H) (quasi-income)
        Lithium-6
Geothermal energy (trapped)

During by far the greatest portion of his existence as a species man has lived off income sources of energy. Only in the past century have the fund sources begun to be exploited on a large scale. Population and standard of living are variables dependent upon energy utilization; both have increased dramatically with our exploitation of fossil fuels, and both are threatened by exhaustion of those fuels within the next few score years. Exploitation of oil shale, tar sands, and uranium-235, as well as new coal technology, can extend appreciably the period of our use of fund sources of energy. Development of breeder reactors based on uranium-238 and thorium-232 will further extend man's grace period and allow for time to control this appetite for energy and to try to develop income sources adequate to the maintenance of a steady-state society.

Breeder reactors, however, will greatly exacerbate the thorny problem of safe management of radioactive wastes. Achievement of controlled fusion reactions and development of practical fusion reactors would not only almost eliminate the radioactive-waste disposal problem but would—if the reaction does not require lithium-

6—represent a quasi-income energy source, because the reserves of deuterium in seawater are so vast.

There is considerable difference of opinion over the real cost of nuclear power from breeder reactors. On the one hand, proponents (Weinberg,[72] Hammond,[73] Weinberg and Hammond[67]) speak optimistically of *unlimited cheap energy* which will allow technology to *fix* the social ills of mankind and eliminate the *have not* regions (Hammond[73]). On the other hand, others[74] point to the enormous capital investment required for practical breeder reactors, where the interest on the fuel inventory alone may be the largest single element in the cost of the power produced; to the costs of safe siting, of environmentally adequate thermal effluent disposal, and of radioactive-waste processing and management, not to mention the great hidden subsidies of insurance, research, and development. They cause one to wonder whether the total cost of such power will be *cheap* by today's standards, and therefore whether the power will really be *unlimited*.

The only true *income* source of energy adequate to the world's needs is solar energy. It is also the only large source of energy (whose utilization appears now to be technologically if not economically feasible) that carries with it no serious waste disposal or ecological problems. Furthermore, it is much less dependent, than fossil or fission energy, on the vagaries of geologic occurrence and political control of the primary sources. The main limitation on the use of solar energy will be economic cost. For these reasons, it might be wise to devote more of our present resources to research and development in this field, while we search for solutions to our short-term energy problems.

If one could increase the efficiency with which energy is converted to usable power, one could make an important move toward alleviating energy needs. The automobile is a good example of inefficient use of energy; its overall efficiency is about 5 percent. On the other hand, fuel cells are theoretically one hundred percent efficient in converting chemical energy to electricity, but they do not appear at the present time to offer much hope of large-scale utilization. The most encouraging development is the continuous improvement in the efficiency of electric power generation. Because electric power is growing in importance (a 9 percent per year growth rate in the United States, compared to a 5 percent growth rate for total energy consumption) and appears likely to continue to do so (when the internal combustion engine is finally banned from our major urban areas, about 1990, battery or flywheel powered vehicles recharged by electricity, will probably take over, thus increasing the electrical demand), the efficiency of power generation is of major importance in conserving fuel resources, as well as in keeping the cost of power down.

Not insignificant either is the increase in efficiency of long-distance electric power transmission over UHV lines. Already this makes possible the transmission of power to urban load centers from mine-mouth thermal plants. In the future it may allow siting of reactor clusters in the Arctic or sub-Arctic, where thermal effluent would enhance rather than degrade the environment, and it may allow transmission of power from haves to have nots, without the latter needing to raise the capital necessary for power generation.

It seems clear, as Hubbert[60] has observed, that the ultimate limit on man's use of energy will be imposed by the principles of ecology. "Sooner or later, man must come to terms with his environment and its limitations."[75] It can also be argued that power's cheapness and availability will in the future, as it does now, depend more and more on the capital available to build generating and distribution facilities, and that, in view of the amply demonstrated reluctance of the haves of this world to share capital with the have nots, the gap between the two in terms of energy—the only true international currency—will not narrow, but will grow larger. Or it may be that the haves and have nots will no longer be separated by geography, but that a thin, tough stratum of *haves* will manage or farm the mass of mankind at some level above subsistence calculated to combat disease and control dissent, and that the population will be adjusted to the resources available in order to maintain this calculated level.

I remind you of what Harrison Brown[65] wrote in 1954:

> ... the first major penalty man will have to pay for his rapid consumption of the earth's nonrenewable resources will be that of having to live in a world where his thoughts and actions are ever more strongly limited, where social organization has become all-pervasive, complex, and inflexible, and where the state completely dominates the actions of the individual.

Because we are altering our environment faster than our cultural evolution can provide species-protective constraints on our actions, it seems further arguable that cost, in the broad sense, can be the only constraint on our ultimate use of energy. If our species is to continue with any large fraction of its members living at a culturally comfortable level, a continual rise in the economic cost of power may be good, instead of bad as Weinberg and Hammond[67] assume, for only cost will cause man to budget his resources, to limit his appetite, and perhaps even to share those resources, short of ecological disaster.

SECTION THREE

ATTITUDES

Seeing the trends and their impact upon the resources, the authors of this section react to some of the critical considerations. Ministers of religion—a Unitarian (William Gold) and a Methodist (James Archibald)—indicate the direction religion must go to deal with macroproblem. An admiral (George Miller) discusses world strategy on and under the seas as a human condition, while another naval officer (retired Captain Gilven Slonim) views the world's oceans differently. A specialist on recreation (Thomas Green) addresses the human capability for playing, within the context of this great threat. A sociologist (Elise Boulding) tries to give scope to those who would *overreact* to the magnitude of the problem. A philosopher-historian (Robert Matthews) asks what role the past can and must play in the future. A journalist (Marya Mannes) dreams of the bend of tomorrowland we must have in Urbana, while a futurist (Charles Williams) rejects the conventional tomorrowland in the face of a traditional ecologist's (Lee Talbott) views regarding preserving the natural treasures. A psychiatrist (Paul Wilcox) examines the prognosis for man's psychological alterations, as does educator and park naturalist (Raymond Nelson). A policy analyst and legal mind (Barry Bruce-Briggs) separates the issues of environmentalism versus conservation to give scope to the process taking place in this period of change, as a behavioral scientist. A planner (Harland Westermann) closes the section on the note of what must be done if sanity is to prevail in dealing with the societal change in geography.

The attitudes-diverse-pluralistic portray the ecological dilemma and give more thoughtful proddings to the reader, who by now must be wondering, "so what," "so whither to, . . ."

[CHAPTER NINE]

THE OCEANIC CONTRIBUTION TO QUALITY LIVING

Gilven Slonim

PACEM IN MARIBUS proclaims an ultimate oceanic aim toward man's future quality of life. With weapons of mass destruction threatening to eradicate civilization, the seas take on increased significance toward providing world stability. But whether peace is to prevail, or warfare is to remain the historic reality, the oceans increasingly can serve man in his search for a better life.

At the outset of the seventies this high level Malta convocation, seeking *peace in the oceans*, observed: "Sea transport has been far and away the major cause that has shaped world history; it is from seaports that modern civilization has developed." This finding affords insight to the deeper cultural aims attending man's turn to the sea.

The seas, as a creative force, succor man's highest powers of mind and spirit. The seafarer, as in the past, represents but a fraction of earth's inhabitants. What remains remarkable is the impact made on civilization by this adventuresome minority of world people. During the centuries that man has sailed the World Ocean, the flow of culture, as well as commerce, moved along the lines of communications across the seas. Exploration followed the sea. Colonization invariably moved in the wake of the seafarer's probing into the perilous realm of the unknown.

Today, there is growing realization that man's future is dependent on his knowledge of the seas and his understanding of their dynamic relationship to human society. Through knowledge of the seas man increases his capacity to satisfy his needs, to support his growth and fulfillment of self.

Individuals' aspirations to build a more attractive world for their children are orchestrated in their struggling effort. The quest for better quality of life is universal. What is still lacking is the concept of what precisely is meant by *quality living*. To determine the sea's portent to serve mankind an understanding of what, in essence, constitutes the higher life must first find expression.

Among the new insights needed is comprehensive knowledge of our dependence on the oceanic world; the dominant portion of our planet.

Quality, at the root of philosophic enquiry, manifestly means different things to different people. Yet, today, the term is at the tip of nearly every tongue, whether futurist, city planner, environmentalist, politician, housewife, or college professor. A heightened crescendo is reached with the conservationists' new-found environmental concern. Lest the quality mode of modern living, at the outset, become a mere cliché, precise humanistic aims must be conceptualized and realistic parameters must be patterned for the pursuit.

The contribution of the oceans, in its substantive aspects, must be woven into our thinking. The seas possess an infinite variety of opportunities for the fulfillment of human potential. Models of human activity on land and on the sea—the entire spaceship earth—can afford a realistic departure point, an incentive, in the drive toward building a better future in its fullest humanistic sense. Mere semantics fall far short in seeking the great goals of the future—in quality living. However lofty the espousal of purposes in our daily utterances and in writings, an uncharted course is a careless way to go about creating better conditions for future enjoyment.

We are obliged to deal with human existence in its most substantive aspects. With an overview of this same substantial sense, the seas hold great promise, with the proviso that man break tradition with his land-bound thinking. Human wants, encompassing the intellectual and philosophic dimension as they do, require that we learn to think anew to gain the full measure of understanding of the treasures that are ours for the knowing in realm of the oceanic world.

At the heart of a better existence is the satisfaction of human wants. But, the problem is as much psychological as it is physiological. Freedom from fear, just as freedom from hunger, is at the base of fuller living. Though material satisfaction is often placed as the first order, the enrichment of life is the core of quality improvement. As the frontier of the future, the seas give promise of serving each of these ends.

A new-found attraction to the oceanic environment reveals this prospect. Seventy-five percent of Americans already live along our coast lines and the Great Lakes. In his book, *The Year 2000*, Herman Kahn[76] predicts, by the turn of the century, the growth of three great megolopolises: the first would extend from Boston to Washington; the second from Chicago to Pittsburgh; and the third from San Francisco to San Diego. All will "show their maritime origins." They will probably "contain roughly one half of the total U.S. population including the overwhelming majority of the most technologically and scientifically advanced, prosperous, intellectual, and creative elements."

With this growing concentration of people along the shoreline their ultimate enlightenment as to the ecological-economic-political importance of the seas to their well being seems assured. If it is leisure that is attracting our people to a closer relationship with the seas, assuredly an educational dimension must follow within the wake of regaining the involvement that was the foundation of the American heritage.

The Constant Struggle to Survive

Life near the sea, or at sea, induces basic changes in life styles and in one's mode of thinking. Action sustains the dynamism of living, passivity falls short as a mode for a fuller life. Action characterizes the life of the sea. For the seafarer, pitted directly against the elements of nature, the struggle to survive is constant.

A person's self-esteem requires productive action. One's well being in world society is gained through the skillful use of one's productive capacity. However desperate one's efforts to gain increased leisure, man's productivity, the cornerstone for true quality living, sustains the strength of his self image. The flow of ideas toward productive growth keeps one vital and alive. These fundamental considerations account for the increasing attraction for people to the world of water.

Anne Morrow Lindbergh's poetic blueprint, *Gift From the Sea*,[11] humanistically sums up the capacity of the World Ocean to add depth to the quality of life:

> The morning swim has the nature of a blessing to me, a baptism, a rebirth to the beauty and wonder of the world.

Starting with this morning plunge, the grace of new worlds for constructive endeavor is gained. The oceans stimulate one's creative capacity while stretching the intellect toward new horizons of self-fulfillment. Just as the seas spur effort, in the dynamic context of true growth, bonds with the community of people are strengthened through pursuit of the sea.

The base of a *warless world* must rest on international understanding and the discipline demanded of humankind for centuries by the oceans wherein the seas have challenged the human race to rise above itself and unite.

Oceanic Recreation—A Fuller Future

Affording a *baptism* for our mushrooming population, today's trend shows an unprecedented recreational attraction to the sea. In the wake of the exodus toward the sea, an intellectual wave toward more profound understanding surely follows. Added educational dimension gives the greatest prospect for fulfillment through our oceanic endeavor. New knowledge is already unlocking expanding fields of personal and professional pursuit as new, nearly limitless oceanic opportunities tending to serve the betterment of mankind unfold.

As Mrs. Lindbergh infers, the present concentration of people along the sea coasts, the waterways, the lakes and rivers is part of groping for quality in their lives—now nearly frantic with the intensity of change. This phenomenal attraction to the water environment arises from increased leisure, a by-product of affluence, the initial quality consideration being enjoyment. Though recreational attraction triggers the trend, mounting overpopulation and the attendant quest for space, both physical and psychological, sustains the drive.

The United States is currently experiencing one of the most rapid rates of sustained population growth in the history of mankind. Lincoln and Alice Day in *Too Many Americans*[78] predict a doubling of our population during the second half of the century, and they point out that recreational use of public lands has more than trebled since the end of World War II. "More of these facilities, if not absolutely essential from the standpoint of physical survival, are certainly essential from the standpoint of the quality of life," they write. Despite the immediate tempering of the alarmists' concern by the recent spectacular decline in the one to five year age group, the population growth warrants continued concern, and ways must still be sought to cope with the population explosion.

The Oceans—Cushion for Overlive Tempo

Beyond the search for enjoyment, the oceans encompassing some three quarters of the earth's surface offer a way to buffer the crescendo of the *overlive* tempo within crowded world population centers and a cushion for the constant land compression. This geographic shrinkage, coupled with an abundance of free time, poses one of the most crucial problems of our twentieth century superindustrialized society. For the first time since the days of ancient Greece and Rome we enter an Age of Leisure, and the search now is to find freedom to enjoy the pleasure of ample time. Quality overtones attend the problem of what to do with mounting spare time—and increasingly, the turn to the sea is to solve the dilemma of leisure hours, to parry rapid change, and to capitalize on the cushioning qualities afforded by the seas' nearly limitless space. More and more people, relieved of the drudgery of routine work through technological advances, seek the pleasure of seabased recreation. Already thirty million Americans swim in the oceans, eleven million are saltwater sport fishermen, and eight million are recreational boat enthusiasts. The increase in outboard motors, from 2.8 million in 1950 to more than 6.1 million by 1961, reflects their mounting water wonderland mobility. The magnetism of the sea mirrors the intensity of their drive to find pleasure. Americans spend one eighth of their take-home incomes on recreation, an amount comparable to the billions appropriated for national defense and education. Is there any wonder *small boats have become big business* in the modern wealthy world?

With the shift from the work ethic to the ethic of pleasure, patently, recreation emerges as an end consideration in quality living. But beyond the frantic race to find pleasure, fulfillment of self remains the great human goal. This new lure of leisure, in itself, creates sharp social and sociological change. Throughout the nearly two centuries of American history, work, for most people, always served as the central interest of life. Now shorter work weeks and the press for retirement at fifty-five creates a mounting need for creative constructive activity to serve the betterment of self rather than one's deterioration. In reorienting our outlook from an Emersonian *perennial nobleness of work* to a *homo luden* pursuit of pleasure, the sea, as a catalyst, enhances man's self esteem and dignity throughout the quality process. In our quest for quality we will seek new conquests, new struggles, and new reasons for our existence; and the oceans of the world can function as a significant stabilizer in the handling of leisure and as a *tour de force* in marshalling our resources for fuller control within our nature. Ever increasing recreational use of the seas bring changes in attitudes and in patterns of living, as well as philosophic perspective. The intensity and delight of a father-son team of scuba divers etches this truism on the mind of even a casual observer.

However grateful Americans may be for machines to do their work and computers to do their thinking, the offshoot of automation regrettably has been the decline of pride in individual work. Liberated free time can lead to the deterioration of self and erosion of resources, unless education reverses the insidious trend. Freedom, coming as it does with the concomitant compression of space, hangs on a hair ready to destroy the very substance from which quality in our lives can be derived. In this uneasy balance the turn toward the seas looms singularly significant, for we learn how well we handle our spare time foretells where we go from here. Mass production became the far reaching spin-off from the nineteenth century Land Grant College program. Today, the Sea Grant College program, established as an oceanic counterpart in 1966, in advancing oceanic understanding and the role of water recreation in alleviating the tension-created ills of mass production process, promises an equally spectacular role.

Tone for Future Living

The higher values, the philosophic-psychological-spiritual dimension of living, are accentuated in determining what constitutes the better quality of life we humans seek. In each category the seas possess a precious potential for adding tonal quality evident symbolically in the zest gained through oceanic activity. Water sports condition one's physical tone. A sense of security, as well as serenity, is gained through involvement in the sea. Beachlife, basically, is vitality restoring, a tension releasing tonic—it antidotes the pressures of a fast moving world. One is able to explore, create, meet others, achieve recognition, compete, or fulfill at sea. Through learning to exhibit our true selves in sea-borne experience, we find a valid test of true value. The ever present consideration of safety, with survival constantly at stake, sustains psychological tone. Visualize the anguish of a person over board in a hurricane swept sea, or even on the calmest day for that matter, to grasp the basic life and death reality of everyday life at sea. There is a daring and dash in heavy weather sailing that peaks the personality. Life at sea stimulates imaginative thinking. Alert and involved, one's ideas flow. There is mental motion, a foundation for creativity—and *doing more with less*. At sea the accent is on action!

On the land, however, passivity is creeping into our lives. The doers of yesterday have now become the viewers of today. However impressively promising, as an instrument of education, television is the chief passivity creating culprit. As TV viewing hours increase, and the national average is now nearing seven hours each day, a sedentary mentality sets in, detracting from the normal drive toward personal achievement. Nor is this passive trend solely confined to television: it spills over into the sports and music, the arts and education as people watch with mounting defiance, challenging the media to *amuse me*! Alas, sand lot baseball has now become an ancient art. So too, the piano-playing, song-singing home fests of the pretube era.

Isn't one's quotient of quality, the feeling of being active, alive and vital? Cannot one consider activities which detract from the realization of the individual's full potential the antithesis of the real values which make life a truly worthwhile experience? Unfortunately, an entire generation reared by television, as a convenient baby-sitter, now moves into the national mainstream. Through a new relationship with the sea, a more activist orientation can be regained and with it, reassurance. To do is to grow.

In *The Year 2000*, Herman Kahn and Anthony Wiener observe, "If the middle third of the 20th century is known as the nuclear era, and if past times have been known as the age of steam, iron, power or the automobile, then the next thirty years may well be known as the age of electronics, computers, automation, cybernation data processing, or some related idea."[76]

Lord forbid!

Seeking an Age of Aquarius

Let us look instead to the next three decades as an age of aquarius. To regain freedom from machines, let us break the bondage imposed by mechanization. Let us generate an innovative oceanic wave of confident creativity. We need to regain the freedom from ills imposed upon man by forces depriving him of quality in his life rather than the passivity and pride destroying activity imposed by electronic marvels. This is not to ignore the conveniences of electronic progress, nor the educational advance gained through modern teaching modes. But, in coming face to face with the question of life's quality, the key consideration remains whether the industrial gods of ostensible progress will continue to be worshipped to the neglect of the human spirit.

The seafarer stands, with a foot in each world, astride of the progress-producing technology, yet always in command of his or her own fate. From his vantage point in emerging civilization he has been a productive force, giving the world many of its industrial breakthroughs. Electric generators were installed aboard ship for a full twenty years before they came into use ashore. Refrigeration was aboard battleships nearly a quarter of a century before it came into use on the land. We produced steel for ships a half century in advance of putting the first steel girder in city buildings.

The Seas as a Great Teacher

The seas already have proven themselves a great teacher in engineering, navigation, and mathematics. Indeed, the seas have forced us to use the capabilities of the mind in order to survive. The mode of thought of those who sail the seas, and their behavior patterns, differ markedly from those of the landed individual. This signals the seas portent to influence future living.

R. Buckminster Fuller, the great innovative mind of our age, as an advocate of a world man and an architect endeavoring to build a world that will work, observes:

> Now there have evolved some new conditions for man and strangely enough as a consequence of our own Navy. The fundamental something I find is the great difference between the ways of thinking about the seas and about the land. It is in no way understood by our world society at large, 99.9 percent of man being landed. And, I find that even though the Navy thinks in a characteristic way, they themselves do not realize the difference in the way they think from the way the landed man thinks.
>
> At sea everything depends on doing more with less, and the doing more with less that came out of the Navy and air has changed the world.[79]

Despite dwindling resources, he points out, in this century a higher standard of living than any kind before is enjoyed by 40 percent of the people. The way we got to taking care of 40 percent of the people is not contained in our economics books, "not a word, not a line, not a chapter," Fuller adds, "It is not in the general policy either." The "doing more with less" is what is hidden away!

Seeing what is opening up on the oceans for man, Fuller emphasizes the curve of doing more with less, from which all unexpected is fallout of the competent, long distance thinking, bringing the blessings of the sea to mankind. Based on this closed cycle spherical thinking, Fuller contends, "Our survival depends upon the kind of thinking that has come out of the sea."

The Oceans—Pathway to the Future

From the dawn of history all that is adventurous and inventive in man has responded to the challenge of the sea. Certainly the utility of the oceans toward giving man a more munificent existence—a better quality of life—must be weighed in the futurist's scenario sketch of *Where we go from here.*

The increasingly complex problems of confronting the modern world encompass the spectrum of human endeavor; the most pressing however, just as Mrs. Lindbergh observes, "fall in the category of man's relationship to man." The conflicts of our times are, indeed, central. Today, despite its promising portent, there is a mounting crisis in the oceans. With problems of pollution, Senator Gaylord Nelson exhorts us to "Stop Killing the Oceans."[80] There is also the pressing need to meet the burgeoning maritime challenge and to regain a competitive oceanic posture. To meet these threats will require education and understanding. There must be a return to the same sound thinking that provided the nation its early sinews of strength to build future greatness.

Unless we preserve our oceanic heritage, the seas can no longer serve us. Indeed, the seas must be saved through environmental integrity and responsibility in our prod for future progress, for the creative strategies for shaping change can readily be constructed through fuller understanding of the oceans and their enlightened use. The seas promise solutions to many serious problems that beset twentieth century people in their struggle to sustain their drive toward a meaningful, productive, enjoyable, and rewarding life during the last third of this century.

The seas relate with eminent directness to people's forward thrust and their future orientation. Maritime history, just as the sagas of the sea, provide a rationale for people looking well forward toward advancing progress. The seafarer, of necessity, is a foremost conservationist. By instinct, experience, and education they deal in boundary-less global terms: they project their thinking well into the future as they prod for greater safety, as a cornerstone to survival and dominance in the unnatural environment. To infuse the citizens of the world with comparable perspective can, indeed, be the most vital contribution derived from the sea. Few have developed this thesis with more convincing clarity than Buckminster Fuller, who accentuates the importance of man understanding the thinking and methodology of the seafarer to profit equitably from the world resources available for their satisfaction.

Resources in the Sea

Population growth is becoming a global problem of crisis proportion. If there are already 1.5 million hungry people in the world, the potential of the oceans to combat famine and despair contributes to the betterment of life. People throughout the world depend increasingly on sea food to meet their dietary needs. The promise of fishmeal protein concentrates and kelp for those living in hunger is but one oceanic potential to meet the resource needs of mankind.

Ambassador Arvid Pardo of Malta[81] developed striking comparisons of relative resource availability between the sea and the land for the United Nations. In his survey of seabed mineral resources the Ambassador found the seas hold one billion tons of aluminium, enough for twenty thousand years at the 1960 world rate of consumption. This is compared to the known land reserves of one hundred years. In addition, 385 billion tons of manganese are held by the oceans, enough for 400,000 years as compared to one century reserve contained in the land. In a more critical area where only a forty year reserve of cobalt remains in the land, Pardo estimates 5.2 billion tons of cobalt are immersed in the oceans—enough for 200,000 years. There is a 150,000 years' supply of nickel reserves in the oceans—only a one century reserve on land. The Ambassador's comparative index of resource availability shows conclusively that people in the future will become increasingly dependent upon the resources of the seas for their survival as well as for the contribution of the seas to human quality of life.

Unlocking the Wealth of the World Ocean

To unlock the wealth of the World Ocean fascinating fields of human endeavor unfold. Man in his turn toward the sea, attracted by the might and the mystery of the world of water, is already directing mounting effort toward tapping the resources of the oceans while prodding for progress in laboratories ashore and at sea. This overall effort in oceanic research, not alone in oceanography, which surprisingly did not achieve major proportions until the last world war, but in all of the sciences of the sea, will provide the springboard for human betterment in the world of tomorrow.

But beyond the water piks, the swift Chris-Craft cabin cruisers, water beds, and missile-firing ballistic nuclear submarines and catamaran sailboats that are creeping into our lives daily to spell betterment of physical living and security, there will be a whole family of spin-offs from today's oceanic research. Cities on and under the sea will follow. Under the ocean restaurants are being constructed in the Virgin Islands, the first indication of things to come spelling greater enjoyment—a more comfortable existence for future generations through increased understanding and more direct involvement with water.

With swifter ships to take us across the oceans on air bubbles at speeds in excess of 100 knots, our material wants can be satisfied more quickly and our strategic needs met more fully. The revolution in oceanic intermodal transport stands to affect the pocketbook of citizens more markedly. These will come along with other things that we do not know about today, as we translate our leisure into idea education, and as a spin-off from more resolute research in the water environment. The seas, as we can readily see, relate with eminent directness to man's forward thrust and to his future orientation, to the delight of the macro-historians.

The New Educational Thrust

With growing recognition by all but arch-apostles of the past, that our educational process is showing signs of becoming archaic, students sense the educational process has less relevance, and a dramatically new kind of education looms in the offing. It demands new intellectual approaches to turn today's crises into tomorrow's opportunities. Through the medium of multidisciplinary oceanic education, the new thrust toward deeper insights and a more comprehensive grasp of our great globe and complex endeavor is within reach. This innovative educational process can become basic not only in *helping people to survive, but to crest the wave of change;* to grow and to gain a new sense of mastery over their own destinies. It can become the test of the relevance of future education in meeting our opportunities.

The oceans affording this new dimension of understanding can become the predominant medium in our management of change. Our increasing involvement in the oceans means altering our larger patterns of life, so that a radically new orientation toward the future will emerge. To the extent that we bring the oceans into our thinking, as well as into our lives, a marked measure of success toward making our world work will be gained. Already there are strong indications that our new-found attraction to the seas will stimulate development of an intellectual dimension with equal intensity. The emerging new ideas, new approaches, new educational creativity stemming from the increasing attention the oceans command will result in an entirely new educational approach relevant to the citizens of tomorrow. Great centers for oceanic advancement are being charted by educators. These centers can attract the scholars and scientists, as well as students, in a noncompartmentalized, multidisciplinary quest of learning and the lore of the sea. The nerve center of the new oceanic oriented pursuit of knowledge will, in turn, serve as the springboard for studies and research in the environment of the sea.

World universities at sea are part of the future planning process to teach students the seas in the environment of the World Ocean, where the geo-economics of the oceans can be learned while living daily with the global geographic facts of life which accentuate the humanities of the sea as well as the sciences of the sea. Global oceanic parks will be constructed at the interface of the beautiful land and water environments worldwide, and these parks will also become centers of ocean learning for people of all ages, all nations, all colors, all religions. They will be linked by multichanneled educational television to make the learning process truly global in nature and to bring the peoples of the world into closer communications through the intellectual vitality stimulated by the oceans. To program the oceanic research requirement of mankind a Manhattan Maritime Project is envisaged, and maritime industrial parks will develop at urban universities near the great industrial centers of the nation as their orientation bespeaks of the Great American Dream with a sprinkling of salt water.

Oceanic Cushion for Future Shock

That Alvin Toffler in his brilliant book, *Future Shock*,[4] should turn to the oceans in search of the antidote to the shock systems he reveals in our society accentuates a largely overlooked quality consideration. Toffler proposes a starting point for getting out of the *hurricane's eye* of change through indoctrination of youth in the oceanic environment:

> even now we should be training cadres of young people for life in submarine communities. Part of the next generation may well find itself living under the oceans. We should be taking groups of students out in submarines, teaching them to dive, introducing them to underwater housing materials, power requirements, the perils and promises involved in the invasion of the oceans.[4]

Manifestly, the potential the oceans possess for conditioning and cushioning *Future Shock* lies in three broad dimensions: geographic space, psychological dampening, and futuristic education. In calling for a starting point, Toffler himself may not entirely comprehend the conceptual blueprint in his suggestion for future education to bolster our increasing relationship with the environment of the sea. He accentuates the role of the specialist in the super-industrialized society of the future. Yet, paradoxically, his entire thesis supports Buckminster Fuller's contention that a plurality of generalists are needed to make out future world work. The vast, nearly limitless laboratory of the World Ocean is tailor-made to train people for their world of tomorrow. If the seas are to teach us anything, it is that our strength is not in our muscles, our strength is in our minds. If quality life in the future is to depend upon psychological accommodation to these changes, then the seas serving as the educator of tomorrow's generation will unquestionably achieve a societal service of the utmost significance.

Caviar, steaks, and salads, though served with bubbling champagne, do not necessarily connote high quality of life. Yet, succulent, well seasoned salmon caught on sportsman's rod, crisply fried at rivers-edge campsites, convey a zestful involved way of life. In each instance the measure is intensity of living and the vibrant satisfaction of a fullness of existence beyond Macy's bargain basement values. Nor is the gross national product a true measure beyond that of mere affluence. The real test of quality can never be realized through financial fluidity any more than in meeting material needs. Quality is spun from the satisfaction of human wants cycled through emotions moving us toward physical and intellectual self-fulfillment. The delicate quality that places the extra pinch of pepper inevitably is philosophic and founded on true values.

New Discipline Oceanic Education Launched

The readiness of the oceans to serve mankind in a fuller sense in the future, most interestingly, is reflected in the emergence of new multidisciplinary thrust in the American educational process termed Oceanic Education. The intellectual vision of the recognized educator Edgar F. Shannon, Jr., President of the University of Virginia, is observed in the launching of this new educational discipline through his announcement of a new pilot research credit course in continuing education titled the *Humanities of the Sea Course,* in co-sponsorship with the Oceanic Educational Foundation. Dr. Shannon announced the course in this premise:

> Man's future is dependent on his knowledge of the seas and his understanding of their dynamic relationship to his society. In no facet of education do the seas receive sufficient curriculum and program emphasis to impart comprehensive knowledge of the dependence of mankind in the World Ocean. Even in Maritime Nations the disparity between the land and the sea in research, and scientific and scholarly studies is pronounced. Historically, those nations that have carried trade have prospered. Yet, the interrelation of maritime activity with a nation's economy is not well understood. In this aspect and in the political, scientific, ecological, recreational, cultural and other areas, education and research are necessary to the fulfillment of mankind.[82]

Dr. Horace M. Kallen, distinguished philosopher of the New School of Social Research, who lectured on *Peace, Prosperity—The Philosophy of the Sea* at the University during this maiden maritime course, gives this definition of the new discipline of Oceanic Education:

> It should consist of teaching the people from childhood on through the nation's schools of all levels: What the oceans are; how through the history of human culture, they have affected life and growth in civilization as resources for certain kinds of food, medicines, minerals—as avenues of transportation and cultural communications. What role the oceans play in the religious thinking of the world's people. The balance sheet of oceanic help and harm. The dangers from the works of man-pollution and the tide as they menace the composition, the life, and the land-water relationship of the oceans—and ecology. Oceanic education should facilitate adding to this knowledge and rendering it a part of the funded mentality of all our people. Toward these ends, it should make possible new professions, new vocations, and new careers, parallel to the innovations on land and in the air.[83]

In William Wordsworth's, *Lines Composed a Few Miles Above Tintern Abbey*, a grasp of oceanic quality emerges:

> A sense sublime
> Of something far more deeply interfused,
> Whose dwelling is the light of setting suns,
> And the round ocean and the living air,
> And the blue sky, and in the mind of man;
> A motion and a spirit, that impels
> All thinking things, all objects of all thought,
> And rolls through all things.[84]

How well Wordsworth describes this the World Ocean belonging to no person, but the priceless possession of all mankind. The seas call constantly for excellence to meet its tasks, and yet refresh as they discipline minds of man. For quality of life unequivocally stems from one's mind, and it is in this realm that the oceans will make life a fuller, more worthwhile, more profound experience.

[CHAPTER TEN]

TOMORROW'S RELIGION

WILLIAM GOLD

W E ARE TOLD that religion is changing. The question is, is it changing enough? Is it changing in basic ways that will make it a creative factor in helping us solve the problems which confront us, or is it merely changing in superficial ways that are designed primarily to recoup membership losses and bolster sagging attendance figures?

To be sure, the mass has been set to jazz and to rock and roll, but the message is still the story of salvation purchased by blood sacrifice. The gospels have been printed in newspaper format, with plenty of pictures, but they are still the story of a Jewish preacher of two thousand years ago trying to deal with the messianic hopes of his friends and neighbors while assuring them that the world was coming to an end. The churches have tried all manner of approaches in an effort to minister to people, but by and large they still insist on ministering in terms of a concept of human nature that is at odds with contemporary knowledge.

To some the situation seems hopeless. The church should be written off as irrelevant and religion left to go its own way while science and technology wrestle with our burgeoning problems. One sympathizes with such views. Yet there are tremendous forces resident in religion and various religious organizations. Suppose they could be related to solving the problems through basic reforms. What steps would be necessary?

People have always faced problems, and religion has usually been one of the tools they have employed to try to interpret and solve the problems. Sometimes the interpretation was made to serve as the solution. Thus, when people sought an answer to the question of their origins, the stories they created did not really prove anything, but they did provide answers. Unfortunately, once people became relatively satisfied with the answers, they began to grant these special status, and it became difficult to change the answers to adjust to new evidence.

Thus, one of the biblical stories of creation granted man an original state of perfection from which he fell, through disobedience, to the divine will. The resulting *sinful state of human nature* has been a basic concept in much religion, education, discipline, and punishment. Today, in spite of considerable evidence that we are born neither good nor bad, we continue to labor under the guidance imposed by some primitive storyteller's imagination.

We need to recognize the origins of religion in human needs. Regardless of how it is verbalized or ritualized, religion consists of the attitudes and beliefs and values a man or woman uses to relate to his or her world. One has to meet basic physical needs in order to survive. Certain rules and regulations have to be embraced in order to live with others. Certain interpretations have to be formulated in order to deal with them.

In times past, when fewer people shared the world and moved about less in doing so, local cultures had a degree of homogeneity. Generation after generation shared the same setting, experiences, problems, hopes, fears, and religion. The same religion sufficed for generations because the world they experienced remained much the same. Interpretations of the unknown remained unchanged because the unknown remained pretty much unchanged. Value systems endured because the problems they dealt with endured in much the same form.

It made sense to condemn birth control and abortion when a high birth rate was essential to the preservation of the tribe. It was equally sensible to claim a unique relationship to one's god if some binding force were necessary to hold a tribe together. It was reasonable to invest particular religious beliefs with divine authority when they remained valid so long that their human origins were lost to history.

For most of human life on earth most men and women have lived much in the manner of their ancestors. Their individual, private, subjective worlds of experience have had much in common. The more they intermarried, the less they travelled, the more they sought to hold fast to traditions handed down from generations past, the more nearly their individual worlds matched.

Since their religions were devised to enable them to explain their experiences, those who shared similar worlds could subscribe to the same religion. The more people there were who found a particular religion meaningful, the more authoritative that religion would seem to be. Of course there were changes during the years, but the changes occurred at such a pace that religion could evolve and still seem to remain stable or even absolute.

Then technology began to speed up the process of change, and with greater changes occurring faster and faster, fewer people found themselves sharing the same world. Increased mobility lessened the likelihood of one's staying in the same community where one's father and grandfather lived. Rapid industrialization and urbanization created new worlds for the younger generation even if it elected to stay in the same place. Improved health conditions prolonged life and increased the population. Today we not only have more people in the world than ever before; we also have them living in more different individual experiential worlds. We have moved from a period where the majority in any given culture shared similar backgrounds, and thus lived in similar worlds which overlapped rather than impinged on each other, to a time when more and more people live in dissimilar worlds which are crowded closer and closer together and which necessarily conflict with each other because they lack many of the common elements which would enable them to overlap. A classic example of our dilemma is to be found in the *golden rule* which appears in one form or another in each of the great living religions.

In a homogeneous culture where the individual worlds experienced by the culture's members tend to have much in common, the epitome of consideration for others is to treat them as one would like to be treated. Under such circumstances, one could reasonably expect that others, sharing one's own experiences and values, would appreciate being treated as one would wish to be treated oneself.

The golden rule was an excellent guide to cooperative living in cultures where individual worlds tended to be similar to one another. As long as cultures did not exchange members in great numbers, and as long as cultures did not change themselves very much, the golden rule worked satisfactorily in most human relations. In fact, its longtime validity and widespread acceptance have tended to make it seem like an absolute.

Then technology made its vast contributions to life's possibilities. Cultures changed rapidly, not only from generation to generation, but even within a generation. More and more people moved about more and more. Old barriers to socialization and marriage began to fall. The individual worlds which impinged on one's own world became more and more different from one's own world—and even from each other. Under such circumstances, to treat another as one would wish to be treated might very easily constitute an insult rather than a compliment. The golden rule, cornerstone of human relations for centuries, became increasingly inadequate.

Americans, cherishing democracy, sought to bestow it upon the rest of the world, but many of those to whom we offered our greatest discovery were not interested. Some of them did not even understand what it was we were trying to give them.

Parents, cherishing hard-won amenities, sought to pass them on to their children, but in many instances the children had grown up in worlds so different from their parents' that their values were ordered by different priorities. As a result neither generation was able to convey respect by trying to treat the other as it wished to be treated.

Even as religions' most practical guideline was thus being discounted, its more ephemeral concepts, which had once served practical purposes, were also losing status under the impact of our enlarging knowledge. Deities who once served very useful purposes as the acknowledged controllers of various forces lost stature as we found better explanations for the course of history, the shape of the weather, and the success of our crops. Rituals which once provided a sense of security were found to do so because of the individual's response to them rather than because of their own innate validity or any divinely ordained power they contained. Symbols which inspired awe and devotion were analyzed in terms of psychological conditioning rather than attributed supernatural power.

As our knowledge of the universe grew, our control over our individual personal worlds also took new forms. Although we have not achieved anything approximating full control of our worlds, we have gained enough control to cause us to begin to question the degree of control exercised by any god. This beginning doubt has had devastating effects.

It is almost axiomatic that a well developed religion must be a coherent whole to meet all of the contingencies possible in the world to which it ministers. One of the best examples of this in our time has been Roman Catholicism. It was so well thought out and put together that one could hardly think of a question that had not already been anticipated and answered. Given a well ordered Roman Catholic world, Roman Catholicism was precisely what that world's owner needed. And so millions of Roman Catholics grew up in Roman Catholic homes, attended Roman Catholic schools, belonged to Roman Catholic scout groups, joined Roman Catholic veteran organizations, and lived Roman Catholic lives. Their religion may well have seemed to them to be composed of absolutes because it was so well adapted to their needs.

Then, bit by bit, cracks began to appear in the walls which protected the Roman Catholic world. The spirit of ecumenism permitted contact with other faiths, acknowledging by implication at least that there might be other paths to the truth. Age-old customs, which had seemed irrevocable, were adjusted to meet changing needs, causing shadows of doubt to fall on still other practices which had seemed immutable. The Pope, realizing that the authority of the Roman Church was being threatened, has sought to stabilize matters by standing fast on certain teachings. Unfortunately, he has chosen for his understandable purpose such areas as birth control and celibacy where the logic of past conditions no longer seems so reasonable. So we see in the Roman Church today some of the turmoil that occurs when an *infallible* religion that has remained relatively stable for a long period begins to try to adjust to a world that is different from the one it has interpreted so long.

Similar adjustments are occurring in other churches. They are less noted because they are less spectacular. Sometimes they are less spectacular because they have been in process for some time. All of this is to point out that inherited religions, well adapted to the time and place of their origin, and only slightly less well adapted to the slowly changing circumstances of intervening years, no longer relate adequately to rapidly changing conditions; and therefore no longer can command the loyalty and devotion they have received in the past.

This situation is both necessary and regrettable. It is necessary because we cannot turn back the clock and eliminate the changes wrought by science and technology. It is regrettable because religion is losing influence at the very time when people need new guidelines to help them find their way in changing worlds.

In what direction should religion move in order to fulfill its mission in helping people live life to the full in these days of rapidly changing society built upon a vast technology? To begin with, religion must be satisfied with relative truths, even as is science. Unfortunately, religion has so oversold the idea of its authority in terms of certain absolutes that the promoting of relative truths seems a poor substitute. Once religion has begun to update its teachings on a regular basis and people find that the constantly revised teachings are more reliable than the old dogmas, relative truths will be accepted, and they will afford a much more stable basis than absolutes accepted half-heartedly. Further, religion must realize the growing necessity for each individual to grow a personal set of beliefs. Individual worlds call for individual religions.

The job of the church in the future will not be to seek to impose uniformity of belief, but to reconcile diversity of belief so different people living in different worlds can relate to each other harmoniously. As a step in this direction, the church, making use of the information available, will switch from emphasis on saving souls to emphasis on creating souls. If we consider the attributes of human life which distinguish it from other forms of life as being at least in some ways representative of this *soul*, it is increasingly obvious that both humanness and the *soul* are the products of humans living together.

Much as we might prefer to think otherwise, we are not born human. The infant is born with a potential for achieving those qualities which we consider the hallmarks of humanness, but their development is an acquisition, not an inherited possession. Language, conscience, upright gait, *human spirit,* all come from associating with other humans. This fact accounts for the long period of time it took for humanness to develop and the further fact that varieties of humanness were able to mingle and enrich each other only in comparatively recent times. If humanness were inherited, its quality should have been high from the beginning. As an acquired characteristic, it has had to be learned generation by generation, and its varieties might easily be lost or minimized.

As an acquired characteristic, humanness has been related to the quality of the humans from which it was acquired. If religion taught them that they were innately evil, the resulting attitudes could hardly help having a depressing influence on the quality of humanness they passed on. Of course this may have been beneficial to the church since it helped to create a demand for the salvation which religion has traditionally offered. But the time has come when the church must put aside the task of saving souls for some hoped-for hereafter and concentrate on the creating of souls for life in the now. This it can do by inaugurating educational programs designed to help adults understand their humanness and how to transmit its best features to future generations.

Mankind still seeks fellowship. Mankind still desires guidelines with which to interpret human needs and experience. The church and religion can continue to minister to mankind. But to do so, they will have to accept the fact that the changes wrought by science and technology have changed the nature of our worlds to such a great degree that superficial alteration of past practices and window-dressing disguising of old rituals no longer suffice.

The religion of the future must once again draw upon all of our experiences in order to provide guidance for their enjoyment and use with a minimum of conflict. The complexity of this task in the light of our continuing changes in society means that religion must be ever renewing itself. The security that it offers will no longer be the security of changelessness. Rather it will be the assurance that change can be for the better.

[CHAPTER ELEVEN]

THE CHURCH, PEOPLE, AND THE FUTURE

James P. Archibald

THERE ARE TWO opposing attitudes prevailing in contemporary religious thought. They are identifiable in an exchange between the master of ceremonies of a television *talk show* and the famous Harvard Divinity School professor Harvey Cox. The MC asked Professor Cox if he agreed with those who felt that we were witnessing the end of the religious era. The professor replied to the contrary by saying he believed we are in the pre-Christian, rather than the post-Christian era. He then went on to say that religion, which for centuries has been bottled up in air-tight institutionalism, is now breaking out into a new relevance. Many of the institutional patterns will change, and some will disappear.

A comparison of the personal goals of the clergyman of twenty years ago and the goals of the contemporary seminarian are illustrative of this change of focus. Two decades ago most clergymen struggled to perfect their homiletical skills and took pride in their oratorical abilities. They dreamed of the day when they would preside over a congregation which supported an edifice having a large (usually single-purpose) sanctuary, where great crowds would come to hear them preach. The dream was embellished with the vision of a high spire, which could be seen from great distances and be known as the highest structure in the community. Little consideration would be given to the needs of individual neighborhoods, as everyone would need to *hear the word of the Lord.* At least one denomination designed a building that could be built any place. Believing that the needs of all people were alike, they thus sought to reduce the cost of individual architects.

The student completing his seminary training today is more interested in being a leader of dialogue than in monologue preaching. He is unimpressed by the idea of a large congregation seated in rows of pews that are screwed down to the floor, because he views this as merely an audience for a performance. He would prefer preaching to small, but involved groups who pull their chairs into a circle (or maybe even sit on the floor) to plan a strategy for action. He, likewise, is not impressed with a beautiful edifice in which to sing and talk about brotherly love, but sees it as a financial extravagance. He is more interested in human investments than in brick and mortar expenditures.

The changes that are occurring are not the result of any single factor, nor are they merely a desire to be modern. They have come about as a result of the changing conditions of human life, changes which are due to the pressures of many different problems assailing us. Religious leaders, like leaders in other disciplines, cannot ignore them. Each problem is so significant that we tend to look at each one and say, "This is the cause." However, no one problem can be blamed for this rapid change in the human environment, but rather a merging of many complex factors into one all-permeating anxiety that gnaws at the human consciousness.

Dr. George Borgstrom, a leading biologist, in speaking to a meeting of the United Methodist Church's Board of Evangelism, said:

> . . . During the past several generations, religion has been more or less identified with a belief in technology, and we seem to have forgotten that man is a temporary visitor to earth, and we have the duty of guarding the riches of earth.

Dr. Borgstrom's appearance was arranged by the Department of Population Problems of the Board of Christian Social Concerns, with headquarters across the street from the U. S. Capitol. This Board is the successor to Methodism's Board of Temperance, which, twenty years ago, had as its single purpose the abolition of the liquor industry. Today it addresses itself, not to total abstinence from alcohol, but to the problem of alcoholism and also to many social issues which it recognizes as having an influence on human life.

The denomination has officially declared itself on one of the central issues facing mankind which is called a *Population Crisis Resolution*[86]:

> The population explosion brought on by medical and technological advances in the prolonging of life poses for man an unprecedented threat. The strong possibility of mass starvation looms ahead in some nations, with its concomitant of social upheaval. The rapid depletion of natural resources faces many countries.
>
> The quality of our lives is increasingly threatened as runaway population growth places staggering burdens upon societies unable to solve even their present growth problems.
>
> The population explosion threatens rich and poor nations alike. Poor nations find themselves on a treadmill of misery as their population growth offsets to a considerable extent their economic growth. Several affluent nations, like the U.S., though growing more slowly, will still double their population every sixty to eighty years if present growth rates continue.

A full-scale effort must be made to stem the flood. Other religious bodies have declared themselves in a like manner, recognizing the threat that the population explosion is to our general welfare. The rapid acceleration of the individual human being's competition for survival makes people enemies of each other. The waning supply of natural resources, together with increasing technological change and the accompanying pollution of water and atmosphere, puts society on a suicide course.

Scientific and technological advancements have produced factors that religion must cope with. Within a span of but twenty years, the moon has been explored, the laser has been developed, and we have produced birth control pills, vaccines for diseases as serious as polio, and the first drug to correct defective brain chemistry (L-dopa for Parkinsonism). Although the astounding progress in medical research during the past decade has made it possible to prolong human life in many ways, we must realize that this very progress will only aggravate the problem of *too many people* with finite resources for their support. Said Maurice F. Strong, Secretary-General of the United Nations Conference on the Human Environment, "We are now producing more changes in one generation in the natural systems on which our own life and well-being—our humanity—depend than in the whole of our previous history—creating risks which we still cannot assess . . . We are, in sum, in danger of destroying or desecrating the vital resources of the natural environment which we require to sustain us."[87]

In view of this, says Norman Faramelli, "we must not ask where science and technology are taking us, but rather how we can manage science and technology so that they can help us get where we want to go."[88] Senator Robert Packwood, on the floor of the Senate, said:

> If we are really concerned about our quality of life now, and what it will amount to in the near and distant future, we ought to get more methodically on with the task of identifying what we want, and then identifying what human forces we will have to redirect in order to assure the achievement of that quality on a sustained basis. There are many constraints we will have to face up to, and better now than later, as delay only makes the problems ever more difficult to solve.[89]

We must assert the values we want to live by.

The tragic state of our national priorities faces the contemporary religious community as it deals with moral values. In the twenty-five year period from 1946 to 1971 our country has been preoccupied with making war, and the military has devoured more than $1,000,-000,000,000. This continues at the rate of $200,000,000 per day.[90] If the choice of newspaper headlines provides a strong indication of priority in the public mind, the Wednesday, September 22, 1971, edition of *The Washington Post* was certainly illustrative. The day before, the Senate has passed a Draft-Extension Bill without an End-the-War Amendment, after weeks of bitter debate. This is a bill which threatened to disrupt the lives of all the youthful generation for at least two years; however, the morning's headline, and four-column front page picture, dealt with the transfer of the Washington Senators baseball team to Texas. The questionable Vietnam election procedures, the drug problem of returning GI's, the infamous black market, all point to the detrimental effects of pouring out our national resources to make war; but, ignoring all that had been said in this regard, Congress passed legislation that affected a whole generation, and the newspapers, reflecting the public interest, considered it of less importance than an athletic event.

Recognizing these problems—advancing population with depletion of natural resources, accompanying pollution, competition for survival, and the general populace's unconcern about priorities—one must ask whether religion can still speak to the needs of the day and to the changing needs of the future. Perhaps this can best be envisioned by looking at the Church's past, evaluating its ability to be flexible, and examining some current trends.

Ours is not the first era in which people have asked these kinds of questions. The so-called Dark Ages were so dark that there was barely enough intellectual light to produce a questioner, to say nothing of a solution. As recently as two hundred years ago, religion was enmeshed in such theological webs that it was almost completely *other worldly*. The corruption that impregnated the Christian Church during the pre-Reformation era makes it almost unidentifiable as a church in our contemporary understanding. In almost every era there have been the prophets of doom who have insisted that they were witnessing the imminent death of religion. Some of these have been extremely knowledgeable people like Marquis de Condorcet in the eighteenth century[91] and Pierre Joseph Proudhon[92] in the nineteenth century, as well as the famous predictions of Karl Marx,[93] particularly in his early writings.

While institutional structures and attitudes have changed, and will continue to change, religion will not disappear. Basically, humans remain religious, for some of their basic psychological needs can only be met with a spiritual emphasis. Those qualities that were evident in mankind in his early evolutionary history are qualities that are inherent in the most sophisticated of modern man.

A chronological study of the scriptures which guide the Church shows a distinct growing process in our understanding and is illustrative of the kind of change that will continue into the future. It took at least 17 hundred years for the material which has been compiled into the modern Christian Bible to be written. The emphasis in the earliest portion is on justice (rewards for goodness and punishment for evil), which was to be rigidly enforced. The later portions, however, show a distinct change of focus, to that of love and forgiveness.

Though no new material has been included in the canon, religious people are still pursuing this growing process. The ethical questions dealt with in the ancient Commandments still provide us with a foundation for a personal moral code, but modern man is finding new ways and new vehicles to express his religious commitment. The scriptural emphasis on compassion serves as a guide to those who transfer that ancient mandate into medical research, social service, population control, educational challenges, etc.

Rather than asking whether the Church *can* speak to this era, one needs to ask whether religious bodies can be sufficiently flexible to *allow* religion to speak to contemporary humankind. The flexibility that provides for human adaptation is essential to a religion that is to survive. The emergence of *situation ethics* is an attempt to provide this dimension. One illustration is the drastic change that has been seen in recent decades regarding abortion. While there are those who are still rigidly quoting the Commandment, *Thou shalt not kill,* there is an increasingly large number who are insisting that, in order to make a responsible ethical decision one must take into consideration the plight of a deformed child or the conditions under which an unwanted child must live. The Protestant Church of today stresses only *responsible* parenthood.

The attitudes regarding divorce are being looked at in a like manner. There are those who maintain that *till death do us part* eliminates all divorce, but there are others who stress that inherent in the Judao-Christian religion is the concept of forgiveness and the recognition that human error is possible. They would compare the tragedy of divorce to the greater tragedy of maintaining a hate-producing relationship.

This flexibility lifts religion to an intellectual dignity that is above the definitions given by its critics, who see it merely as a hold-over from our irrational superstitions. Because it is adaptable and reasonable, religion has a future.

The late Bishop James Pike described our society as having a declining interest in the Church, but an increasing interest in religion. The first part of his statement might be questioned, in light of the fact that in the United States church membership statistics may not give a complete picture, other factors cannot be ignored. For instance, books such as *Honest to God*[94] and *Situation Ethics*[95] have demanded wide publication, and the recent *death-of-God* controversy stirred great interest. The so-called *Jesus Movement* and popular religious productions such as *Jesus Christ Superstar*[96] have attracted the attention of America's youthful generation—a generation which seems to be searching for something to give fulfillment to their more spiritual yearnings. The addition of courses (if not complete departments) dealing with religion on college campuses is a post-World War II phenomenon that cannot be ignored. Some of these are in schools which had neglected the subject until the present era, when students have demanded it.

Another trend of the modern Church is that denominationalism, certainly in Protestant Christianity, is fading. The issues which once divided the Church into denominational groups are insignificant in light of the problems that confront everyone's struggle for survival. Denominations are becoming administrative and social entities, rather than representations of individual beliefs. Theological seminaries are cross-pollinating students and faculty denominationally. The world mission enterprises no longer compete or duplicate each other, for the major efforts are coordinated to eliminate this practice. Sectarian enterprises are yielding to Councils of Churches on both the national and local levels.

With the current trend toward individuality, it would seem fair to assume that the so-called *underground Church* movement will continue. Rather than having a Catholic or Protestant affiliation, or a denominational bond, these groups are bound by a specific need and a common means of religious expression. Most of them are small, intimate groups, meeting in homes or facilities that are less formal than the conventional church building. Thus far, most of them are in urban communities, though not determined by geographical neighborhoods. They are dissatisfied with the luke-warm sense of mission and need more than the sociability of a *friendly neighborhood church*. Generally speaking, their members have lost faith in conventional church structures and feel that theirs is a subtle protest against those traditions.

Another change that will be a part of the religious scene of the future is that its structure for existence will not be merely in the framework of a worshiping congregation. Though this framework will continue in various forms, religion will increasingly find expression in various mission groups. Perhaps the most familiar counterpart on the contemporary religious scene is the Salvation Army, whose purpose is to serve the lower socioeconomic groups in our society. A less familiar illustration might be the Washington, D.C. organization know as FLOC (For Love of Children), which grew out of the experimental ecumenical Church of the Savior and seeks to find homes for the homeless children of the city. Other mission groups might be in the form of choral societies (like the Mormon Tabernacle Choir) or those finding religious outlet in some other form of art.

An organizational religious structure that may supplement the worshiping congregation in the future may be the research team, such as the newly formed Institute for the Study of Human Reproduction and Bioethics at Georgetown University. This will bring Catholic, Protestant, and Jewish religious thinkers together with social and physical scientists and physicians, to conduct coordinated research into the ethical and scientific aspects of human reproduction, now that medical technology has made possible instances where people will be reasonably tempted to *play God*.

Being aware of the pressures that problems of human survival present, and having the new and varied religious organizational structures, people will also have a new kind of religious belief. Rather than being dependent on sacraments, liturgical forms, or traditional creedal statements, the religious person will find his way into a religion that is based on his own personal spiritual search. It will have less mysticism and more of an ethical emphasis. Perhaps this is best illustrated by the changing attitude of those who wear the clerical garb. Twenty years ago they wore vestments and behaved in ways that would set them apart from the laity. Today they are seen on the picket lines, in peace vigils, or socializing with the people they serve. Their activity is in every social stratum and seeks to have influence far beyond religious circles. The sacred and the secular, in the closing years of the twentieth century, will become more unified.

T. J. Gordon,[97] speaking before the Conference on Religion and the Future, said:

> Churches today are more than custodians of the symbols, rituals, and cultural history of the religions which they interpret. They are (or have been) welfare agents, educators, acculturators, employers, medical healers, sanctifiers, social directors, instruments of social status moralizers, hope givers, politicians, and social critics.

This broad influence is waning, however. The old concept of the *parson*, meaning *leading person in the community*, or of the rabbi—*the teacher*—is being diluted, as other, better equipped professions emerge and other agencies meet the needs which previously were exclusively the responsibility of the Church. This is as it should be. The Church should be the stimulant, but not necessarily the doer of every good deed. Educational institutions at all levels were begun by the churches and synagogues but can be more efficiently operated by the government, with the much larger financial resources that powers of taxation make available. A similar phenomenon can be seen in the health and welfare systems. This puts the Church in the challenging position of perceiving needs and stimulating the channels for solution.

Gordon[97] pointed out, at the previously-mentioned conference, that society's perception of the role of the Church in questions related to specific moral behavior is also changing:

> Less than ever before, it seems, do values of society stem directly from the Church. People now follow other drummers.

> To be sure, today's value systems are being built on the base laid by Judao-Christian principles, but what dimensions will they assume in the future, and what will be the Church's response to these unfamiliar modes which grow from new technology and the popular ideologies?

One of the factors which must be recognized as rising on the religious horizon is the variety of religious cults that are dependent on manufactured stimulants, a by-product, in large measure, of the youth-drug culture. The origin of such groups goes back into the centuries, but their prominence is only recent. Some within the conventional religious community insist it is only a passing fad, but only time will determine this. The Native American Church, which now numbers over 200,000 members, has made a sacrament, in corporate worship, of the eating of peyote (derived from a small cactus which is sliced and dried), believing that by so doing they absorb part of the power of God, since God put the power in the cactus to begin with. Other psychedelic churches operating in the United States which are dependent on drugs for religious experience must be recognized by the perceptive observer, particularly as the prospects of wider drug usage becomes more socially and legally acceptable.

Professional religious leaders have been reluctant to acknowledge that the Church has played a role in community life as the social and recreational center. Though it has always insisted that this is a secondary function; the quilting bees, church suppers, and bingos have filled many leisure hours and, particularly in rural areas, have constituted a community's primary social activity. This may be an increasingly important function in the future as leisure time becomes more abundant. Personal income is rising three times as fast as the population, and gadgets continue to replace the need for human hands. Multiple-family homes are housing an increasing percentage of our population and demand less of their occupants. If the welfare of the whole person is to be a consideration of the Church, the use of leisure cannot be ignored.

The changes in sexual mores have created new demands upon the Church. While these changes are polarizing the opponents and proponents of change, such developments demand that religious people look at their own basic ethical standards of human acceptance and brotherhood and less at their traditional legalism. Within a decade, we have seen homosexuality transformed from total rejection as *immoral* to acceptance of *gay* congregations by established denominations. The stigma that was once attached to divorce is being replaced by sympathetic programs of marriage counseling and the organization of such groups as Parents Without Partners and Divorcees Anonymous. There are some signs of greater acceptance on the part of the Church of communal living.

The increasing rate of mobility seen in our society is an issue to be faced by the religious community. Today the average American family moves once every five years, unlike a generation ago, when our predominantly rural population lived on farms that were originally homesteaded and passed from one generation to another. The study of future growth patterns indicate that this migrant pattern will continue to develop. Some forecasters are saying that we will see as much construction of new buildings in the next fifty years as we have seen in the entire history of our nation up to this point. This migration also means that established communities will undergo social change and that their needs will change.

Perhaps we will see history repeat itself. The earliest portions of the Old Testament were written by those who lived in a migratory culture, their place of residence being determined by the condition of the pasture. They devised a portable house of worship, called a *tabernacle*, which could be dismantled and taken with them or adapted to the needs which the time demanded.

We are going to have to look at our *real estate hang-up*. All across the country, we find congregations burdened by the existence of huge, single-purpose sanctuaries, once filled to capacity; but today, victims of community change, they stand almost empty though still demanding tremendous maintenance. A modern adaptation of the ancient tabernacle, or the use of prefabricated, multipurpose buildings will undoubtedly come forth.

In the year 2000 religion will still be a part of the human scene, if it is able to remain relevant to the issues of its day, is intellectually compatible with each generation, and finds new channels to accomplish God's will. It will die, or at best, have only historical significance, if its goal is no more than self-preservation.

[CHAPTER TWELVE]

MAN'S WORK AND LEISURE*

THOMAS GREEN

IN THIS COUNTRY there has long been an understanding of how
people are supposed to relate to the world of work, but the fact is
that society may be embarking on a new period in which a different
view toward work is emerging. There is a shared assumption, a widespread belief on the part of many people, that the future holds for
us an era in which one of our fundamental problems is going to be
the fact that life is not work but leisure. If you put the problem that
way, it presents some grave social, political, and psychological problems. In this connection I would like to suggest three propositions:

1. If leisure be thought of as a kind of time (time away from work,
or *free time*) then the prospect is highly probable that for a great
many people there will be, in the years just ahead, increased leisure for
some, and less leisure for other people.
2. If leisure be thought of as the opposite of work, then leisure
probably will not be available.
3. If leisure be thought of as a state of character, then there will be
no more leisure in the future than there is now, nor than there has
been in the past.

These are complex issues, so let me take them one by one, and elaborate on each.

Leisure as Free Time

If you think leisure is *free time*—and this is the popular conception

*Presented at a conference on Human Ecology at Jersey City State College, Jersey
City, New Jersey, April 23, 1971.

—then the prospects around the corner are that we could have a society in which there could be a great increase in leisure. Think of it in a very conventional way. Let me propose a couple of exercises by which one can determine exactly what the prospects are likely to be for such an increase in leisure. For example, one may ask, is there going to be a very rapid decline in the average length of the work week in this country? Will this provide more leisure?

First, is it true that the length of the work week will decline? Like most assertions of that sort, there is evidence on both sides. The fact is that the average work week in this country has not changed much in the last fifteen years. Since 1955 the average work week has gone down at a rate of about an hour a decade. If one takes that rate and projects it into the future, a leisure society will not be realized at all by the year 2000. In fact, such a rate will not provide anything significantly different from that which now prevails. If one looks at the work week as it is currently formulated, it can be seen that the rate of decline from the beginning of the century—or say, from 1905— has been so great that if that rate increases, or even continues, people will not work at all. However, since the possibility of people not working at all is implausible, it would be more reasonable to assume that the rate of decline in the work week will be somewhere between the maximum level seen between the beginning of the century and 1940, and somewhat less than the level that exists presently. If this line of thinking is followed, one comes to the conclusion that a work week of about thirty hours or a little less could occur in due time.

There is little particularly reasonable about this line of argument. This is primarily because the validity of the information one receives about the length of the average work week makes judgement about the length of such a week quite precarious. Judgements based on the types of workers in the labor force show this to some extent. Probably the greatest increasing group of workers in our society is what we call the professional-managerial. And they certainly do not have more leisure lately. In fact, this group seems to have less leisure. So, if one looks at leisure related to a certain labor class or kinds of workers, these figures regarding greater or lesser amounts of leisure do not clearly indicate that there is going to be a leisure society.

Now we could try a second exercise. Suppose one sets some kind of a reasonable target for population growth and for economic growth, and then makes some assumption about the rate of productivity of this projected population. Make all figures very modest. Say that we will have 210 million people in this country by the turn of the century (that might be a little high on the basis of current figures, but a few years ago we thought pretty low). Suppose we think that we could get a gross national product of 2.2 trillion by the end of the century. That would be an average per capita income of something over six thousand dollars per person—twice what it was in 1965. That goal is pretty modest. It could be achieved very easily in this country. Then let us compute how much labor it would take, how many people, how much work, how much the labor force should be expanded, how many people have to work to reach that target by the end of the century. You could, with somewhere between 1,300 and 1,500 working hours in the year, have 33 percent of the work force employed and reach that target. In the past, the work force has been running close to 40 percent.

In other words, an option is available in this country for reaching some very high economic targets with relatively few people employed full time. You can mix up the variables I have been talking about—population size, gross economic products, greater productivity—and derive information that will tell you in what proportions a population has to be employed to obtain a certain economic target. For example, the population employed could go as low as 20 percent of the labor force. There is a very well laid out set of estimates on these variables in a book by Herman Kahn and Anthony Wiener, *The Year 2000*.[76] The book tells exactly what choices are available. While it is my opinion that Kahn and Wiener's figures are inaccurate, they are sufficiently close so that the reader is able to see what the choices are.

In order to examine these possible choices, there is a third exercise one might do. Make a little chart. On one corner of the chart put down the number of hour per day. Enter next to those figures different figures that you might want to invent about the length of vacations. Now calculate the number of work days that people spend and the number of days off that they spend in a year. Then multiply these figures, and the resultant will represent the total work hours that would occur. When this is done, one can figure out what would happen to the five-day week, eight-hour day (that would be a forty hour week) and what would happen if one had a two-week vacation, four-week vacation, or six-week vacation. These variations are important, because the increase in leisure in this country is going to have very different social consequences *depending on the form in which it comes.* You can reduce the average length of the work week 20 percent by cutting it back one day. But it would be much more interesting if the same amount of free time could come as a six-week vacation, or a three-month vacation. Those alternatives have very different social consequences—they mean very different things from a behavioral point of view, for such alternatives would influence how people live. Do the same thing with the five-day week, seven-hour day (that's a thirty-five hour week). The interesting point is that any combination of a four-day week and four-week vacation will produce an absolutely even split between the days people spend working and the days they have off—given vacations, days, weekends, and so on. I find it interesting that any combination of a four-day work week and four-week vacation will produce something like 182 days on the job, 182 days off. The point that I'm trying to make is that whether you look at the length of the average work week, or whether you take some complicated economic forecast as you find in Kahn and Wiener's book, or whether you just sit down and make up this little chart, you will discover that all these methods of arriving at some estimate of the future begin to converge. They converge on the possibility of about a thirty-two hour week in which exactly 50 percent of the year can be spent doing something else.

It is very clear to me when I follow that line of thought that in this country, with very modest effort, such a situation is quite attainable. It is quite possible for people to modify their time for making a living and doing something else which might be called work and leisure. Whether it is likely that this will be done depends on some other things. It depends on human beings—whether Americans will be willing to forego some of the psychological demands or disciplines of work in order to experience the results of some other kind of life.

Leisure as the Opposite of Work

In thinking of leisure as free time—that is, time off from the job—then the prospect is very great that leisure will be an important option for Americans within the next twenty years. However, if you think of leisure as the absence of work, which is currently the way leisure is viewed, I suggest that there will not be any leisure. For three hundred years in our historical and cultural assumptions about the nature of work in western culture, we tended to associate the idea of work with jobs. We associate the notion that the work a human does is what he does on the job. The idea that a person's work is to be found in the job really is a distinctly modern idea.

Think of the prospects of a world without any work. I am not talking about jobs. The basic notion of work is predominantly that human beings expend some energy and that the expenditure of such energy is not fruitless. There is some result that has some stability and an enduring quality. The word *work* is ambiguous. Work is a product; it is a net result, the end of one's energy. Work is also a process. We do not use the word *labor* in the same way as we use the word *work*. Labor is not something that produces a result. Cleaning the Augean stable, because of the biological nature of things, is an endless task. Dish washing is done only in order to create a situation in which the task needs to be redone. When we talk about people producing works, we are talking about them producing things that appear to constitute some modification, some impact, some stable relationship to a stable world that will sustain those works. What we mean by *works* in the arts is an opus, a piece of music, a painting, or a piece of pottery. Works can also be a political order, a civic task, or the formation of the family. To think seriously that a world will ever exist in which there is no work, is to think of a world in which there is no civilization, because the root concept of a work (in the sense in which I am talking about it) implies that life be lived in a way that something significant comes out of it. There is a marvelous passage in the *Bhagavad-Gita*[98] which states the matter succinctly and absolutely correctly: "Without work the world would collapse." That is to say, the world that we know is a world which in many ways is the product of human effort. A world in which there is not any work would be a world without houses, dishes, or thousands of other things. If we are to have a world in which there are not any artifacts—no nails, hammers and tools—there would be no man-made civilization.

If leisure be thought of as the opposite of work in this sense, there can be no leisure in the future. Indeed, what has been said here suggests that the agenda for work to be done in the years just ahead is vastly greater than most of us have the energy with which to cope. People sometimes think that because *jobs* may become less important, *work* is going to pass out of the world. I suggest to you that this is wrong. That is one reason why it is not very important to talk about whether the work week will decline, or whether we can reach a certain economic level with fewer people and fewer hours involved. It may, in time, be recognized that the work we are called to do may have little to do with the jobs by which a living is earned. That indeed *would* be a different world, but it would not be a world of leisure.

Leisure as a State of Character

There is no indication that this concept of leisure as a state of character is going to grow more popular, although it might, since one lives with the eternal hope that human beings will somehow muddle through. Let me suggest a couple of points connected with the idea that leisure is really a state of character. In Greece, which is where the idea got started, the word was used to refer to school and learning. The word, as employed by the Greeks, was *skota* (which is the root for the word *school*). This is to say, school is leisure; or at least one part of school is leisure. But what does one do with leisure? One does what one should do—learn. That is what leisure is; leisure is learning. It is interesting that there are two words related to this subject in the classical languages, Greek and Latin. In Greek there is the word *skota*, the opposite of *aschola*, or *bus-i-ness*. The basic concept for the classical world was leisure not work. In Latin there is the word *otium* which means leisure; *negotium* is its opposite which means work. The *denial* of leisure is what work is. In the ancient world, leisure was the prime thing that counted. The denial of leisure, the absence of leisure, was the only way to express what was meant by work (in the sense of *job*).

The basic problem is that there seems to be no way of thinking about leisure as a positive good. Leisure is thought of as the opposite of work; not work as the opposite of leisure. Notice what is said about leisure. The problem with leisure in the modern world is how to use free time. It has been suggested earlier that there are two mistakes in that question of how to use free time. In the first place, the problem of leisure involves how to reach the point where it is necessary to *use* time, for time is not something that would come up with that notion of leisure. One can go to the next step and say, the educational problem of leisure is to help people to learn how to use their free time profitably. The tendency is to make leisure a work concept, and also a capitalistic concept. Such a notion has no connection with what the ancient Greeks meant by leisure. In other words, the basic notion that the ancients had to deal with was leisure, and that was a human ideal. It was a description of what man was supposed to become. In the modern world the root of the notion is work. We are a work dominated society, and the problem is going to be not that we do not know what to do with our leisure but rather that we do not know how to conceive of the problem. We conceive of it only in terms of categories that are appropriate to work; hence we tend to say that the problem of leisure is to know how to use one's free time profitably.

I would like to suggest to you just one last point. Sometimes when people go on vacation they try to relax. Sometimes they go fishing. I remember spending some time on the lake of Minnesota when I was younger. It was perfectly obvious there that some people engaged in fishing acted as if their whole life depended on catching fish. They would motor up and down the lake trolling for long hours, really working at it. They worked at their leisure. Then there were other people who did not really much care whether they caught fish. It was not that they went fishing without any care for catching fish, but they would just as soon catch them and put them back. Notice the difference between these two—there is not any objective difference between their ways of fishing. It is a very fundamental difference in the way in which people learn to relate to what it is they do. Only the latter of these two characterizations I have given you is one that fits the notion of leisure. Such persons may let time pass. Indeed time is not a factor to such people.

It is only in a work dominated world that we can say such things as, *Time may pass;* you can save it, you can store it up, you can spend it, you can count it, you can record it, and all that. Some day, maybe if we do not have to be so driven by making a living, that is, by our jobs, we might raise a generation which decides really it is not that work is not important, it is just that some way or other a truly human existence might just become possible if we could learn to relate to our activities for their enjoyment. In fact, that might lead us to develop some other kind of activities—some other works.

It seems to me that this really is a prospect, and it would constitute in many ways a sort of revival of the ancient notion of what it is that we are to be. In fact, that is what Plato and Aristotle thought. I might indicate to you, by the way, it is not alien to the American theme. There were people like Thomas Jefferson who understood this full well.

[CHAPTER THIRTEEN]

PROTECTING OUR NATURAL RESERVES: A ROLE FOR PARKS*

Lee Talbot

Concerns with the environment are playing an increasing role in the viewpoints and the attitudes of the people of the United States, as well as those of people throughout the world. Our government is now committed to the principle that environmental considerations must be given adequate weight at all levels of government decision-making, planning, and action. This principle prevails regardless of whether or not those environmental considerations can be quantified in dollars and cents. Therefore, in this decade of the seventies things *are* changing.

We have heard much of systems in this meeting. We can devise systems, but the main point is that we are *part* of the systems, *part* of the world ecosystem, and as integral parts of a biological system, we are dependent upon it. It seems to me that this is the point of departure for an evaluation of the future role of parks relative to ecology and ecological needs.

Parks mean different things to different people. We have a park system which ranges all the way from city squares to Yellowstone and Yosemite. We also have preserves, some of which are kept as

*Presented before the World Future Society, Washington, D.C., May 14, 1971.

purely scientific preserves and others used intensively for one kind of recreation or another. For the purposes of this presentation, I will use the definition of parks which is in the World List of National Parks and Equivalent Preserves, prepared for the United Nations by the International Union for Conservation. This reads, in part: "To qualify as a national park or an equivalent reserve, an area should enjoy general legal protection against all human exploitation of its natural resources, and against all other derogations of its integrity resulting from human activity." The significance of this definition is that these areas should be truly protected.

Human activities are changing the whole face of the earth at an increasingly rapid and pervasive rate, and these changes take place in a series of ways. There is a spectrum which ranges from direct total changes, as for example, from cultivation, urbanization, transportation systems, and artificial lakes, to the indirect effects of activities such as grazing, lumbering, or the effects of pollutants and the use of pesticides. All of these factors are altering the earth's surface, and its ecosystems. For those who have tried to get away from any signs of human activities, and for those who are sensitive to factors altering the ecosystems, it is almost impossible to escape signs of human interaction with the system. It is not at all out of the question—in fact, it is highly probable—that within a relatively short time (by which I mean just a few years), except for areas that are intentionally protected, the whole earth's surface is going to be modified. I am not saying that this is necessarily bad, but it is a fact. Therefore, the ecological significance to human welfare of protected parks stems from their identity as islands of natural ecosystems in a sea of modified environment.

There is a series of important ecological reasons for maintaining these *islands*. In the first place, they provide ecological reference points by which we can judge the changes we have wrought in the rest of that kind of environment. This is extremely important, and two quick examples can explain why. First, in a natural area remaining in the midst of a large area changed by man, it is possible to study the ecological systems and to compare the natural processes of productivity with the productivity in the modified area. Historically, as we use and modify lands for human production by grazing, plant production, forestry, and so forth, the productivity frequently tends to drop off after some years or decades. This process continues until the reasons are discovered and remedial action is undertaken. The best way—and in some cases the only way—to find out how things have been changed so that the productivity can be increased, comes from having unmodified areas, *ecological reference points*, where we can compare and study these processes. The other side of this coin is that, as the composition of the environment is polluted or changed, for example, with the addition of mercury or DDT, there is need for base-line areas where one can learn what is the natural background level of these substances. I think the recent experience with mercury shows the importance of having this sort of information.

Parks can serve as natural laboratories or museums for study. It is possible only to study a living ecosystem while it is *living*. Humankind is really still at the threshold of learning what makes the world tick biologically. Knowledge of ecology still is fragmentary. This knowledge is exceedingly limited. Sometime, we shall reach the point where we can model ecosystems and predict ecological effects. However, to achieve that capability, it is essential to have living examples of ecosystems to study. This is a continuing need if the human race is to know what is going on in the environment in which it finds itself.

Another major reason for maintaining park areas, with their protected ecosystems and component wildlife and plants, is to maintain diversity. It is a basic ecological principle that diversity contributes to stability. This concept can be illustrated by the analogy of a bank account. Suppose you have a fairly large family with all members working in the same firm and suppose that these incomes are all put in the same bank account. If something happens which affects that bank or those jobs, the family is in real trouble; all the family eggs have been put in one basket. On the other hand, if the family is diversified—it has a series of jobs in different areas and banks in different places—it would take a very major disaster to wipe out all the jobs and banks.

Another value of park areas is that they provide gene pools. Parks, in this sense, serve as storehouses or living museums. That is, they maintain the stocks of plants, vertebrate, and invertebrate animals, which may get wiped out elsewhere in the rest of the modified landscape. This storage function is exceedingly important, because humankind has only domesticated a tiny percentage of the available plants, and a still smaller percentage of the available animals. Among this high percentage of species unused so far, the human race may very well find the stocks for the plants and animals that can provide us food security in a future where world food supply is a matter of grave importance. Further, gene pools are also needed to strengthen what is already available to the peoples of the world. Those of you from California may know about the walnut trees. The genetic structure of the native California walnut provides the security, the strength, and the resistance to disease needed to grow walnuts in California; yet, the English walnut, which is the tree that was brought here, is the one which produces the greatest yield. The English walnuts when planted failed to survive or be productive. If the California walnut had not been available at that time to hybridize with the English tree, today there might not be a walnut industry in this country. To give another example of the importance of a gene pool preserved in our parks, several years ago in Indiana the horticulturists succeeded in growing tomatoes that were beautiful things—big, juicy, tremendous. The problem was they grew so big that these tomatoes split: their skin was too thin. The horticulturists cast about and in Brazil, discovered a wild seed, a wild tomato, that happened to have genes for a thick skin. By combining the two, Indiana now has a very important crop of tomatoes which grow big and juicy but have a strong skin and whose skins do not split. For these reasons—and of course, there are a series of others—the establishment and maintenance of the worldwide system of parks for gene pool reservoirs must be considered ecologically essential.

At present, the world park system which has been referred to and which is documented in the UN list contains something like 1,200 parks in about a hundred countries. Yet, this is really only a fraction of what is needed. We should not confuse recreation parks with areas that protect pieces of the natural environment. The recreation parks are needed, too. But the protected areas—whether they are called parks or nature reserves or natural areas—are critically needed; and for that kind of a system, we must have areas adequate to protect samples of all of the earth's significant habitats and all of these species of plants and animals. This is a job now being undertaken, but it is going to take some time, and I think this is one of the greatest challenges to the future of world parks.

[CHAPTER FOURTEEN]

DESIGN FOR LIVING—
IN URBANA*

Marya Mannes

M Y QUALIFICATIONS as a futurist are rather tenuous. They rest on a novel I wrote called *They*,[99] which was laid in 1990 and concerned five survivors of *this* era. The government of the young finally took over in 1976, and one of their first laws concerned compulsory retirement at fifty, exile and relocation at fifty-five, and compulsory death (either self or state-administered) at sixty-five.

Since my five exiles had no contact whatsoever with the outside world (either in the book or in the television play broadcast on Public Television in 1971), I did not have to envisage, physically, the society of the future. However, I have always dreamed of what *should* be in a world which most definitely *is not*. Most of what I now see of our country's spiritual and physical environment appalls me. In this, as in many if not all things, I am with the young. It is imperative that we build a new society, new cities, a new humanity. *How*—that awful question—I suppose, is the reason we address ourselves to this matter in this book.

In the next few pages I will include suggestions for new ecosystems for the aging, which I guess means where our doomed elders are going to breathe decent air and see green trees in the cities of now and the future. To this direction I would like to throw

*Presented before the World Future Society, Washington, D.C., May 14, 1971.

out a few ideas, not only about the needs and functions of city parks, but about a general obsession of mine. It concerns the really large park systems and their future. I am passionately convinced that the national parks must be saved, not only from the realtors but from the habitual depredations of that wild and undisciplined herd called Man.

It seems to me an inexorable law that the more people who have access to the wild beauties of nature, the less of these remain. The marvel of wildness, or wilderness, crumbles after invasions of people in cars, bearing gifts of garbage. And though this may sound anti-egalitarian, I would institute certain statutes and restrictions to remedy this devastation.

No cars, trailers, campers, jeeps should be allowed beyond the outer portals of a national park. Those who are physically able and really *care* about wilderness should walk, carrying their camping needs on their backs. Those either too old or too young for long or steep distances might rent the equivalent of a golf-cart (noiseless and hopefully gasless) for their journey. Each person or party entering the park is to be issued a large plastic bag for litter, to be left at certain pick-up points indicated on the park map or at the park exit. Patrolling rangers finding any violators are empowered to collect a whopping fee.

What I am getting at is simply this: the glories of nature can only survive the presence of those who crave them enough to forfeit the comforts of home. Wilderness is not a *recreation area*. It is a Revelation Area.

I do not believe there is a divine law sanctioning open access to everything for everybody for any purpose. I do believe, on the other hand, that blessings such as virgin nature belong to those who love, respect, and nurture it. The rest can look at television.

One more thing about both big national parks and city parks, of any size, in winter; in fact about snowbound land anywhere, all snowmobiles not used for specific purposes—and recreation is *not* one of these—must be banned. The snowmobile is the newest unmitigated disaster.

Now, about city parks. A community still fortunate enough to have within its incorporated borders tracts of open country and water capable of sustaining wild life and plant life should preserve these, as they are for future generations, confining all other building—commercial or private—to areas with a low yield of natural resources. This is obviously easier said than done and harder still for the big cities that have sprawled over vast areas of land like creeping cancer—Los Angeles, for instance.

The Angelenos, of course, think nothing of driving a hundred miles to get out of their suburbs; but densely congested cities, like New York or the other huge center ghettos of our nation, would have to undergo such massive restructuring that it would be simpler and more appropriate (as a futurist) to talk about what new cities would ideally provide in the way of intro-urban escapes to nature and peace.

New York, of course, is saved by Central Park, that magnificent concept of Olmstead and Vaux actually creating natural beauty in the middle of a city, three miles long and over a mile wide. That this glory is being steadily eroded by negligent masses was the subject of a recent piece of mine in the New York Times. In it I suggested that several areas of quiet beauty, like the Bethesda Fountain and other lake-edges, be reserved for the older generation and for those unable to endure steel-bands, loud harangues, freak shows, or garlands of garbage.

But for most cities I have two visions of a park system serving the needs of both the old and the very young. It is based on a few rare enclaves in New York, one of the loveliest of which is Turtle Bay. Here is an entire square block in which the houses enclose a long rectangle of common garden for the use of the tenants. Similar blocks in new cities would share with the city the planting and tending of trees and bushes and grass, the collecting of litter, and hopefully, a playground and at least one fountain.

I would pattern these new city communities on this general plan, requiring that no house in the block be more than eight stories high, that each block contain a day nursery, a clinic, and an apartment house of small efficiency units reserved for older people of modest means who cannot afford expensive nursing homes. Ideally, these would be relatives or friends of tenants of this block; near enough to visit, separate enough for independence.

After visits to superb residences for the old in Sweden and Denmark, I am firmly in accord that older people should not be cut off from the daily familiarities of their community. Since the streets in the big cities are cruel to the frail, this inner park would bring them in contact with other ages and other kinds in a natural manner, instead of a forced and often degrading grouping of age.

I would also like the future suburb to be designed on the same general lines: individual houses surrounding an acre of untampered land where the children as well as their elders could meet and play in easy normal contact. Certainly, this is a kind of commune, but I am fairly certain that the present system of rows of houses with one small plot of grass in front and one small yard in back—the single family stockade—is one reason for the massive boredom of the young and consequent flight from home. What on earth can you do, whom can you meet, on a piece of grass surrounded by cement walks?

This nuclear family idea must be either jettisoned in the future, or modified by a series of much closer and self-governing communities *within* the structure of a city consisting, hopefully, of no more than 100,000 people.

Americans must be convinced that the daily relation of people to the natural world is absolutely essential to the quality of a humane and liveable society.

Whether on foot in the wilderness, or sitting under a tree in a small city enclave—free of the tyrant auto—people must grow from birth to learn and love the land that sustains them.

Otherwise, we are finished.

[CHAPTER FIFTEEN]

ENVIRONMENTALISM VS. CONSERVATIONISM: AN ISSUE FOR THE SEVENTIES?*

B. Bruce-Briggs

For a century American conservationists have been fighting a long and difficult struggle with limited resources against heavy odds of indifference and special interests, so it is understandable that they have been enthusiastic at the promise of massive reenforcements offered by the burgeoning environmentalist movement. At last, after years of being a few voices literally crying in the wilderness, they perceive that the public has gotten the word and is responding. With the support of the environmentalist movement, conservationists can now reasonably expect to further their aims of preserving America's natural environment. Clearly, the advent of environmentalism offers immense opportunities to American conservationists, as represented by such established institutions as the American Wildlife Federation, Sierra Club, and the National Park Service. However, it is not so obvious that the environmentalist movement has the potential of at least being a deadly enemy of traditional conservationism. Environmentalism could threaten the hard-won gains of conservationism.

One can identify two general positions in the environmentalist

*Presented before the World Future Society, Washington, D.C., May 14, 1971.

camp: the first can be described as *superconservationism*, that is, the position which favors and promotes taking the historical conservationist concern with maintaining natural areas and widening it to the larger environment. Hopefully, environmentalism would encourage treating every national area as if it were a National Park. To some degree everyone would be a ranger. Apart from a few devoted (and unpersuasive) enthusiasts who would dismantle or demolish our industrial culture, these *superconservationists* recognize that compromises will have to be made, even though they hope and will make every effort to assure that compromises will be as much on the conservationist side as possible. But there is another position in the environmentalist camp, the *ecosystems* position. These people talk in terms of a *total world* system, *integration* of man and nature, and the like. It is this position which could be the enemy of conservationism as we know it today.

The historical conservationist position made a clean separation between man and nature. Over the past one hundred years, through careful education, conservationists have propagated the belief that these areas are sacrosanct and not to be touched under any circumstances. To use an urban example, the extremely powerful lobbies organized to protect New York City's Central Park from *improvement* is an ideal case. The conservationists have felt it necessary to conserve these valuable natural and historical assets by creating in the mind of the people that they are clearly different things from the rest of our industrial culture. A park or other conservation area is seen as a sanctuary, a reservation, or a refuge, cut off from and protected from predatory man and his culture. The ecosystems approach recognizes no such distinction. Everything is part of the whole. *Ecosystems* people recognize that tough choices and compromises (*trade-offs* in the jargon of the systems analyst) will have to be made based upon rational analysis of costs and benefits. But we know from experience with military and other systems that final decisions are seldom made purely on such *rational* criteria; more often, key decisions are the result of personal, institutional, and mass interests and/or values. Such decisions are *political* rather than *rational*. Acceptance of the ecosystems approach could threaten the achievements of historical conservationism.

What if the environmentalist movement has the effect of eroding the existing distinction between the conservation areas and the rest of the environment? First of all, it is certain that if conservation areas become less sacrosanct, then it becomes more conceivable to do other things with them. It is not too bizarre to speculate that if you were taking a *total systems approach* to preserve the environment, it might be that the result of cost-benefit analysis and trade-offs would lead you to place certain things within existing conservation areas. Perhaps, Yosemite might be an excellent spot for a sewage treatment plant, or Gettysburg might be a superb dump. We select these extreme examples merely to show the possibility, though we hardly think that these themselves would ever be touched. Still, the ecosystems' view tends to blur the distinction between *conserved* areas and the remaining historically *exploited* areas.

But does not the present widespread enthusiasm for environmentalism indicate that a blurring of distinctions between conservation and other areas would be to the benefit of our blighted total environment? Surely, at least in the short run, but despite the great current enthusiasm for environmentalism and its deep public support, which cannot be underestimated, we must recognize that to some degree, at least, this enthusiasm is faddish and potentially rather shallow. Being for the environment has come to be rather like being for motherhood and the Flag, but it is not clear how much people are willing to pay for environmentalism. Unfortunately, we know that a high regard for nature is a relatively recent phenomenon limited almost entirely to highly educated, prosperous classes in the Western world. Historical man, living at the margin of existence, grabbed all he could from nature. From the American Indian with his slash and burn agriculture, to the robber baron and his stripmine, anything went in the struggle with nature. And historically, nature was not considered to be beneficial, noble, or beautiful, but rather an implacable and potentially ugly enemy who was always dangerous. The peasant, painfully grubbing his life from the soil, did not sing the praises of the stony hills; nor did the seaman, his life threatened by storms, praise the sea; nor did the farmer or ranger think it was necessary to preserve predatory or competitive wildlife.

One way to look at our historical relationship to conservation is to consider that mankind has fought a war with nature, lasting hundreds of thousands and perhaps millions of years. With modern technology, about a century ago we won that war. Having won, we can afford to be magnanimous, and can also afford to take a more tolerant view of the attributes of our defeated adversary. A good analogy is the relationship between the white American and the American Indian. Having defeated the Indian, we cooped them up on reservations, so that, among other reasons, we might go and look at them and appreciate their virtues. Similarly, our parks, conservation areas, historic preservation areas, and wildlife preserves are reservations for defeated wildlife, mountain scenery, and what few relics of the past have survived our onslaught. Many ecosystems advocates hope we will achieve the harmony the Indian is alleged to have with the environment. But the opposite may also occur—an ecosystems approach promises (or threatens) the complete domination of humans over nature.

Even today, conservationism is necessarily limited almost entirely to the prosperous industrial nations. It would be foolish to tell a Peruvian earthquake victim or a Parkistani monsoon survivor about the glory of nature and the need for maintaining the balance of nature.

Even in our own society, among our fairly prosperous middle American lower middle classes and working class groups (with the exception of the very large numbers of hunters and fishermen) the respect for nature goes not very deep. The unfortunate behavior of many of our citizens in our national parks and recreation areas speaks for their somewhat ambivalent attitude toward nature. On the one hand, they wish to enjoy it, and on the other, they do not wish to pay very much. Some are not even willing to pay in terms of enough effort to drop a bottle or can in a litter basket. Similarly, it is not clear how much people are willing to pay for a whole environment. A recent survey asked people how much they would pay in cash to clean up the environment, and the average answer was on the order of one dollar per capita, a far cry from the 115 billion dollar bill projected by the Environmental Protection Agency.

A recent example in the New York Metropolitan area beautifully illustrates this point. The Consolidated Edison power company has been attempting to expand its power generating facilities in the

New York City area. Every type of facility that they have attempted to build within the last five years has been opposed by local groups on the grounds of fear of air pollution, water pollution, nuclear aversion, and in the case of the proposed Storm King project, conservationism. Meanwhile, power shortages are becoming more acute in New York. Very few New Yorkers enjoy the unspoiled beauty of the Storm King Valley; every New Yorker needs power. No New Yorker wants air pollution. The implications are clear. Something is going to have to give. To a certain extent, most Americans support conservationism, but they have other values as well. What if the choice was between maintaining the natural beauty of some area at the cost of having insufficient power available to watch television? A lot of tough choices like these are going to have to be made. Unless some reasonable compromise can be found, Storm King or some other natural feature may well be sacrificed for the benefit of the total system.*

These potential adverse effects of environmentalism are likely to be compounded by certain excesses of some environmentalists. There is unquestionably a lunatic fringe in the environmentalist movement which is strongly hostile to all the manifestations of our industrial society and culture and in a few cases even is avowedly politically revolutionist. Perhaps the most extreme group are the advocates of *ecotage* which, despite its outwardly noble rhetoric, is plain and simple terrorism. Doubtless, these people will be hunted down if they get much beyond the talking stage; but more likely to discredit the environmentalist movement are people who work within the law, but make extravagant demands without regard to who is going to pay (financial, as well as other costs) and how much. The New York example cited above is an excellent instance

*A recent editorial in the *New York Daily News* is extremely revealing: "Dim the lights, switch off the appliances when possible because the source of juice, Consolidated Edison, is balancing precariously on the brink of calamity. It has already resorted to voltage cuts, and selected 'load-shedding'—cutting off power to some localities—may not be far away.

"It's just too bad Con Ed can't really be selective when and if it pulls the plug by casting into darkness those super-preservationists and ultra-environmentalists who have helped create this shortage by roadblocking efforts for an orderly expansion of power resources."

A few months after this editorial was written a power failure in New York cut off all television.

of this indifference to the overall effect on the public. If, because adequate power cannot be provided for New York (or any other place) because of conflicting claims of various environmentalist groups, whose fault will it be if a hundred should die, or millions should be seriously inconvenienced by a power failure? More important, who will be to blame?

Perhaps these remarks seem unnecessarily pessimistic, but it would not be the first time that a positive and definitely beneficial movement could overreach itself, go too far, and provoke a severe counter-reaction. It might be good policy for conservationists to support environmentalism, but at the same time, take care not to become irreparably intertwined with it. One position might be to take something like an ecosystems approach to the present exploited areas, but keep it absolutely clear that Yellowstone and Valley Forge are extra-special places, not to be *systematized*.

[CHAPTER SIXTEEN]

NATURE AND THE NATURAL STATES OF TOMORROW*

Charles Williams

I N LEADING UP to what we now call the emerging macroproblem (a major dimension of which is the crisis of the ecology and the environment), we must examine a crisis of the human spirit itself. There are a number of oversimplified classifications into which we can put the basic trends. One of them is man's image of himself and of nature; and the relationship all of these images have to the present ecological crisis.

It is useful to think about four basic categories of man's image of nature:

1. Nature is a threat to survival and/or existence and hence has to be overcome. (There are surely aspects of nature that fit that criterion.)
2. Nature is a material source to be exploited—to be exploited to the maximum degree. We have had an extraordinary record of success in carrying out those attitudes toward nature in western society.
3. Nature is a deterministic system that is simply to be accepted and then we adapt to it as a part of it. (Much more amenable to eastern culture than to western culture.)
4. Nature is a source of enjoyment. This is where parks fit into the system. People might envisage nature, not as enjoyment in the

*Presented at the World Future Society, Washington, D.C., May 14, 1971.

raw sense, but as a source of enjoyment in the sense that it asks the human race to protect certain areas so that people can go out and be among trees, among wild animals and fish—those things which human beings took for granted before they were living in artificial environments.

Going on to man's relationship with nature, I have put down three things that I think are meaningful in the context of this discussion.

Man started (in terms of human history) having to relate directly to his *natural* environment. It was the laboratory of life, and people were very close to nature in everyday life.

We have progressively gone toward an *indirect* relationship with nature, made possible by the intervention of technology. More and more, proportionately speaking, we do not really farm the soil nor do we realize the dependence that we have upon the soil because there are so many intervening systems between us and that kind of activity.

Direct contact with nature occupies such a small percentage of the people that our dependence upon nature has become removed from everyday consciousness.

Human beings are moving now, particularly in some of the futuristic architectural design, toward what might be called artificial nature—that is, synthetic nature. If we cannot return to it—to nature —then bring it to us; but bring it to us in synthetic form. For example, futurists will speak of buildings with computer program control systems to change the walls so that one can change the feeling that one has, several times a day, if one wishes. You can sit in your office and *feel* that you are in the middle of the wilderness or you can even smell it, sense it, or hear the sounds of nature. These are, of course, only being talked about and are only on drawing boards at this time. If I were making a forecast now, I would say the probability is weighted that we will begin to try to recapture nature into our everyday life through synthetic means rather than by moving back to real contact with nature. We have a special problem: an organizational problem of how to handle the intervening technology which we are going to develop.

Going beyond that, man has made nature a commodity. For example, even the Park Service is now a consumption industry. We do cost-benefit studies which show how much people are willing to pay to stay in the park areas as a means of determining whether or not the parks are in fact being supported and enjoyed and so forth.

Turning now to man's image of himself, I believe several significant changes combine to make up a fundamental long term trend. Our image of ourselves has been changing. Let me just suggest how. Copernicus told us we were not the center of the universe after all. Darwin said, "Not only that, but you're not even divinely or uniquely created." Freud said, "Not only that, but you're not even rational." Modern behaviorists say, "Not only that, you're not even spiritual." Technologists are about to tell us, sometime in the future, "Not only are you none of those things you thought you were, you're not even the most intellectual process because artificial intelligence is going to exceed that." There is little question about these changes in self-image. And more and more people are, I think, shifting toward the concept that not only are we none of those things we once thought we were, but there's nothing metaphysical about us either—we are only a series of chemical reactions, stimulus and response, etc. At the same time, even though we cannot measure it very well, you find social psychologists giving you a general consensus that we have something called a *crisis of the spirit*, alienation, anomie. Is it any wonder?

I think there is a relationship between these trends. There is little question in my mind that we have a crisis of nature—our ecological problem. We have simply got to change, not only our concepts of nature and our relationship with nature but also the systems that we have structured by which we intervene in natural processes, if we are ever going to be successful in solving the ecological problems.

Furthermore, we have a crisis of man. In the very near future we are going to have to decide what viewpoint of the nature of man we are going to stake our claim on and say, "*This* is *not* negotiable." That image of the nature of man must be structured into some kind of protective system, at least equivalent to the protections of the Bill of Rights—the inalienable right to be a human. The problem is that such a protective system cannot be like a normal judicial system which never acts until after the fact—until after some offense has been treated.

In terms of determining the nature of man, we have two basic categories that we can decide upon. One is that we are only animal; that we are fully behavioristic, deterministic creatures. Within the coming decade we may decide that all this business about parks does not make any difference because we will be able to manipulate much more efficiently, much more economically, and in a much less painful way all of the aesthetic pleasures which we now consume as enjoyment in the parks. We will not have to travel anywhere to get them.

As a second alternative, if we should say that we are something more than that—that we have a spiritual, metaphysical quality—then we come back to the question of the twofold role of nature, supporting physical life and as an avenue through which we can discover the spiritual life. I think it would be fair to say that if we went back to study the individuals who have asserted that we do have a spiritual existence, we would find that a great deal of their evidence came from what we call *communion with nature*. And I would argue that if we want to accept that proposition and could synthesize it in order to change our definitions of the role of parks, we might be able to move beyond the role of parks as they are conventionally described—as *pleasure grounds*.

It would take at least three things in order to make this possible. *First*, an entirely new philosophy is needed—what Victor Ferkiss[100] called a *new naturalism* but going beyond naturalism and coming very close to what I would simply call spiritualism and theology and philosophy of the nature of man in his spirit. *Secondly*, we will need a new economics because it is not likely that we can carry those philosophies into the operational programs and practices which govern the basic trends unless we can find some way to make the calculus that we use to determine the social transactions incorporate the noneconomic aspects of the transaction as if it *were* economic. I would simply call this the *post-Keynesian* economics. It's no more outlandish than it would have been for some economists when we still had a barter system to say, "You know, we really need a standard medium of exchange." It's not much more farfetched than that kind of a statement would have been at that time; yet I do not know of any economist at the present time that may be working at that level. *Thirdly,* we would need a new technology. If we had all of those things, we would need a new institutional adaptability, because it is equally clear that the institutional structures that we now have would have to be pursuing and seeing their pursuit of social viability in the context of different roles.

If we did these things I think we might evolve a synthesis of the technology which supports life and nature in a context of a park and in that sense return to something like Eden. My intuitive sense is that mankind would be much better off if we could. If we could dare to *imagine* it, I would suspect that we could *create* it.

[CHAPTER SEVENTEEN]

INFLUENCING INEBRIATES*

RAYMOND L. NELSON

IN THE BEGINNING was the earth.
The swirling mass of gasses slowly crusted with rock. The rains came and oceans formed. Then, from somewhere, somehow, came life. Two billion years had passed, a span of time far beyond the comprehension of man.

Then another two billion years went by. Untold numbers of different forms of life came and went. The waters teemed, then the land. And the forms that came, came briefly, adapting to a cyclic pattern of time and dependency and change.

Finally, yesterday, came man. Equipped with a powerful brain, his reasoning powers evolved with a rapidity that soon surpassed the rhythmic pace that had flowed steadily for eons. The basic law of adaptation no longer seemed relevant. "Why," reasoned the reasoner, "should *I* adapt when I can make *other* things adapt to me?" And in a brief flash of time the synchronized patterns of billions of years was interrupted.

Reason produced power, and as inevitable as cyclic night and day, fear was replaced with a confidence that immediately spawned arrogance. For the first time in the history of the earth the basic law that sacrifice was a requirement of existence was challenged, found wanting, and discarded.

*Presented at a conference on Human Ecology at Jersey City State College, Jersey City, N.J., April 23, 1971.

The first sip of this elixir of power made man a drunk. His tools, produced by the elixir, and in turn, producing more elixir, are now appearing in astonishing numbers. Convincing himself that he is now in complete control, his numbers are skyrocketing. He gorges himself on a banquet of finite natural resources. He is truly *high*.

But, any system that has steadily chugged along successfully for billions of years will react unfavorably to being revved up, especially if the amount of revving is appreciable and suddenly applied, which is the case. It is no wonder that the system coughs, skips, and sputters.

A few people have heard the sputtering, and a few of these have peered closer at the system. What they see has sobered them, and they have cried out in concern. But how do you get a drunk to listen? Do you plead with him? Do you threaten him? Do you reason with him? Do you insult him? Do you imprison him? Do you ridicule him?

For many years I have been trying to communicate with drunks, and I frankly admit that I have been outstandingly unsuccessful. So much so that there are times I wonder if *I* am the one who is drunk.

I doubt if it would surprise anyone why I have tried to be an influencer of inebriates. It has something to do with that religious term, *laying on of hands*. A half-century ago when I was a boy in Concord, Massachusetts, I was blessed, or cursed, depending on one's outlook: I knew an old man named George Warren who had known Henry David Thoreau when Warren was a young boy. Thoreau had the keenest of ears. He heard the discordant notes of the old system that others could not, or would not, hear. Thoreau taught Warren how to hear; Warren taught me.

Thoreau wrote. Warren spoke. I have tried both. From the evidence all around, none of us has had much success, and I the least of all. Perhaps the reason the other two have been more successful is that they have realized more clearly than I that there is no such thing as teaching, only learning. They paid more homage to Emerson's words: "Man may teach by doing, and not otherwise." Thoreau and Warren lived their beliefs, daily and completely.

However, what little I have learned through my *teaching* efforts I want to share. I can do no more. I will do no less. And that, to begin with, is my definition of *teaching*.

I believe that the road to learning begins with awareness, takes a fork to commitment, and finally branches off to action. The last two roads—commitment and action—are individual and personal, as Pogo knows. A teacher, at first to his frustration, can accomplish nothing for anyone else in these areas. In fact, any attempts he makes to force anyone onto the roads of commitment or action will always do harm, never any good. This limits the role of a teacher to the first: awareness.

Since disciplining is difficult. Especially so when you, too, have been born drunk and feasted completely on a diet of intoxicants for both mind and body.

An environmental teacher has but one subject, one message; humility. It is a humility that extends far beyond considering only our own kind. It must include every other thing in the system, be it living or not. A grain of sand, a drop of water, a leaf, mosquito, snake, or bug demands a respect and love, in both quantity and quality, that we usually bestow only upon ourselves. Impossible? If it is, then the old system, after a few more coughs and sputters, will settle down to its old, old rhythm . . . minus man.

However, if for no other or better reason than self-interest, I believe that an environmental teacher can help others of his own kind to relearn humility. That our students are habitual drunks merely makes it a bit more difficult. I believe we must approach our drunken students on an emotional, not an intellectual basis. *Madison Avenue*, our present-day, sophisticated hawkers, know and practice this. And can anyone question their success? We, too, must use this method, but in doing so we have to strive for just the opposite goal: *Madison Avenue* wants to get us drunker; environmentalists want us to become sober.

It is easy to approach drunks . . . most of them are friendly folk. But once the environmentalist gets close, the difficulties usually begin. The drunk, accustomed to having more and stronger intoxicants handed to him by those who approach him, does not want anyone to take it from him. When this happens, the drunk usually changes immediately from a good-natured slob to something else. Angered, he becomes unpredictable, often dangerous. And this seems to be pretty much the general picture today.

Both the *haves* and the *have nots* are drunk. The *haves*, clutching tightly to their champagne diet of jets and steaks and super-eights, are determined they will never give it up. At the same time the *have nots*, reeling under the influence of their rot-gut, are clawing at the *haves* in an effort to get a swig of champagne. Into this melee has rushed the environmentalist trying to outshout the combatants, yelling: "You're both wrong!" If he is heard at all, both the *haves* and the *have nots* growl the same thing at the environmentalist: "To hell with you, baby!" Result? Lousy communications.

Is there a better way? I think so. First, a rewording of the message. Instead of shouting: "You're both wrong!" I would prefer to borrow words from Freeman Tilden, one of the few true teachers I know. Tilden puts it this way: "It all comes down to a simple choice: *voluntary or involuntary austerity.*"

There just is not enough to go around. It would be difficult to find enough of the necessary items for existence for an appreciable length of time if all of us were sober, impossible if we remain drunk. The *haves* must give up much of their materialism, the *have nots* will have to settle for much less than they are demanding. Once the elixir of materialism is gone, mankind will become sober. But the *great reasoner* has been drunk for so long he finds it impossible to believe he *has* to give up anything. Only when he *wants* to, will he. Which leads to the final step of possible, effective, environmental teaching.

For this final step I return to Thoreau and Warren. These men knew exactly what Emerson meant when he said: "Man may teach by doing, and not otherwise." The environmental teacher must also understand and believe that, if he is to be effective, he must act. He does not talk he acts. If he talks at all, it is merely to answer questions. As words can never do, the environmentalist communicates by his acts, that *he* has walked the three roads of learning: awareness, commitment, and action. If he cannot do this he cannot teach.

Will it work: I believe it will, if anything will. For a little proof I shall offer a poor example: myself. Thoreau, Warren, Tilden—at long last I now join you.

In the end will be the earth—with or without man.

[CHAPTER EIGHTEEN]

THE ROLE OF THE UNCONSCIOUS MIND IN THE FUTURE OF MANKIND*

PAUL H. WILCOX

SIGMUND FREUD was able to formulate so many insights into human behavior by using the concept of the unconscious mind that, that concept is now widely accepted. However, a number of therapeutic methods have achieved practical success in many individuals without involving the conceupt of the unconscious mind in explaining the methods. This has led some authorities to challenge the validity of the concept. This is where semantics enter into the issue. The meaning of the words *unconscious mind* depends on the definition. Biologists are generally agreed that the problem of evolution should be broken down into three aspects, viz., the fact of evolution, the course of evolution, and the cause of evolution. Thus, we can also divide the problem of the *unconscious mind* into three aspects, viz., the existence of the *unconscious mind*, the patterns of change in the *unconscious mind*, and the methodology of influencing changes in the *unconscious mind*.

The term *unconscious mind* implies that there is a component of brain function that goes on without simultaneous conscious aware-

*The content of this paper has received elaboration in Reference 101-111.

ness. If we can accept the term *unconscious mind* as a label for the sum total of brain function which does not produce information that readily flows in and out of consciousness, we are able to differentiate it from the conscious mind plus the so called *fore-conscious mind*. The latter is defined as the part of brain function which does readily feed in and out of conscious experience. In other words, the fore-conscious contains those memories which are readily available to the conscious mind but at any particular moment are not in conscious focus.

By these definitions, it can be said that there is an operational concept of *unconscious mind*. The next aspect immediately poses problems. Based on our definitions it is not possible to introspect directly about the *unconscious mind*. Therefore, how can we expect to discover the patterns of change in the *unconscious mind?* This is where, in an operational sense, the third aspect, namely, the methodology of influencing changes in the *unconscious mind* yields clues as to the patterns of change in the *unconscious mind*. In passing, it may be of some interest to point out the analogy with *potential energy. Potential energy* can only be measured in terms of kinetic energy transforms. Likewise, any spontaneous change in the *unconscious mind* is not measurable because, using the black box concept, all we can measure are resultants of the forces at work in the black box. By definition we cannot measure any of the unit intrinsic forces. However, we can measure in some degree what forces we put into this black box and can compute changes which emerge from the black box in terms of the input forces and thus speculate about the transforms that take place in the black box.

The triad of Id, Ego, and Superego is a Freudian psychoanalytic picture. The Id is an elemental emergent drive which arises in the deep unconscious foundation of the mind and seeks expression in the conscious mind in multiple patterns. However, time and circumstance lead to various patterns of taboo so that an unconscious control system develops, namely the Superego, which at the unconscious level blocks certain aspects of the Id from entering into consciousness. This control system is also called the unconscious conscience. In contrast, the conscious conscience is described as being a part of the conscious mind.

If we postulate that the unconscious mind operates at several levels of increasing degrees of organization, the Id would be at the most primitive undifferentiated level as an emergent driving activating force.

I would like to propose that at a very primitive level, but more differentiated than the Id, is a drive which I would like to name the unconscious confabulation drive. This would be defined as the tendency to systematize information and to bridge gaps in the information. This is such a complicated process that we might be tempted to identify it as one of the *higher* mental processes. However, let us give it the characteristic that it operates at all levels of life in terms of the primitive tendency to interpret any and all input stimuli as either helpful or dangerous. It thus serves to try to preserve the living protoplasm at all levels of organization against external dangers, as well as to orient the protoplasm to helpful influences at all levels of integration. To make these statements brings into focus the amazingly complicated implications of the defensive and synergic reactions to outside influences at all levels of living substance. At the most primitive level, it means that there is some way for the protoplasm to evaluate whether a given impinging stimulus is more likely to be favorable to it or more likely to be unfavorable to it.

I think it is fair to say that we are still far removed from an understanding of this process at the cellular level, including the intricate level of chromosomes. At the very limits of electron-microscopic magnification, we still find forms and boundaries and patterns of stable organization that hide the vast empty spaces of the atom. Therefore, let us accept the reality that we are still filled with puzzlement as to how the system is actually organized. The term *unconscious confabulation drive* is a grossly anthropomorphic formulation for a universal characteristic of living tissue, by which the living tissue attempts to survive in the face of universally incomplete information. The interface between the living cell membrane and the chemicals which come in contact with it provides information which leads to survival behavior in the cell membrane. At no time could that cell membrane have more than an infinitesimal bit of information as to what are the forces around it and as to the meaning of those forces. Bewildering as it may seem to us, still the evidence is that the living membrane attempts to preserve itself against external influences with only scraps of information available. There is evidence in immunity phenomena that the cell can learn methods of defending itself from attacking chemicals, if the concentration of the foreign chemical is not too great at the start. Anthropomorphically, we could say the cell wall learns how to chemically defend itself against attacking chemicals if it has time to do so.

I have spent this time on these details of the microcosm to bring out the universality of this defense system which I have labelled macrocosmically as the *unconscious confabulation drive*. This is an amazingly complicated process, and yet it enters into the brain organization as probably the most primitive of the organizing forces. The reason I use the term *unconscious confabulation drive* is because in certain severe organic mental illness patterns, the term confabulation has been accepted as the label for the tendency to fill in gaps of memory with made up (imaginary) information. I have thus taken this term out of the context or organic psychopathology and have given it a very general meaning to describe all the processes of living tissue at all levels which tend to consolidate the information available and organize a reaction as if the information were complete. If the completed gestalt is sufficiently close to the reality, a survival pattern results. If not, varying degrees of failure to survive become manifest. If the system is such that it can correct the information quickly enough, then survival patterns can replace the nonsurvival patterns of response in varying degrees.

At the human brain level this *unconscious confabulation drive* is also expressed in the power of abstraction and generalization. Thus the human being is *aware* of his dilemma in the face of the unknown. When the forces affecting his experiences and actions are too complicated to be clearly discerned, he is prone to attribute these influences to *luck, life,* or *fate*. This universal recognition that there are forces affecting us which are beyond our control and beyond our exact prediction is the experience around which the person constructs his concepts of God. In other words, his unconscious drive to confabulate prompts him to construct a God concept to relieve his feeling or something missing when he faces the unknown. Any of an infinite number of God concepts may at any given time in an individual fulfill that needed gestalt feeling and carry with it the sense of certainty. However, we only need to survey some of these different concepts to recognize that any individual's sense of certainty, *faith*, or *belief* does not prove anything at all except that it is possible to have such feelings.

The preceding sequence carries the concept of *confabulation* from the activities of the cell membranes through to the highest level of the longings of the human brain to solve the mysteries of the universe of which we are a part. This concept involves that aspect of the living process that attempts to fill in the gaps of information. It should be understood that this is an abstracted component of the total living process and that many other formulations are possible. At this point I wish to outline another universal principle of living tissue which certainly overlaps the *confabulation* drive but is probably more organized. This is the intrinsic self-healing tendency of living tissues. If I cut my hand, it tends to heal. If I break a bone, it tends to heal. What does the doctor do? He cleans up the cut and perhaps puts in a few stitches and the cut heals better, but the doctor does not do the healing. Nature does the healing. The doctor may straighten the broken bone and put on a cast, but again nature does the healing, not the doctor.

When it comes to the brain we find that the brain provides an extremely complicated information system. The tissue healing property of the brain is one aspect. However, there is a functional aspect of the brain wherein it seems to have a mechanism for organizing ideational defenses. I have taken the liberty of calling this the ISSOT, i.e. the *i*ntrinsic, *s*pontaneous, *s*elf-*o*rganizing *t*endency of the brain or mind. My assumption is that this operates in the unconscious mind as well as in the conscious mind. Certainly, there is some overlap between this operational concept and what I called the *unconscious confabulation drive*. However, the latter is a general tendency to bridge gaps of information, while the ISSOT is perhaps more complicated because, like the self-healing tendency at the tissue level, it tends to repair disturbances in terms of previously laid down patterns. However, the ISSOT can also be conceived of as a sort of an on-going reviewing system that tends to redo previous patterns when new experiences do not fit the previous concepts well enough. These statements bring out the close relationship between the ISSOT and the unconscious confabulation drive, but I wish to stress that ISSOT is a special function of the brain which is most easily recognized in the human brain. It is as if the human brain has reached a degree of complexity, so that some kind of higher level reviewing system develops which is, as might be said, a quantum jump beyond what is evident in subhuman brains. However, we may discover that if we can supply the dolphin with a tool comparable to the human hand that it may have comparable powers of abstraction and generalization. At any rate the ISSOT is the dynamic tendency of the brain to adapt to the conditions to which it is subject, and to organize the thoughts and feelings in ways which favor survival. Thus we can say that the ISSOT is the very complicated operation of the unconscious confabulation drive at the brain level. This is an on-going process which does not wait for the intervention of the physician. However, the brain is subject to many complex interferences which decrease its efficiency. The brain physiology is modified by a wide variety of chemicals, and the ambient patterns of the brain function are influenced by the various life experiences in the complex process of memory development.

It is open to speculation as to how old the child has to be before there is significant manifestation of the power of abstraction and generalization, but it seems to be present quite early. At any rate, many aspects of childhood behavior indicate that abstraction and generalization are early characteristics of the human brain. The child's complaints of *you always* or *you never* are examples.

Going back to the black box symbol, we need to remind ourselves that the actual unconscious organization is open to question, but our speculations can be evaluated in terms of how useful our deductions are. With this reservation, I wish to propose that at a level below the level of dream consciousness there is a level of differentiated drives which are organized around words in terms of unlimited abstraction and generalization.

The law of the control of the unconscious drives can be formulated as *Thou shalt not do this or that,* but it puts in something the Bible leaves out, namely *unless you have a good enough excuse.*

The potential for these differentiated drives must be present in the fertilized human ovum, but it is difficult to decide when in the squence of development their attachment to generalized word concepts begins. For example, a drive which certainly has its parallels in animals, easily seen in the young as soon as they become ambulatory, is the impulse to explore. The parent animal exercises protective restraints over the young while they are learning some boundaries of safety. The human being is more persistently exploratory than the subhuman species. This becomes manifest in the wish to be free from both internal and external controls. This example of the abstraction and generalization of a drive as experienced in the human being becomes one of the most dynamic psychological forces we have to manage. This drive may be labelled the chaos drive because when the wish to be free from both internals and externals approaches fulfillment a horrible experience occurs, namely the experience of chaos which includes a feeling of total insecurity. Thus it can be said that there is no such thing as complete freedom, but there is such a thing as limited freedom at a price. Thus the challenge is what freedom do you want and what price do you want to pay for it. I am free to drive my car down the road, but I am not completely free. I must obey the mechanical laws to keep it on the road and I must obey the traffic laws in order to stay out of jail. If I accept these reasonable limitations, I can drive along with a sense of freedom. If I am fretting about these limitations I lose the sense of freedom. It is an easy step from these generalizations to see how this drive which is a dynamic part of each individual must be constructively managed in order for mankind to survive and retain the modulated feelings of freedom without which life loses much of its feeling of meaning.

Another drive which possibly is slightly more differentiated than the chaos drive may be formulated as, "I unconsciously want to kill everybody and everything all the time." However, when we add the control factor, it reads as follows, "Thou shalt not kill anybody or anything at anytime unless you have a good enough excuse." Most of us figure that for a mosquito to light on us is a good enough excuse to justify killing it. It becomes increasingly difficult to find acceptable excuses to kill larger creatures but obviously there are acceptable excuses for many people in terms of hunting in hunting season. In war to many people it is acceptable to kill the enemy provided he has not surrendered.

It is difficult to face the implications of the universal kill drive. You and I and every living human unconsciously wants this unlimited power with its power of destruction. Without this wish man cannot master the universe. What started out as the primitive life and death struggle in the primitive jungle, which has been re-enacted on every battle field since the beginning of history, has become the unconscious wish to kill everybody and everything all the time. This is because of the power of the mind for abstraction and generalization.

What shall we do about it? Shall we stop the unconscious mind from wishing to kill everybody and everything all the time? I am sorry, but that is not only impossible but also undesirable. There is no other alternative. Either we live with this destructive force and control it or we destroy ourselves. This is the Pandora's Box that science has opened. Can we control it? I do not know, but it be-hooves us to try to learn how to control it. Space mastery is a pos-sible outlet. Can we turn this unlimited wish for power away from each other to outer space? The greater the mind the greater the concept of power and the greater the danger if that power is mis-used. The solitary killer in the night streets of New York City is only a minor threat to us. The real threat is the team of men at the control panels which can set off atomic suicide. Every one of those men, no matter to what nation he belongs, ours or some others, has an unconscious wish to find a good enough excuse to unleash the terrific power he has at his finger tips.

What is our solution? We need to train people with the con-scious knowledge that their own kill drive must be properly man-aged in order for us to be safe. Secondarily, when these people are so trained, they can be trusted to help teach others to control their kill drives. At last we are at the brink where human brotherhood is forced upon us. The white man no longer has a monopoly on the supreme power to kill. If we do not respect the intrinsic human value of all races and people, they will turn against us with their kill drives, as we have been turning against them, but now no longer dare to do. You may feel uneasy with a black man, a red man, or a yellow man as a bed fellow, but you better make him your bed fel-low or he may kill you in your sleep just as you may kill him in his sleep.

In so far as we properly manage this power drive so that we gain mastery over nature and limit our actions toward other human be-ings, we can survive and progress in this modern technological world.

Let us remember that other people as well as ourselves are not expendable.

Another universal drive which reflects the influence of the sensory nervous system can be formulated as, "I unconsciously want to submit to everybody and everything in every way all the time." The same law of control applies, namely, "Thou shalt not submit to anybody or anything in any way unless you have a good enough excuse."

Other drives could be formulated as follows:

I unconsciously want attention from everybody and everything in every way all the time.

I unconsciously have sexual feelings toward everybody and everything all the time.

I unconsciously want to own everybody and everything all the time.

At this point there may be a transition to a more complex formulation. The drive to own is one thing and the belief that I do own is another thing. There is evidence of an unconscious universal ownership feeling. The infant seems to assume that anything in reach is his. He does not have to be trained to know what *is* his. He has to be trained to know what is *not* his. Human beings automatically feel they have a right to take anything in the universe if they can grab ahold of it, unless there is clear evidence that it is already owned by somebody else. We do not hesitate to take possession of the moon, but we are on guard for danger signals arising from some other creature which might own it. Not having found any evidence of extraterrestial creatures on the moon, we merely consider what rules we make regarding ownership patterns by other human beings. So far the astronauts have not discovered precious metals on the moon, but if some mineral were discovered which would be valuable enough to travel to the moon to get, the race would be on, unless adequate rules were already formulated.

Another unconscious drive which is organized on the belief level may be worded *the unconscious delusion of grandeur and irresistibility*. This can be conceived of as having its roots in the first six months of the baby's experience. At that time the baby does not even have to know what is the matter with him in order to be fixed. The signals, "Wah! Wah!," suffice to bring to his aid an intelligence beyond his comprehension. As he grows older he learns that the magic no longer works that easily. However, if the parent *spoils* the child by trying too hard to satisfy his whims, the child does not learn the appropriate reality limitations, so he expects more than is possible. Sooner or later the spoiled child is a crying child. This unconscious delusion of grandeur and irresistibility normally remains in the background of our inner experience and probably plays a complex part in the religious experiences which have been described in various ways as a transcendental feeling of unlimited being, which leads to illusions or delusions of identity with God. It is a fine line of distinction between using this experience as a basis of faith, trust, humility, in the face of the vast unknown and using it as a pathological delusion of grandeur, such as of being God.

Once one conceives of these mechanisms in the unconscious mind, it is not difficult to recognize the emergence of power crazy persons on the world scene. It is helpful to realize that those individuals are not basically different from the rest of us. The difference lies in a difference of control and modulation patterns. Our basic training needs to take into account these forces are in all of us and must be managed, or disaster results. Yet if these drives were absent, people would not be people.

The drive to deceive is manifested in two planes. It is the outside boundary of the Ego by which Ego deceives the outside world about various thoughts and feelings that may be in the conscious mind. This is usually thought of as *self control*. On the boundary between the conscious mind and the Superego (the highest level region of the unconscious mind) the layer of deception serves to deceive us as to what is in our unconscious minds.

Thus we have reviewed briefly the concept of differential layers of organization in the unconscious mind from the Id to the conscious mind. It would seem reasonable that understanding these forces in the individual can throw light on the behavior of individuals in their circles of influence from local to global patterns.

The patterns of management of human affairs are related to how human beings modulate their drives. As mentioned before the ISSOT has a great deal to do with how each of us manipulates the world around us. There are a variety of disturbances which interfere with the appropriate operation of the ISSOT. One of these disturbances can be labelled *unconscious superstitions*. A superstition, as used here, is defined as a *false belief that something is doomed to happen*. When the unconscious mind has a superstition, it does not know that it is false, and it treats is as a belief. Any concept which is organized in the brain as a belief is one which we want to preserve and defend. The unconscious mind is able to give up a superstition, provided it is convinced that it is false. Herein lies the problem. How can we penetrate to the unconscious mind to convince it that its superstitions are false? I have chosen to label any method that succeeds in reaching the unconscious mind in a way that changes it, *psychopenetration*. We are up against a confusion because if at any moment we are aware of an idea, that idea is no longer unconscious. However, there are some patterns of response which indirectly indicate that something is influencing the conscious mind from the unconscious mind. For example, take the phrase, "I unconsciously feel that everything is doomed to be worse than it is." Most people say that that statement is false for them. However, some people claim the statement feels true and it may take a considerable effort and special formulations to change the person's feeling. Therefore, it can be said that in the presence of an unconscious superstition, the unconscious mind blinds the conscious to the contrary evidence. There is evidence of other methods used by the unconscious mind to try to preserve its unconscious false beliefs: for example, the unconscious mind may give the conscious mind compulsions to do things which tend to fulfill the superstition, not because it is really doomed to happen but because we actually do something to bring it about. The unconscious mind also may attempt to preserve the superstition by producing nightmares which symbolically fulfill the superstition. Still another manifestation may be psychosomatic symptoms that symbolically fulfill the superstition.

To summarize: the unconscious mind is an operational concept and the development of methodology for producing beneficial changes in it is an imperative for modern man, if he is to survive. The concept that the unconscious mind operates in ascending levels of complexity gives us a framework for analyzing the divergent patterns that emerge in consciousness and in behavior. The drives which have been formulated are mediated through the individual, but the interpersonal reactions from small groups to large groups enter into the excuse systems which release the various forces in the unconscious mind in the multiple patterns of life.

We have reviewed some of the forces which human beings draw upon from within themselves, and these forces are essential to being human, but they can destroy us unless properly managed. If properly managed they provide the means of man's mastery over his destiny and the destiny of everything he touches. To paraphrase the Bible one might say "man shall inherit the earth and the fruits thereof," but something now must be added, namely, "and the responsibility therefore." No longer can we depend on the regenerative forces of nature below the level of the human brain to save the earth and its subhuman creatures from man and his errors. Man has now so filled the earth space, that his actions, good or bad, wise or unwise, become the main determinent of what happens around him. It is now already within his power concept to blow the moon out of the *sky*, either to blow it to pieces or to change its orbit. The challenge to us echoes and re-echoes that we must learn to modulate the forces within us so that they are expressed in controlled power patterns, controlled so as to serve a dynamic constructive purpose for mankind and his universe.

[CHAPTER NINETEEN]

ENVIRONMENTAL IMPERATIVES OF STRATEGY

George H. Miller

As our population grows, consumption of energy and other resources grows even faster. People are becoming more concerned with the effect of this steeply ascending cycle on their environment. How can the natural goodness of our air, our water, and the land itself be preserved from the wasteful throw-off of modern society?

On the military side there is equal concern for the side-effects of modern weapon technology. For example, has anyone calculated the total permanent loss our country would sustain, in terms of devastation and pollution, from the explosion on U.S. territory of one megaton-size nuclear weapon? Or ten such weapons? Of fifty? Or one-thousand. The single most important fact of military life today is the large and growing stockpile of nuclear weapons in the world. As citizens, all of us hope and pray that these weapons will never be used. But hoping and praying may not be enough when the very existence of the country is involved. One's entire national security must always place special emphasis on preservation of the nation. Consequently, those responsible for national security will wish to take *all* steps necessary to prevent nuclear attack on our country.

Uppermost in many people's minds is concern that some aggressive group of nuclear zealots may one day launch a surprise nuclear attack on the United States. The military strategist must therefore look coldly and objectively at every possible way a potential aggressor might attempt to do us in. Strategies and deployments must be devised which not only defend against such an attack, and retaliate thereafter, but even more important, *prevent* it from being launched in the first place. Here is where the military strategist and the environmentalist can and must make common cause.

In identifying steps which can be taken to prevent a nuclear attack, one must understand what motivates an aggressor to initiate war with a surprise attack on his victim. A review of a number of such attacks in modern history shows that the primary motive for initiating a surprise attack is high confidence on the part of the attacker that he will thereby gain a decisive military advantage. To gain such an advantage over the United States, an aggressor must be certain he can destroy the major portion of the U.S. nuclear weapons force which could retaliate against him.

The accepted formula for nuclear security is deterrence. But what might seem to be adequate deterrence from our point of view may not necessarily deter a ruthless opponent obsessed with achieving a decisive military victory. As long as there exists the military temptation to achieve decisive advantage through nuclear attack on the U.S., deterrence through threat of retaliation (*after* he has launched his attack) may not be enough to insure national survival. Thus, in addition to the deterrence through-threat-of retaliation approach, our deployment and strategy must be such as to make it physically *impossible* for him to achieve decisive military advantage through such an attack—no matter what he may try. The would-be aggressor must be persuaded to think and plan courses of action other than nuclear destruction of the United States. Remove the temptation for such an attack and the aggressor is forced to other avenues to achieve his military advantage.

Anyone who contemplates the geographical structure of our earth cannot help but notice the vast expanses of open ocean touching our shores, to the east, south, and west, and extending over most (70 percent) of the earth's surface. One also cannot help but notice the relatively limited extent of U. S. land geography. In fact, one might suggest that the U. S. is as land-deficient with respect to the nuclear weapons of today as England was with respect to the weapons of

World War II. Our limited land geography virtually compels us to place more emphasis on sea-based deployments, merely to achieve the degree of geographical separation between urban-industrial and offensive weapon complexes that the Soviets achieve in their far more extensive land area.

In addition to more emphasis on sea-basing, our nuclear posture, both land and sea, should stress mobility. The reason is clear. To execute a successful surprise attack, an aggressor must prepare detailed targeting plans *in advance*. He must know precisely where each important target is located and the details of exactly how and in what time sequence it is to be destroyed. Such detailed pretargeting can only be accomplished against fixed targets. In the Pearl Harbor surprise attack, for example, it was the airfields and the ships tied up in the precisely-located berths in Pearl Harbor itself that were attacked. Ships operating in nearby waters were not attacked.

Because of the requirement for precise, detailed pretargeting, it is virtually impossible to pretarget and destroy a large force operating at sea with the same speed and degree of confidence with which stationary targets can be knocked out. Mobile targets such as ships at sea must be located and continually tracked before they can be attacked. Such tracking tends to provide warning to the victim that an attack may be imminent, thus providing time to take defensive measures to defeat or neutralize the attack. Since it is virtually impossible to execute a successful, massive surprise attack against continuously moving forces, like ships underway at sea, their survivability can be measured in hours and days, rather than the minutes it would take to destroy non-mobile forces. Now, the time required to reduce a victim's major weapons to ineffectiveness is approximately the time which the victim government would have to appraise the situation, examine options, and make decisions. Thus, if the survivability of one's nuclear offensive force is measurable in minutes, a government's decision and response time must also be measured in minutes. The longer one's major weapons can retain effectiveness under attack, the more time a government has for decision-making and appropriate, rational response.

Deployment of the majority of U. S. nuclear offensive missiles and bombers outside the U. S. would reduce the value of the United States as a primary, time-urgent military target. It would force the aggressor to allocate more effort to weapons other than ICBM's aimed at the United States. And if the weapons are sea-mobile, their increased survivability would give the government more time for decision-making and appropriate response.

Historical experience shows that human beings, and governments as well, require considerable time to recover from the shock of major surprise attack and respond in a manner which best serves the common good. Thus, a deployment which assures adequate time for decision and intelligent response is an essential element of credible deterrence.

Even if one were to accept more emphasis on sea-basing as the best way to go, there is a time element which must be taken into account. The massive buildup of nuclear missiles aimed at the United States has continued into the seventies. Our own nuclear buildup has been confined to upgradine present missiles and maintaining present deployment patterns. The implications of the current Soviet effort to increase their strategic weapon superiority can best be portrayed by recalling some of the recent statements by U. S. Defense officials. Americans have been warned on a number of occasions that by 1974 the Soviets could achieve the capability to knock out 95 percent of the strategic weapons based in the U. S. When such a capability is achieved, those elements in an aggressor's government, who were influential enough to have this vast nuclear missile program funded, may one day urge that it be used. On the basis of the warning by our Defense leaders, it would appear that the United States has until 1974 to readjust its nuclear deployments, so as to reduce the value of the United States as the prime target for nuclear aggression and make it impossible to gain a decisive military advantage by such an attack.

But even though an opponent may not be planning to launch his nuclear strength against our country at this time, there are other ways he could use his superior nuclear leverage to pry concessions from the U. S. and its major allies, and prevent them from taking more limited actions in their own vital interests. Precedents for this form of nuclear blackmail are already part of the historical record. In the early fifties, for example, U. S. resolve to have *no more Koreas* led to our adoption of the concept of *massive retaliation*. Our government at that time took the position publicly that any nation which threatened U. S. or NATO security interests would run the risk of massive nuclear attack. The crucial test of U. S. *massive retaliation* came in the Suez crisis of 1956. As the crisis deepened, the previous U. S. threat to retaliate massively caused the Soviets initially to take a cautious attitude toward Egypt's take-over of the Suez Canal. After a period of increasing tension, a high U. S. official announced publicly that the U. S. did not intend to *shoot its way into Suez.*

This tended to ease tension, at least from our point of view, and assuage the fear of nuclear war which was building up in Western nations. At the same time, it served as a signal to the Soviets and others that (a) Suez, long regarded as of critical importance to Western security, was no longer considered among vital U. S. interests and (b) that the U. S. had backed away from massive retaliation as its main military deterrent against aggression, and had indeed deterred itself from taking more limited action in support of allies by the fear *massive retaliation* generated here at home.

The year 1956 thus marked the beginning of what can be regarded as the Soviet strategic breakout, from the historical confines of the Asiatic land mass into competition for world power and influence. U. S. failure to maintain its firm position in the Suez crisis led aggressors to believe that they could safely compete for influence in strategic areas formerly regarded as of vital importance to the West. Their tremendous Soviet merchant marine and naval buildup began soon thereafter. The U. S. nuclear threat had lost credibility as a deterrent of limited, nonnuclear aggression action.

It was not long after the Suez crisis that Soviet influence was penetrating the Western hemisphere, in Cuba, which is located in an area most critical to the security of the United States itself, and astride the Atlantic Ocean approaches to the Panama Canal.

In the early sixties, with a friendly government installed in Cuba, the Soviets sought to convert that island into a base for nuclear missiles aimed at the United States. As the Cuba crisis developed, U. S. military leaders, according to Theodore Sorenson's account,[112] recommended to the President that U. S. forces bomb and invade Cuba. The President, apparently on the basis of other advice, decided to postpone bomb-and-invade actions and instead prevent the entry of Soviet ships carrying missiles into Cuban ports. This was termed a quarantine, and it caused the Soviets to remove their nuclear missiles from Cuba. As a result of this noncombat action, the need for ground combat in Cuba never arose.

Unfortunately, we did not persist in our quarantine, and Cuba still remains a hostile politico-military strong point in the heart of the Western Hemisphere. Nevertheless, U. S. noncombat action in the Cuba crisis is one of the few, and perhaps one of the most noteworthy, examples of U. S. use of its nuclear and naval superiority to resolve in its favor, without war, a very serious international situation. But as has been the case many times in recorded history, the winner in such instances tends to glory in his past victories, while the loser learns all the lessons and sets about correcting his mistakes.

The current Soviet campaign for world influence and control is perhaps one of the most comprehensive and successful of recorded history. In this campaign we find a common denominator, the Soviet merchant fleet. It is the Soviet merchant fleet, supported by their Navy, which is in the vanguard of their drive for world influence. The Soviet merchant marine, fishing fleets, scientific ships, and naval units are being coordinated at the government level, operating as instruments of foreign policy. It is the Soviet Merchant Marine which establishes the political bridgehead, builds up trade, and carries the weapons to arm and sustain the satellite armies which fight the Koreas, Vietnams, and others yet to come.

The Soviet Union today is in the midst of a massive buildup, not only of nuclear weapons, but of their naval and merchant fleets as well. Under the shield of their anticipated nuclear superiority, their Navy and commercial fleets will be available to serve as the spearhead of an aggressive foreign policy. Indications thus far suggest that *peaceful aggression* is likely to continue on the assumption that Western nations will be deterred from initiating significant counteractions. Thus, the worldwide campaign for influence and control is being furthered—without direct Soviet involvement in fighting.

Meanwhile, post-World War II Western responses to world crises have been characterized by a greater tendency to lead with land combat options. The subtle, subversive preliminary campaign and gradual arms buildup for *wars of national liberation*, which precede the call for U. S. troops, often-times have gone virtually unopposed. Since World War II, U. S. land forces have been deployed overseas on a large scale and have engaged in extensive land conflict on two occasions. But, it is not called war. Maritime options, such as interception at sea of military supplies before they reach enemy-controlled territory, on the other hand, have usually (with the exception of the Cuba crisis) been cast aside with the allegation that they constituted *acts of war*. Also, since World War II, it has become popular in our country to regard ships as things of the past. It was so easy to sink them, we were told; they would be virtually swept from the seas. The impression was given that hereafter most overseas transportation, military as well as commercial, would be carried on by other means.

As time passed, however, events suggested that America had become the first victim of this kind of theorizing. For, while many Americans expected ships to disappear from the seas, world trade and surface shipping began, and is continuing, to expand at a very rapid rate. The ship construction and sea transport business moved overseas, as foreign nations began to build ships and compete for a greater share of the world shipping market—including our own foreign trade. Thus foreign nations are now reaping, at our expense in many cases, the revenues from this expanding world shipping market, which continues despite predictions to the contrary, to carry over 98 percent of the continuously-expanding world overseas commerce. Meanwhile, our own merchant marine gradually declined into obsolescence.

Our nation, with its relatively limited heavily-populated land geography is now faced with an unprecedented buildup of Soviet nuclear and maritime power. The momentum of the Soviet buildup could be matched by our country only by a high-priority effort over a period of several years. We are behind, and it will be very difficult to catch up.

As for the nuclear threat, it is more important than ever to do everything possible to keep the conflict away from our shores. Toward this end, the United States is compelled, as never before, to compensate for its limited land geography by turning to the seas for additional nuclear weapon deployment area. The sea deployment component of our nuclear weapon mix should be such as to eliminate any temptation on the part of an aggressor to seek military advantage through nuclear attack on our country.

But while it is of utmost importance to the survival of our country to prevent a nuclear holocaust, this is not enough. We need to do more than we have in the past to avoid being dragged into unwelcome wars of any kind. This means that more needs to be done to strengthen our know-how and capacity for peaceful competition. Our maritime options need to be developed and utilized on a continuing basis in furtherance of foreign policy by peaceful means. We are now in the process of bringing our troops home from Vietnam. If we are to keep them home, we shall need to make better use of our naval and commercial fleet assets in winning the peace.

The Nixon low-profile doctrine for Asia[113] and the President's Merchant Marine program of 1970[114] are significant steps this Administration is taking to emphasize and strengthen our country's effectiveness in peaceful competition. If given the support and direction they deserve, they will increase our capabilities for keeping the fighting away from our land environment and for winning the peace.

If the low-profile doctrine for Asia of the 1970's had been applied to our nuclear weapon deployments in the 1960's, the current unprecedented nuclear threat to our own country probably could have been avoided. Hopefully, there is still time to readjust, to optimize our nuclear deployments, to use our sea-oriented geography to best advantage, and to take all other measures to reduce an opponent's temptation to initiate a surprise nuclear attack on the United States. Here is an area in which all citizens working for a better United States, and indeed, a better world environment, can lend their support.

[CHAPTER TWENTY]

MYOPIC VIEW
FROM OLYMPUS*

Elise Boulding

A MERICAN FUTURISTS need to be scolded about three habits to which they have become professionally addicted: the habit of global-style ethnocentrism, too much reverence for existing data banks, and the habit of using a rhetoric of competence that masks the problems of competence.

Ethnocentrism in Social Model-Building

The global ethnocentrism is an unintended by-product of an honest effort to think about the planet as a whole. To describe the macroproblems of the planet within the frame of reference of a particular Western sequence of experience, however, is about as appropriate as for the Australian bushman to describe the problems of the planet in terms of his own experience of desert life. The Australian bushman has a very sophisticated technology of environmental utilization, given the resources he has available. He knows how to find food and water and how to deal with distance, time, space, and heat in very remarkable ways. His knowledge, however, is useful in a very limited range of settings. Our knowledge covers more settings, but our cognitive map of the planetary sociosphere is still very inadequate.

*Presented before the World Future Society, Washington, D.C., May 14, 1971.

This is serious, because the resources available to us for social change are limited by the thought models used to describe and label them. The intellectual reality constructs of the scientific subculture of the West make quite a few resources unavailable to us, including large chunks of human experience codified in nonwestern historical records, the possibility of living in multidimensional time, and a frugality orientation that alters consumption patterns.

Model of Frugality-Oriented Social Systems

Interestingly enough, there are certain highly specific conditions under which frugality as a social resource is available to us. The analogy of the spaceship earth, first used by Barbara Ward and Kenneth Boulding, points to the circumstances under which we admire and are willing to develop the techniques of frugality. The nomadic role, for example, evokes this type of frugality.* While in the broadest sense, we earthlings are all space nomads, in practice most people acquire their sense of the significance of frugality from newspaper stories of the problems of compressing survival equipment into a tiny ship for the long journey to the moon and back. This is why the spaceship image can convey the need for frugality, even if it is not enough to alter behavior patterns. More mundanely, most people's adventures with nomadism involve traveling with a carefully packed camper trailer. A more austere form of this adventure is found among backpackers who spend solitary summers in high mountains living on what land and stream offer. The Outward Bound Program[115] is a popular device for training the children of affluence for austerity. Some counter-culture styles offer interesting examples of an ethic of frugality. The implications of these counter-culture patterns for changing life-styles of the middle class are not yet clear. Under what conditions does the experience of affluence lead to an ethic of frugality? We need to know more about the dynamics of the frugality-inducing process.

Macro-system models for a society based on frugality have been developed both by Ghandhi and Mao Tse-tung. Western economists have laughed at the various special campaigns launched from time to time in China, from the back-yard furnace movement to the *save bits of string* campaigns, pointing out the high costs of this

*This has been true historically, and even at the height of their affluence the great Mongolian Khans, Kubla Khan and Ghengis Khan lived simply and traveled light.

type of resource conservation.[116] While these particular campaigns may indeed have been inefficient, the importance of developing a technology of local power development and household resource conservation is at least nationally recognized in China. The technologies themselves may take a while to develop. Gandhi's Village Development Model involves increasing the food intake and level of physical comfort in the homes of a village simply by applying new (and partly very old) simple-tool technologies to existing resources in a village, with a bare minimum of starter equipment brought in from outside. It is, in fact, a more sophisticated version of the Chinese bits-of-string approach, and some European economists are belatedly beginning to see the possibilities in this non-western model.[117] (Unfortunately the Indian government in its passion for modernization Western-style has rejected this decentralist approach.) I do not hear very much serious discussion about Indian and Chinese development models in development circles in the United States. Frugality as a life-style exists in special compartments in our social thought, but is not available as an option to be seriously considered in a consumption-oriented society.

Parochial Data Banks

In addition to the global ethocentrism that enables us to envision one pattern only for world development, we have a Euro-North American reverence for a certain set of UN-nurtured international socioeconomic data banks. This leads us to measure the length of our noses more and more precisely, with less and less understanding of an elusive concept known variously as *welfare* or *quality of life*, especially in its international comparative aspects.

> In the early days of cross-national comparative work no one questioned the use of the highly industrialized nations of the west as the yardstick by which all other developments could be measured. With the primary focus on poverty, disease and malnutrition, economic productivity was naturally the developmental goal. Thus economists and demographers alike worked increasingly with concepts of levels of industrialization, literacy levels, infrastructures and readiness for change (including readiness for population control). As take-off points become increasingly hard to predict in purely economic terms, more attention came to be paid to "soft" variables, and the publication of Russett's *World Handbook of Social and Political Indicators*[118] was a kind of landmark in presenting hard and soft variables

side by side, as they related in development. Adelman and Morris[119] went much further in quantifying "soft" variables, using informed but subjective judgments on a range of political and social factors which they theorized would relate to development.

Although Adelman and Morris deplore the implication in their choice of indices that the western model is *the* model of development, and suggest there could be others, there is in fact no way that such other models could be recognized, using their indicators. Thus we are back to the question of how we can define welfare levels so they can include other styles of living than the urban western style.

Sametz,[120] building on Kuznets[121] work, suggests ways of recalculating the GNP so that the *costs* of industrialization, in terms of public and private expenditures which must be made to provide for old wants now harder to meet in technopolis, should be subtracted instead of added to the GNP. He would also add non-monetized production to the GNP, which would in his estimation double the GNP of predominantly non-industrial societies. (This would add to GNP in industrialized societies too, but far less.) The longer we use the unrealistic traditional method of calculating GNP, the longer we postpone accurate description of welfare levels. The complicated arithmetic of cost-benefit analysis, applied to the major sources of pollution in industrialized societies, cannot yet be easily translated into overall corrections to the GNP. Even without doing that, however, Sametz' corrections would substantially improve our estimates.

A grasp of ways to revise GNP estimation procedures represents one major recent insight into assessment of welfare. The recognition of obstacles to social mobility and equitable distribution of social and economic resources is another. The UN *Studies on Levels of Living*[122] make it quite clear that overall levels of industrial and educational achievement are not in themselves predictive of further economic growth. The crucial factor is degree of rigidity of social structures, of cultural and religious barriers that may prevent some groups within a society from taking advantage of educational and/or job opportunities.[123]

The goal of the project to which the above-quoted memo refers is to develop national welfare profiles that will take account of new concepts of GNP (gross national product) and of the interrelationships between opportunity structures and social structures that determine access to opportunities, while minimizing ideological bias in measures of political development. The idea is to get away from a rank-ordering of nations on any one dimension of development, and to make a multidimensional presentation of the state of each society in such a way that planning can proceed according to the preferred values of that society.

It is difficult for us to broaden the agenda and examine alternative concepts of welfare and quality of life. On the whole, we think of ourselves as being *locked in* to a high-technology society with the only imagined exists involving an unthinkable return to the past. The feeling of being locked in is a result of the acceptance of a peculiar unilinear theory of development that postulates such a tight interlocking of physical technology and social patterns (the urbanization-industrialization-communications-network theory of development) that we are convinced we can only go where urban-based technology will take us.

The Data Banks of History

Here is where history as a social resource can help free us. Complex communications networks have evolved in the absence of urbanization, as the horseback empire of Ghengis Kahn demonstrates. This empire undertook the first mapping of the kingdoms of Europe when the local princes could not even find their way to each other's castles.[124] Pluralism and decentralized control is possible even with large-scale administrative systems of empire, as the millet system of the Ottoman Empire demonstrated, allowing a variety of religions and political subsystems to exist within an overall Moslem administrative structure. A passion for learning can exist without a large-scale planned educational technology when people have the idea that knowing how to read is advantageous,[125] as the sudden flourishing of lay teachers of the Three R's outside the cathedral schools of the medieval European church demonstrated. A passion for experimentation with the building of new societies can exist without governmental subsidy by monarchies or parliaments, as the countless adventurous bands of Hittites, Celts, Phoenicians, Greeks, and other Mediterranean people showed in the second millenium BC, in organizing do-it-yourself utopian expeditions all around the Mediterranean.[126]

A passion for experimenting with forms of household organization and kin patterning is endemic in human civilization, and the storied variants in primitive tribes are only a tiny fraction of the arrangements that have been tried. The two-hundred-person communes of the European middle ages make our young people's counter-culture experiments seem tame.[127] Humankind has developed many patterns for dealing with varying population densities over the past ten thousand years, and seven thousand years of experience with urbanism is no small heritage to draw on. Almost any kind of family or communal experiment that is being tried today has been tried over and over again under varying conditions—nomadic, settled rural, settled urban, seasonal migration utopian colonization.

In short, the innovative spirit was not born in the West and is not dependent on modern technology. Furthermore, there is no one-to-one correspondence between environmental resources and culture, any more than between technological resources and culture. Tightly-packed and environmentally deprived Japan and the Netherlands would never have made it if they had depended on physical resources. Their chief resource was social ingenuity. Assuming that we are all potentially as ingenious as the Japanese or the Dutch, we are free to borrow social technology from India, Japan, China and elsewhere—technologies that were developed in totally different contexts but which can be adapted. Our main problem is to inventory all the existing social technologies so we knew what we have to draw on. This we have not done because we think that what we have is all there is.

The BLTMT[76] is a millstone around the neck of the West. There is nothing inherently wrong in projecting Basic Multiform Long-Term Trends, as long as we include all the forms, but a reading of futurist literature only gives us the Western variants.

Why this emphasis on borrowing from other social technologies? Are we really so badly off in the urban West, apart from some impending mineral shortages that can be solved by a combination of consumer education and new scientific discoveries? Maldistribution of existing resources is after all a solvable problem. Development theory tells us that the increase in individual rationality and social competence that modern urbanization makes possible will lead to a society both more equalitarian and more afflluent than the one we have now.

The Mythology of Competence

In spite of the comforting doctrines of development theory, we are ambivalent on this question of competence. We think we have it, yet we fear we do not. Our fear of being locked in by current technologies indicates our uncertainty about our competence. There is good reason for this uncertainty. On the one hand, although we have been able to develop very complex, large-scale systems of administration of physical and social resources in Europe and North America, there seems to be some evidence (in the United States at least) that at this moment we are unable to do anything but elaborate on present patterns. We may not be able to deal with structurally generated inequities because we cannot address ourselves to structural change. Roland Warren's article, *The Sociology of Knowledge and the Problems of the Inner Cities*,[128] analyzes the participation of community decision organizations in the Model Cities Program and concludes that all the rhetoric about a redistribution of decision-making power among the peoples to be served by the Model Cities Program led to nothing but a reinforcement of existing structures. After three years of major and well-funded effort, nothing had changed.

Other startling evidence on the failure of social competence is coming from some of my own research on American families. One comparative study of anglo and chicano families in a small town near Boulder that focused on the capacity for warmth and intergrative and adaptive relationships in family and community seemed to point to greater integrative and adaptive skills on the part of the chicano than the anglo husbands and wives.[129] A Colorado field project of the Gross-National Research Studies in the Family that is focusing on the skill with which families take up new life options and make use of social resources to improve their situation is uncovering somewhat analagous material. Low income families are reporting that they depend on themselves, *with a little help from their friends*, to cope with a wide range of problems, from illness to unemployment. Middle class families convey a sense of helplessness apart from reliance on professionalized bureaucratic services to help meet the same range of problems. The other side of the coin of skill in using bureaucratic services may be loss of personal feelings of *copability*. If an increase in reliance on professional services triggers a decline in feelings of *copability* in the most educated sectors, we may have something to be concerned about.

While it is depressing to contrast our mythology of competence with the reality of over-reliance on professionally administered systems that resist structural change aimed at inequities, we can cheer ourselves up by looking at the evidence on the ability of human groups over a wide range of settings to engage in adaptive behavior in the face of changing conditions. For example, in the realm of population control, societies have historically elaborated a great variety of physical and social devices for keeping their numbers at a manageable size, as long as they have had a good reality-feedback concerning their own optimal size. Colonial occupiers interfered with the reality feedback system in Africa and Asia by suddenly changing the scale of social relationships as they involved *a colony* with a mother-country administrative network. It will take some time for the reality feedback systems to get working again in ex-colonial countries.

In all social problem-solving, there are thresholds of perception, and there are patterns of social organization and social communication that enhance the ability to perceive problems and to act on the perception. In short, there are patterns that lower perceptual thresholds. A great deal of modernization-related technology acts to lower such perceptual thresholds, which is why we can identify fertility thresholds[130] for societies based on indices of urbanization, education, and communications networks. Since newly industrializing countries must in addition cope with the problems of change of scale noted above, the indicators by no means predict perfectly, but they are useful.

The same problems of scale that stymie newly-industrializing countries also stymie us. I think that is the lesson to be drawn from the analysis by Roland Warren of the failure of the Model Cities Program, and from similar analyses of other failures in the war on poverty.

There are, however, two approaches to the problems of competence. One is to design large-scale social structures with good delivery systems that equip people well. The other is to focus on decentralized units of the larger social structures. In this approach, one can trace how reality feedback systems operate for individuals from infancy through adulthood to give them the capacity not only for social coping, but also for social creativity. What experiences does an individual have in the family, the local neighborhood and the school as he moves through the various stages of his individual life cycle? There are certain dimensions of human experience common to all these microsystems that affect the ability to function in the larger society. The experience of personal autonomy in a supportive matrix of social warmth is crucial to the development of social creativity, as a great deal of child development research demonstrates.[131]

Failures of the Microsystems of Family and School

I will confine myself here to two examples in the U. S. of inadequate microsystem capacity to develop social competence even in the face of continually rising standards of living. Today's nuclear family has some difficulty in providing the optimum supportive matrix for the growing child. A recent analysis of trends in the U. S. from 1900 to the present at the microsystem and the macrosystem level gives:

> . . . a picture of increasing owner-occupancy of homes and declining incidence of doubling with relatives, which combined with the rising income levels and declining number of children per family (a trend only briefly interrupted by the post-war baby boom) indicates increasing economic security, privacy, and opportunity to give individualized care to children in nuclear family units. Coupled with the decline in labor force participation of children we can view family units as having increasing opportunities for cultural enrichment and personal growth.
>
> Normally these items are thought of as pluses in modern living. It is possible, however, also to view the increase in family privacy and trend to smaller families, and declining opportunities for children to be in the labor force, as a dangerous narrowing of opportunities for meaningful human contacts.
>
> (At the same time) increasing numbers of babies are born outside of the protective matrix that conventional family life provides for children. Supplementary social services make up for this partially, but only partially. The rise in the divorce rate means that increasing numbers of children as well as adults have to pay the emotional costs of family dissolution and reformation. The joint impact of increase in incidence of birth outside of wedlock and of family dissolution rates suggests that the capacity of the home to give nurturance is declining. (There is an) added strain of increasing numbers of women having to provide for the care of small children while they are working, at the same time that day care facilities for small children are declining. The hardest hit of this group are the single family heads of household. This problem must be seen in the context of the decline of the joint household portrayed earlier. Day care centers could serve as substitute extended families if our social values permitted.

Instead they are perceived as a social threat to the family. Participation in the labor force for women could well be counted as a plus if there were adequate child care and home maintenance facilities for women workers, but in their absence this participation is a heavy burden. The relatively static nature of the distribution of occupational categories with respect to the service sector means that there has been no increase in the other possible types of supporting services which could ease the social and physical maintenance burdens of the householder.[132]

Clearly new interfaces have to be developed between public and private structures to provide adequately for the maintenance and loving nurture of individuals in familistic groups.

For the child, the inadequacies of the home as a source of nurture are intensified by the increasing depersonalization of the school environment. In 1900, 80 percent of our schools were one-room schools. Today, less than 20 percent of our schools fall in this category, and small neighborhood schools are the luxury of affluent suburban neighborhoods. With urbanization has come a total age-grading of all life's activities, so children no longer interact with adults except in formal classroom settings or as objects of professional attention in the community. Rising school drop-out rates signal the rebellion of the young against this professionalization of all child-adult relationships. Breaking down the schoolroom walls and recreating an image of the community as an arena for developing new learnings and new social relationships for the child is the main thrust of the alternative school movement. Since most of these experiments are regarded as being on the lunatic fringe of education, we are a long way from creating the interfaces between the social space of the child and the social spaces of the community that will give the child positive feedback experiences in the exercise of social competence outside the manufactured *for children only* environment in which the U.S. specializes.

Nevertheless, there is much reason for optimism. If as futurists we can be faithful to our planetary commitment, and examine the whole range of human resources available to us, great possibilities are opened up. Although we have more problems than we thought we did, we need not remain trapped by our global ethnocentrism, our specialized set of data banks, or our brash rhetoric of pseudo-competence. If we bring a broader repertoire of ideas to the task of coping with increasing scale of human relationships, and give more attention to the public-private interfaces for home, school and local community, we can with our colleagues of other continents contribute positively to the generation of new tomorrows.

[CHAPTER TWENTY-ONE]

A FUTURE FOR THE PAST

ROBERT J. MATTHEWS

WHEN WINSTON CHURCHILL once spoke in the United States, he prefaced his remarks by saying that he was happy to speak about what was now history because he knew ever so much more about the past than about the future. I share that sentiment with Churchill in the present essay. I want to talk about the quality of life in the future, but I know ever so much more about the quality of life in the past. But this is a problem common to all who have an interest in the future of man: we have to use what knowledge we have at present, a knowledge gained from the past, to shape our future. My contribution to the present study of planning for the future will be minimal inasmuch as I wish only to make a plea for the importance of *historical understanding* to this task of planning for the future. Certainly, by this plea I do not want to suggest that there exists a schematic application of the important lessons from history. As Montaigne[133] has aptly noted, *every example limps*, which is to say that these examples from history never fit exactly the situation at hand. Nevertheless, the study of history was for Montaigne, as it was for other humanists of his time, principally a means of achieving that practical wisdom which enables a person to live well in the world. I would like to make a similar proposal in my present remarks on the task of planning for the future.

Planning for the future can be roughly divided into two sorts: short-range and long-range. The former, a mode of knee-jerking, is closely wed to the present *world-state*; it is fundamentally remedial or corrective, responding to specific decisions to modify this present world-state. The short-range plan *implements* a commitment which is most often assumed or adopted elsewhere in the institution or society; in other words, short-range planning focuses upon the *means* of change rather than upon the ends. By the very notion of the ends as remedial or corrective, short-range planning goals are invariably realizable, technologically as well as socially. Social institutions are in that sense quite reasonable: they normally only demand correction of the correctible! The problem for the short-range planner is thus one of choosing feasible means which will realize these preestablished ends. (Insofar as it aims at cleaning up the environment, the ecology movement is a good example of a short-range goal. The decision to adopt *this* goal, rather than some other, has been made not by planners, but by sectors of the society outside of the planning sector. Planning has been charged only with the *resolution* of the acknowledged problem.)

Long-range planning is another question altogether: operating beyond the threshold of the present's effect on the future, long-range planning has the distinguishing characteristic of being genuinely guiding or determining of future world-states. This is not to say, of course, that long-range planning is uniquely determining, but if it is at all effective, the domain of realizable possible world-states is diminished as a result of the long-range planning. Certain world-states possible at time t are no longer possible at time $t + l$ as a direct result of the implementation of long-range planning. In contrast to short-range planning, the planner is here concerned not only with the means but also with the *ends* to be achieved. Unlike in the short-range planning situation, the long-range planner must *choose* which possible world-states will be allowed and which will be eliminated. Needless to say, as potentially powerful and beneficial as this planning is, it is equally dangerous. And as the degree of planning becomes more total, so does the potentiality for good and evil.

In formal terms, the planning-action sequence conforms reasonably well to the *practical syllogism* of Aristotelian logic (the *ends* plus *initial conditions* are premises for the concluded *means*). In addition, such teleological systems are self-regulating by virtue of certain feedback mechanisms. (For example, the thermostat activates the furnace when the room-temperature falls below a certain point; it shuts down the furnace when the room-temperature reaches a specified level.) The regulating mechanism (thermostat) requires a system-independent datum (temperature) by which to gauge the operation of the system. But as long-range planning achieves greater efficiency and more total integration of all aspects of the world-state, the independent datum disappears. When feedback becomes part of the planned consequences, it becomes tautologous and uninformative. Long-range planners are then left with a serious control and monitoring problem, a problem which increases in severity with the effectiveness of the planning. And even where legitimate feedback is forthcoming, it may come too late. In the last decade we have seen firsthand these problems of control. It seems, for example, that President Johnson himself confused generated support for the Vietnam War in the mid 1960's with some sort of spontaneous mandate from the people for his policies. But in large part, what Johnson took to be a measure of the support for his policies was in effect only a measure of the effectiveness of the Administration's pre-planned support for this war-policy. As a counterpart to this example of illegitimate, tautologous feedback, one can point to the ecological crisis as an example of legitimate feedback which was almost too late in coming (or perhaps we should speak of an insensitivity to the feedback). We recognized this crisis only after the cumulative effects of misplanning and nonplanning in such areas as industrialization, urbanization, and resource-exploitation had worked a seemingly irreparable harm.

The implications of this contrast between short-range and long-range planning should be apparent: what we demand of the short-range planner is far different from what we demand of the long-range planner. Not being called upon to choose the quality of life for some future world-state, but only to implement or realize a pre-established choice, the short-range planner need be little more than a technologist. Our nontechnical demands on the short-range planner are minimal, and his (her) nontechnical responsibilities are likewise minimal. With the long-range planner, however, our nontechnical demands are great, and his nontechnical responsibilities are heavy: he *must choose* between the possible future world-states. That this choice is fundamentally nontechnological in nature, that technological considerations serve only as constraints upon acceptable possible world-states, cannot be overemphasized. We Americans suffer from a naiveté, or perhaps more correctly an intellectual timidity, which attempts either to translate the nonquantitative dimension of human existence into quantitative terms, or simply to neglect this dimension altogether. The inescapability of the qualitative dimension of long-range planning is apparent even in the seemingly simple questions of housing and the like. Assuming a certain *scarcity* in the world, logical if not factual, everyone cannot live in a house bigger than everyone else's house. As a result, will housing be built as it is now—shacks to mansions—or will everyone live in identical accommodations? Clearly an *ideological* question, if I may call it that, of *what* to build underlies the technological questions of *how* to build. To expect the *hows* to determine the *what* would appear to be both wishful and evasive! Our demands upon the long-range planner are thus severe: not only must we require sound technological expertise in a particular discipline or disciplines, but we must require as well a Renaissance-type *sagesse* or wisdom which will equip the planner for the qualitative choices which he or she must make.

Long-range planning, in addition, involves what the late Marxist theoretician and philosopher Lucien Goldmann[134] terms a *va-et-vient* dialectic—a going-and-coming—between means and ends. Not only must the planning look *forward* from the present to see what appears feasible as ends, given the available means, but the planning must look *backward* from desired goals to see how these ends might be achieved. In this dialectic between the perspectives of means and ends, hopefully the planner articulates realizable goals—that is, realizable future world-states which best approximate the desired goals. The polar terms of the *va-et-vient* are in one sense of radically different natures, but in another sense they are little different one from the other: the means must be viewed as constraints upon the ends, not only insofar as they represent possible means of achieving the desired end, but also insofar as they represent (and must represent) acceptable world-states through which the society will move on the way to the desired end-state. The choice of means thus poses an ideological problem which the ends taken as ends, do not: what sort of sacrifices in the intervening world-states are we willing to make in order to achieve a specific end-state? And because every end-state becomes in turn itself a means to a subsequent end-state, this question can be rephrased in terms of the more general question of the sacrificing of the immediate good of individuals for the long-range good of the society of individuals yet to be born. Here on the diachronic axis we see an ideological problem which is a counterpart to the question of scarcity on the synchronic axis. Simply put, in like manner as everyone cannot have everything, neither can they live forever. The benefits of life, material and cultural, must be allotted *both* in space (synchronically) and in time (diachronically). Again this task must fall to the long-range planner. What nature has left *en masse*, the long-range planner must allot. Were the planners gods, they might solve this problem of spatio-temporal scarcity by fiat, but as men, they can best be kings. But they will be kings! The question to be asked is whether we can stop short of making them philosophers as well.

By calling forth the spectre of the Philosopher-King, I do not wish to resurrect Plato's Republic, far from it; but the very nature of the increasingly complex technological society within which we live certainly bears the analogy. Within the technological society in particular, control of information and planning represents an extreme power. Control of information implies not only physical accessibility but intellectual accessibility as well: if he is to manage, the manager must be able to understand the information once it is in hand. This demands a high level of technological expertise. It is truly doubtful that competent supervision of planning can be effected by managers lacking in this technological expertise. And by all indications, the planning sequence will continue to grow in technological sophistication, demanding an ever higher level of expertise as the price for its accessibility and control. Whether we maintain an *open society*, to use Karl Popper's[135] terminology, or whether we move toward the stratified Republic of Plato will depend upon whether or not a technological gap is allowed to open between those who plan and those who are planned for. But here again, this is an *ideological choice* which will be made through planning. In the final analysis societies do not remain *open* because of an ingenious system of checks and balances within the government, high school civics texts notwithstanding, but rather because citizens and leaders alike reaffirm repeatedly by their actions the choice of an open society.

Moreover, our only true safeguard against abuse by the planners will rest in their education as well as in the education of the nonplanning citzenry. Perforce the long-range planners must be Philosopher-Kings, but the citizenry must be equally so, if only potentially.

Our goal must be to equip the planner intellectually—ideologically and culturally—for the choices which he must make of future worldstates, choices which will defy quantification. This type of intellectual preparation is more elusive than technological expertise which can be taught in a reasonably straightforward manner. The lay philosopher's distinction between formal education and common sense has an intuitive grasp of this problem. In the introduction to his *Nicomachean Ethics*,[136] Aristotle admonishes the young to return to the theoretical sciences (mathematics, natural science, etc.) until they have ripened a bit through the experience of life; only then will they be ready to study the practical sciences (ethics and politics). Aristotle is no doubt correct that these studies, precisely of the questions which interest the long-range planner as philosopher, demand a certain maturity, but Aristotle also emphasizes the need for a proper cultivation of these interests from earliest childhood. From childhood, the planner (and nonplanner) must be imbued with an appreciation for the importance of these philosophical and ideological questions. Such preparation in our own times must include a firm denial of the positivistic thesis which rejects the nonquantifiable as so much nonsensical metaphysics. Precisely the contrary of the positivistic slogan that *ethical and aesthetic values are not in the world* is true: cultural values are very much in the world; man has put them there through the course of history. The positivistic denial of such values, while passing itself off as a factual description of what *is* in the world, is equally a value-judgment or metaphysics. This outgrowth of the naive scientism of the nineteenth century, while deflating the more odious ideologies against which it did battle, should be recognized as an ideology of intellectual blindness. It recommends that we reject as nonexistent a significant dimension of human existence; it achieves a simplified *Weltanschauung* only at the price of omission of human life's intrinsic complexity and richness.

But how are we to prepare the long-range planner for these ideological tasks? How is this necessary *sagesse* to be developed? At this point I must return to my original plea for an historical understanding of man, for a general anthropology encompassing both the arts and the sciences. (I could have described this study and its resultant understanding as one of focusing upon the *humanities*, but this term is popularly understood as suggesting that certain aspects of our existence are more human than others. The sciences, taken as a human *endeavor* rather than as a body of theoretical knowledge, are equally of importance to this study.) This understanding of man demanded of the long-range planner requires exposure to life for its development. If one were not so short-lived the need for historical study would not be of great importance, but unfortunately this exposure is all too brief, all too homogeneous, and usually quite unreflective. In our early years the task of living leaves little time for reflection and consideration, and when we are older we are often simply too tired. But fortunately we have centuries of historical record and reflection written by diverse individuals who have devoted much time to the task we leave undone. Throughout history these individuals—philosophers, scientists, historians, politicians, artists—have assumed the task of reflection, considering the very sorts of questions which will confront the long-range planner. The questions are, to be sure, never the very same, but they are sufficiently similar that coupled with good judgment they should help the planner in his own tasks. Although he will notice developments and trends which unify long periods of history, the planner will not intuit any *necessary* direction in the course of history to which he may tie his planning. Instead, through this study, he should come to realize that there exists, and have existed, many possible world-states, all satisfying certain basic material constraints on human life, yet all *significantly* different from that one in which he lives. (A valuable lesson for those who come from the homogeneous culture of the American middle-class.) The perception of *other* lived possibilities is irreplaceable: a livable possibility for the future, different from his own, is precisely what the long-range planner must envision and plan.

The attainment of this historical understanding demands a study of greater depth than those which merely *appropriate* a particular historical period for what the art historian E. H. Gombrich[137] terms "a metaphor for an attitude." This antiquarian appropriation is manifested, for example, by the young in the nostalgia for and return to dated clothing styles, by the older in the collection of Early Americana, or by the university classicist in his reverence for the austere Apollonian values supposedly characteristic of Classical Greece. But this appropriation is far too shallow, too incomplete. A true historical understanding demands an intelligent development both in depth and in breadth of this alternative world-state. The incompleteness, for example, of Greek white marble statuary, a metaphor for the classicist's *own* austerity, must be remedied by an intellectual restoration of the high coloration which originally covered this statuary; only then can we begin to really understand the role of this art within the Greek world-state. Only then does the planner begin to achieve this perception of a genuinely complete alternative world-state, the perception of a totality. The incompleteness of the antiquarian mode of historical understanding gives way to the essential complexity and holism of the alternative world-state, a complexity with which the long-range planner in his own tasks will be confronted and will have to come to grips. Under this holistic perception the world state, his, or another, will be appreciated for what it is: a rich but complex interweaving of social institutions, beliefs, habits, values, activities, and the like. Only with this understanding can the long-range planner choose *wisely* the future state of the world. He will recognize the impossibility of piecemeal planning: the choice can well be partial, as it too often is, but its effects will surely be holistic.

History is the record of human action, individuals and societies planning and acting. Through his historical study, the long-range planner has the unique privilege of viewing these earlier planners' choices and decisions, from above as it were, seeing both the antecedents and the consequences of their planning decisions. Recognizing planning to be a very fundamental and very old aspect of human existence, the long-range planner hopefully will develop the tempered confidence in man's ability to plan for his future, a confidence which will be necessary in order that he do well his own task of planning. If this historical appreciation can be achieved, the study of history will certainly have contributed its share towards assuring the quality of life in the future.

[CHAPTER TWENTY-TWO]

THE PLANNER, GEOGRAPHER, ARCHITECT, AND ECOLOGY*

HARLAND WESTERMANN

I THINK IT MIGHT BE PRUDENT for me to begin by letting you in on some of my biases. In the first place, I want you to know that I shall be talking about *human ecology*, but from a very slanted perspective. Secondly, I believe you should be aware of a fact that escapes too many people, and that is, that planning is an art. It is, as of this moment, a rather primitive art—it is not a science. Thus, as a planner, it is not my function to study human ecology. It is my function, rather, to manipulate human environments. And I include in the human environment the man-built contrivances, the social and economic qualities of a place, and the setting provided by nature. These are elements of the human environment in which the planner operates. Quite obviously, people should be included also. Unfortunately, people too often are ignored by the physical planners; and just as unfortunately, too many social planners are unaware of of the limitations imposed by physical realities. Thirdly, I would point out that one should keep in mind that planning, irrespective of who is doing the planning, is a part of a political process. The plan-

*Presented at a conference on Human Ecology at Jersey City State College, Jersey City, N.J., April 23, 1971.

ner does not make decisions. If she or he is capable at all in this art, he or she may, at best, influence decisions. I tell you this because many of my scientific colleagues are political boobies. The tremendous influence that they might exert on improving our environments too often are lost because they fail totally to understand the political process and their respective roles in that process.

With that as background, I would like to get on then to the subject at hand. There now appears to be an increasing number of scholars, representing a variety of disciplines, who seem to think that the decades of the sixties and the seventies may, indeed, mark one of those moments in time which are used by historians to start a new chapter in the events of mankind. You will remember from one or another of your textbooks on the history of civilization that chapter eight was the *Roman Empire*, chapter nine the *Dark Ages*, and chapter ten the *Renaissance*. If we are, indeed, at such a point in history, then future historians are going to have a delightful range of title chapters that they can use to begin this next new period. *The Age of Population Zero*, obviously, *The Age of Aquarius*, or *The Age They Let It All Fall Apart*. Being a more pedestrian spirit and one who is daily intrigued by the possibilities that now are on the horizon, I would hope that some future Louis Mumford would be able to write a chapter called, *The Age of the American City-States*. Somewhere on the first page of such a chapter, there has got to be a footnote. That footnote says, "To understand more fully the course of human events and the political attitudes of the latter portion of the twentieth century, see Plato's *Republic*."

I am given over to the idea that some of Mr. Plato's ideas coincide pretty well today with the emerging political attitudes in this country. You will recall that it was Plato's contention that the good life —and I suggest that his *good life* is simply today's cliché, *the quality of life*—could not be achieved as the sum of individual efforts. It was, therefore, in his mind, the proper responsibility of government. It was on the basis that government must play an entrepreneurial role in social development that he established his Utopian concepts. It was Demosthenes who suggested that the good life properly was comprised of three elements. He gave those elements in a very particular and purposeful order: justice, beauty, and usefulness.

My contention is that the Romans subverted this initially by substituting law for justice. They destroyed beauty rather totally, despite the fact that they had monumental architecture. I would point out also that they had around Rome their *cordon mal-sanitaire* which has existed, in one form or another, in every city since. I submit that in the ages that follow it was usefulness that became the prize. The Hanse and its intrusion into the affairs of state is simply another recording of that attitude. That we lost justice is a matter of historical record. One need only to look out the window to see that we have a warped sense of beauty.

Now if I sound like a pessimist, put it out of your mind, because I seriously think that we may just now be turning a corner. I hear the word *justice* and the word *beauty* with increasing frequency, and somewhat louder than before. And that is a remarkable change because from the inception of this nation we have been a growth-oriented, a usefulness-oriented, society. At a national level our success indicator has been a somewhat dubious measure called gross national product, a device to measure increases in usefulness, or productivity, if you will. As a society, we have been taught to believe that an increase in this national productivity of 5 percent or 6 percent per annum was an ultimate measure of success, and therefore, it was a thing we must attempt to achieve. Such a record of success became part of our political philosophy and our political platforms. At the echelon of local government, we continued this because we were concerned with new industries, population growth, increased retail sales volume, and on and on. Thus, the realities of politics at any level of government —and that means getting back into office next term—dictated that growth measures become a fundamental political input. Pray tell me, who, prior to today, could have been elected on a platform of *justice* and *beauty*. Despite the fact that a successful political organization was one which could demonstrate such growth (such usefulness), governments themselves did not participate in a direct entrepreneurial role. Regional growth was realized most fully when state and local governments played a totally passive role. This allowed the *American free enterprise spirit*, the unfettered opportunity to develop the country according to their concepts of usefulness. And, government became a partner in that it supplied ancillary services—in that it failed to use restrictive legislation.

I have no intention of giving you still another recitation of all the ills besetting our communities which have developed because of these attitudes. I simply point out that, in developing under a concept of passive government—that is, one in which police powers are not exercised; in which corporate economic opportunity is privileged; in which other values are submerged—we have arrived at a situation in which today 90 percent of our citizenry is urbanized in communities which the Urban Coalition has described simply as *an American insult spawned by neglect*. Eighty percent of our population lives on 2 percent of our space. The problem in the past has been horrendous; but we are today growing and urbanizing at somewhat over twice the rate we did in the period 1900 to 1960. If present trends continue, a great bulk of our population is going to live in already-forming major conurbations such as megalopolis. We have then already arrived at a situation which is an outrage and which quite obviously demands change.

Let me try quickly to outline where I think we might be going. Fundamental to reestablishment of the three elements which might guarantee an acceptable quality of life is a change in our concept of measuring growth and development, and a change in our concept of governance, especially at the state and local level. Arthur Burns has told us that new measures of GNP, which now are being devised, will include the social cost incurred in economic development. When these costs are demonstrated in a pragmatic fashion, as opposed to simple rhetoric, I feel we are going to see a number of changes in political philosophies and in attitudes. We have, essentially, two development problems as I see it. At least from the planning perspective, these problems can be tackled only if there is now a distinct change of attitude and change of role in decision making at the local level. On the one hand, we have cities which do not work in any acceptable fashion. It seems to me that we have two options available for making them work. The first of these is to rebuild them so that they accommodate vastly increased numbers of future people. Our technocrats—and unfortunately, these include many planners and architects—tell us this can be done. They are saying that we now have the engineering technology to achieve some satisfactory future level of existence. What disturbs me mainly about these people is that they rather automatically substitute *should* for *can*. The fact that we *can* do something does not mean it is a best choice. To add to our confusion, we seem to have a number, an increasing number, of exiled Italian and Greek architect planners who are in the country, wandering around like minstrels, telling us that we ought to build now a great megastructure between Lynn, Massachusetts and Atlanta, Georgia. And even the mayor of New York City is not satisfied with the present level of his catastrophe. In these first years of the nineteen-seventies, he wants to add more commercial space by piering out over the river.

In my way of thinking we have achieved enough chaos in our cities. We should begin to question how additional growth can possibly aid in improving the quality of life within these places. An alternative, one which finally seems to be getting some serious attention, is to centralize our population into smaller workable clusters. I mentioned a moment ago that we had two development problems. In addition to our metropolitan problems, we quite obviously have not achieved the Utopia in rural America. Selective immigration of population; ultraconservative political attitudes, which have been responsible for a lack of modern updated development; and a once-productive agricultural population, which today has declined to something about 4 percent of the total (and, if we were to remove the marginal and submarginal farmers, probably 3 percent) add up to the fact that Appalachia is a great deal more widespread than we are led to believe.

Thus we are confronted with a paradox in which our over-populated cities are subjected to even greater growth prospects because no one is doing something to change the trend. At the same time, our rural areas desperately need growth if they are to achieve acceptable standards. A potential solution to both metropolitan and rural problems may lie somewhere in the area of the new towns concept, a new concept of human ecology. However, simply building some number of new golden ghettos such as Reston and Columbia seem to be a questionable future national settlement policy.

If we consider the geographic structure of local political units in most of our states, we see regions which are far too small to command the space and the resource needs of a modern optimally-size urban community. Growing numbers of states are now beginning to recognize the need to amalgamate county governments into new geographic regions which are large enough to support small clusters of urbanized populations with an adequate resource base of water, air, open space, and other fundamentals which can improve the life style of an individual. This seems to suggest that human population should not be greater than the carrying capacity of the region they occupy. It's a range management philosophy, I am told. But yet, if we have done this in range management, I see no reason why the concept is not valid in the case of human population. I am rather proud to say that the Commonwealth of Virginia, in delimiting its 234 separate, fighting, small political units into twenty-two planning districts, may have taken a first step which is going to demonstrate a way of achieving an acceptable settlement policy. In each of these twenty-two planning districts, adequately sized decentralized clusters of urban population can now be developed, that is, if the legislature will act to encourage a new settlement policy, and if in so doing we do not overtax the carrying capacity of that region in terms of space and natural resources. And that means that at some point we must have the capacity to say, "no more growth." And if we can develop, along with this new structure and function, a new sense of governmental responsibility for achieving a high quality of life (which means that the government at the state and local level must become an entrepreneur), then I think we may have created truly a new concept of human ecology.

I submit that the realization of a sensible pattern of human settlement, which allows for a high quality of life, requires the development of a new breed of human ecologists. It is my opinion that the geographer, the architect, and the planner, collectively, have the know-how to initiate a new concept of *city-states* which meet our needs.

It can be achieved, however, only if we now will accept that the good life is, indeed, a responsibility of government, as opposed to the responsibility of the individual; and if that government, then, is charged with the task of providing justice, beauty, and usefulness—in that order. Given these many *ifs*, I think we may succeed. I believe this can be accomplished in as short a time as the next three decades, if we are willing to abandon our present passion for over-populated cities and are willing to accept the ideals of the *city-state* in America.

SECTION FOUR

ANSWERS?

In the final chapter of Section Three, the goal was better planning. In the second chapter of Section One the imperative for better and even more dramatic decision was invited. In this Section, Willis Harman speaks to Institutional Change; Russell Rhyne offers means for so effecting this change, devising a method for forecasting alternative futures. Harman and Rhyne, both engineers, humanists, and futurists, beseech the attention of the decision-maker.

Peter Kivy, in this Section, demonstrates the complexity of the meaning of meaning, much less its communicability. Sylvan Kaplan summarizes and raises a question of whether man's duality of mind and emotion permits fusion, perpetuates diversity both between and within the personalities of humankind, and whether the point of no return is reversible.

[CHAPTER TWENTY-THREE]

A METHOD FOR PLANNING ALTERNATIVE FUTURES

RUSSELL F. RHYNE

Introduction

QUALITY OF LIFE is already in jeopardy, as all of the chapters of this book tell us, just a few years after sufficient ease and independence had been gained to let us start to disregard those qualities and focus upon others. Nothing seems apt to make us safe amid the new dangers that success has laid upon us, but ordered approaches to the interwoven problems around us should at least reduce the risks. The topic here, accordingly, is method, with preferences pushed into the background. While there seems to be no reasonable chance that science can arrive in time with workable prescriptions for our woes, reason and analysis can help us all appreciate—feel—the nature and variety of the alternatives before us. Possessing such appreciations, we then can bring to bear that most powerful of human issue—resolving capacities, intuitive judgement.

The author argues here that one key to these concerns is offered by the projection and subsequent use of scenarios describing plausible, alternative lines of evolution of world and local patterns of life. As ecology accepts man and his works within its field of discourse, it will have to talk less about relatively determinant transitions toward some stable equilibrium and refer more often to alternative sequences of patterns—scenarios. The same scenarios that would be useful to the new ecology of man as planning referents also promise to serve a broader need by helping all of us appreciate the options that are realistically open to man-in-the-biosphere.

The scenarios needed are distinctive in several ways, but methods for composing them have been developed. The particular approach described here evolved during a decade of policy research by Patterns and Systems, International, working most recently in support of efforts by the Educational Policy Research Center of Stanford Research Institute to advise and inform members of the U. S. Office of Education. Its applicability to ecology might seem surprising, until one recollects that policy governs both our major disturbances of life patterns and our subsequent efforts to amend our errors. It would therefore be strange if policy analysis and inquiries into quality of life did not end up needing the same tools.

The Need for Scenarios in Quality-of-Life Analysis

Among the many unanswerable questions that surround the phrase *quality of life*, there does seem to be one secure point of departure. The study of that topic should be holistic, attending to whole complexes of relationships as though they were units. The preferability—the quality—of any given circumstance depends upon the whole circumstance (as well, of course, as on the likes and dislikes of the person(s) making the judgment). For one thing, isolated events rarely can have worth in and of themselves; value is a function of interaction. For another, some values always must be hostaged so that others may be gained, and the pattern of compromise and attainment within some broader setting will determine whether the net quality of life has been enhanced or reduced in any given case. Any adequate method for investigating quality of life, therefore, would have to deal with whole conditions and to facilitate comparisons among them.

Ecology offers a natural departure point. It takes holistic treatment of its fields* as its prime rule, and its attention to the nonhuman

---

*A *field*, as the word is used here, is neither a patch of land nor yet a discipline (as in the *field* of engineering). It is defined by the nature of the associations between a variety of variables or entities. A field exists when its components interact in such a way that a disturbance of one usually will induce changes in most others. Also, a field usually is characterized by homeostatic responses, in which interactions among environment brings it into many current quality of life debates. The former is far the more important point, since pollution is only one of many ways in which the attractiveness of life may be diminished, and the methods of analysis to be sought must deal somehow with it and all the rest. Ecology is being whipsawed by the very conditions that bring it into unaccustomed salience now, however. It is notable because it highlights man's involvement with the world around him, but that same intrusion of people upsets many of its traditional concerns and methods. Ecology must undergo a revolution of a sort in order to please its new public or even to live up to its own precepts. The latter is so because its basic credo demands concurrent, balanced attention to all significantly powerful components interacting within one of its fields, and there can be no doubt that we now cause most of the disturbances and also introduce the most powerful corrective forces within the broader, more important fields on earth. Ecology cannot leave us outside without denying its true nature; it cannot bring us in without deeply changing its methods and priorities.

Moreover, the fields that apparently must be considered as whole units are much broader now than in the past, and the refined techniques of what might be called *pond ecology* (in which details of nonhuman species interaction within some limited geographic area are studied) are not so useful when applied to the sociosubsistence problems of earth's biosphere or even to similar problems within a given nation. There is a modern circumstance which aptly has been named the macroproblem.[138] This macroproblem may trace to some primary, underlying cause, or it may represent a less ordered combination of separate streams of misfortune; but in any case we are now embedded in world and regional environments wherein adverse trends seem to be more likely than not to be mutually exacerbating. In the past, one could think hopefully in terms of serendipity—of the good things which might flow from the random

its components tend to contain and minimize the net effects of a disturbance in a kind of self defense that seems at times almost volitional. It therefore often is described as quasi-organic, responding to stimuli somewhat as a living body might. Study of its parts may lead *toward* understanding, but it finally must be viewed as a whole if sound, purposive control is to be effected. An ecological field should take cognizance of all the living species and those aspects of the physical setting that matter in any given location and from any specified point of view.

doodlings of fortune. Now, it seems more prudent to assume that serendipity more often will prove negative, with unanticipated secondary consequences of action being more often damaging than favorable. Whether one looks at population policy, the problems of infant mortality, the growth of national pride, or a dozen other modern issues, it becomes clear that optimal solution of each problem taken alone is apt to contribute to some horror story within a few decades. The kinds of problems in question have combined to form a single field of interaction; feedback has become endemic.

This condition may not already be true of the globe as a whole, but it soon may be. The onionskin of living space that wraps the globe is being disturbed, and that disturbance feeds back upon just those extractive practices that are causing the disturbance, as nations turn defensive in the face of expected hardship for their own people. Resultant inhibitions upon capital formation and trade impede those economies of scale and location that have made the present population seem tolerable in many regions, while desperate efforts to prevent this decade's famine in capital-poor areas may plant the seeds of future calamity.

When one looks at individual regions, the reality of the local macroproblem can hardly be doubted. Whether one attends to highly technological human ecologies (such as those throughout the North Atlantic community and in a few other nations) in which glut is the salient issue, or to most of the rest of the world where subsistence is or soon will be the subject of personal and national preoccupation, each field of concern has become a whole.

Ecology assumed its present form during the brief interlude in which Western people at least, have thought themselves to be above and apart from a world that they controlled (or would control, after finding out just a few more facts). It characteristically studied nonhuman fields of interaction and talked of a *natural* environment that has come to be a little like the Forest of Arden, partly dreams and rarely to be found unless defended within very artificial conditions. Relationships with such fields were relatively well determined, however, and ecology has learned to predict the consequences of disturbances within them as species died away or flourished in nature's permanent war of attrition as changed conditions lowered or raised their relative survival potential. It has become possible to prespecify, for instance, the sequence of stages that will be passed enroute to a new equilibrium after a major forest fire and to have the actual future match quite well with the predicted scenario.

The idea of describing the route to a new and relatively static equilibrium is important here because it looks as though the acceptance of us within a field makes such developments too rare to be important during coming decades. When we and our preferences enter, we tend to swamp the nonhuman forces at work simply because the power of man has grown so great. The work of bulldozers, for instance, preempts the normal processes of erosion, and if *natural* weathering begins to take over after an earth-moving job is done, that process, too, is likely to be superceded by another 'dozer or by a crew of men with grass seed and sprinklers. Disturbances by man, attempted corrections of those disturbances, and further responses to side effects of those corrections tend to govern in place of *natural* forces. Since such activities are sparked by our imperfect perceptions, guided by at best a partial understanding of the forces at work, and mediated through a political process that emphasizes different goals as different groups gain power, the course of change can hardly be expected to settle down. A different sort of scenario is called for, open ended and permeated by the uncertainties of human life.

It might be argued that such only was the case until society became concerned about quality of life and while manipulation of ecological fields by us was thought to be legitimate. It's hard to see that things have changed enough in such respects to make much difference. Each of the achievements that have carried with them things that distress us now were undertaken specifically to improve the quality of life, and they did so in ways we would not want to erase; and any changes that we now undertake will be similar in kind to those of the past. The only really natural environment is the whole, human-influenced one that exists around us, and any deliberate effort by us to modify any part or all of it will be manipulation. The future might not be so bouncy if we were to move more humbly, in awareness of our own ineptitude and with a fuller appreciation that any simple answer must be wrong, but the present mood seems almost the opposite of that. Steady attention to broad fields of interaction and realistic consideration of the compromises along any future path should, however, help steer away from catastrophy and toward conditions that would seem satisfying when attained.

It seems wise to assume, therefore, that ecology's answer to the question "What would happen if we introduced this policy?" cannot be phrased in terms of a route toward some new equilibrium pattern (as it might be in forest management); rather it would have to come out somehow as an estimated difference between one scenario and another. Indeed, since there can be no hope of detailed, reliable prediction of the future without a given policy, the approach should be to consider each of a set of illustrative, alternative lines of future evolution for the field in question, to see in each instance what the impacts of the contemplated policy might be.

Such an *answer* must seem weak and insecure to ecologists familiar with the relatively determinant fields where we are the actors, but it is the most that can be promised, and it would not be so weak, after all, in comparison with other aids to policy determination. Science rarely has offered clear prescriptions for action, even in the rather simple field of family relations. There and in the even more complex fields of concern to makers of more sweeping policies, logic and research help most when they try only to help enhance the appreciations from which judgemental decisions then may flow.

If appropriate scenarios were composed to illustrate the lines of evolution that seem plausible within any given ecological field without specific policy interventions, they would serve directly to expand and direct the appreciation of each decision maker (including the only one with unlimited power, the voter) for the field in question. They would serve the same end indirectly by helping analysts judge the likely impacts of any particular attempted manipulation dealing successively with each original scenario, as suggested above. The needed kinds of scenarios are distinctive, however, in at least three ways:

1. Each projection must be holistic throughout. It must reflect a plausible sort of organic growth through time, with each pattern growing from the one before it somewhat as a web of changing personalities evolves within a good novel; and each pattern (that represents a snapshot of the field at some particular time) must be internally as coherent as the field itself is. This does not mean

that changes must be quiet or subdued, but if they are rough then the costs that normally go with such circumstances should be reflected. Neither does it mean that the pattern shown for any given time need have its parts coexist comfortably; indeed, such comfort seems sufficiently unlikely so that a scenario showing very much of it would be suspect. This requirement of plausible interconnection within the whole is standard through all ecological analysis, but it also is important here because intuition seems only to be able to *take off* from some holistic base, and the purpose of quality of life investigation should not be to give answers but to nourish insight as a precursor to intuition selection among alternative courses of action.

2. Each pattern called out or implied along a scenario should be described in terms such as to facilitate its comparison with any other such pattern. This is important in the original composition of the needed kind of stories, but it also is essential to their optimal use. If someone is to internalize such materials so that they may be grist for one's judgement, it seems necessary in practice that one be able to compare a given field condition quickly and easily with others. Furthermore, if one is to move further and try to visualize the likely impacts of a considered action along one or another of the scenario lines, that too will be made more sure and easy if alternative patterns for the whole field can be swiftly compared.

3. Finally, the scenarios making up an illustrative set of alternative futures for the field of concern should be picked and elaborated with an eye both to plausibility and to the spread of conditions that a prudent planner might be expected to consider seriously. Some plausible cases may be rejected simply because the potential user would have no opportunity to act within them, as may be the case in disaster scenarios; such futures might indeed come about, but there would be little point in making plans or tracing ecological impacts within them. At the other end of the spectrum, some lines of evolution may seem implausible but worth trying for, and appreciation of these alternatives by acting authorities might help spur kinds of manipulations of the human ecology that would help bring them about.

The Field Anomaly Relaxation Method

This call for a particular kind of alternative futures scenario would be relatively empty if no way were known of composing them, but there are such ways, and the rest of this paper is addressed to the description of one that seems especially well structured and well tried.

That method, called Field Anomaly Relaxation (FAR), has

evolved during a decade of practice in the projection of contexts for use by business and governmental planners and the executives who must choose among candidate plans prepared by their staff supporters. As such, it has been applied to the projection of alternative world patterns[139] of a sort that would offer immediate points of departure for any inquiry into overall courses of development for that most inclusive of fields, the earth's biosphere. Having been composed first to highlight opportunities and risks facing U. S. aircraft manufacturers and then elaborated so as to similarly contribute to the insights of defense planners, however, these Projected World Patterns do not now place emphasis upon such quality of life topics as subsistence/population crises, world pollution, or the socioagricultural concomitants of the Green Revolution. Nevertheless, one should expect to find the major definitions of quality of life distributed differently over the earth along each of the scenarios already laid out.

The second application of the FAR method, which will be used to illustrate that method, has resulted in the projection of alternative futures for this country, the so-called Contingent U. S. Patterns (CUSPs).[140] Here, again, the interests of the client for whom this work has been done, the U. S. Office of Education, were such that some kinds of detail that would be of prime interest to a human ecologist have been played down, but still there are evident implications for any who would like to explore the prospects for quality of life here and the compromises that may be faced as we try to realize any given set of such qualities. The aspirations and risks that seem plausible do indeed shift from one CUSP scenario to another, and one's feeling for the race to be run is heightened by consideration of such differences.

The intent here is not to describe the FAR method in *cook book* detail; that already has been done.[141] Rather, by exposing its main characteristics, the author seeks to indicate the extent to which its products may be expected to meet the three requirements for ecologically serviceable scenarios that were listed above.

The method was designed, keeping in mind the same three desired attributes described above: internal, holistic consistency; neat comparability of patterns along any one scenario or from different scenarios; and final generation of a set of scenarios for any given field that would explore both the potential users' interests and the range of plausible expectation.

INTERNAL CONSISTING: The method takes its name from the ways in which the first of these was sought. In it, ideas concerning quasi-organic fields, such as those adduced throughout the first half of this paper, were linked with methods in engineering mathematics, wherein answers from one approximate solution of a problem are fed back in as assumptions to start a similar round. The latter approach, one version of which has been named the Relaxation Method, permits continuingly closer approaches to entire self-consistency within a physically determined field (such as the distributions of stress and strain within a solid, or the pattern of air flow and pressure around an airplane wing), as each successive repetition of the process results in smaller and smaller differences between input assumptions and output answers. By yoking such methods along with social field theory, a qualitative version of the Relaxation Method has been produced, weaker but with wider scope. In it, each cycle of inquiry produces more refined bases for detecting anomalies, wherein field components do not seem to fit together. Hence, the name Field Anomaly Relaxation.

In order to make the process reasonably regular, in spite of the lack of crisp definition of many of the elements to be dealt with during the investigation of world or national fields, a four-step cycle has been used. Also, to reflect the need for balanced attention to sweeping appreciations and component analysis in any treatment of complex fields, two of these steps emphasize synthesis and two analysis:

1. *Step 1* begins with an initial impression of the answer that is the final goal, namely a view of the spread and character of future alternatives for the field that is being studied. As Kurt Lewin wrote some thirty years ago[142] ". . . to find what one would like to know, one should in some way or another, already know it." Lewin, the master in this subject, goes on to suggest tentative, initial trials to learn the nature of the field, followed by increasingly exact and confident treatment of the same materials. The steps of the FAR method are designed to do just that, as the whole cycle of four is repeated time and again. This first step is appreciative in character rather than analytic.

2. *Step 2* will be discussed in greater detail below, in connection with the goal of neat comparability. Here it is enough to say that a

taxonomy is developed that is consonant with the view of the future formulated in Step 1 and suitable to the condensed description of any of the field patterns deemed plausible within it. This step clearly belongs on the analytic side of the diagram.

3. *Step 3* also is concerned with parts more than with wholes, but no one of the four, in fact, is purely one or the other. In it, various manipulations of the taxonomy from the previous step are carried through to generate and then filter out a few especially plausible alternating combinations of factors from an inclusive list of all of the thousands of field patterns implied by taxonomy. While the process is not rigorous (so that some rejected pattern descriptions prove worth bringing back later), this cuts the problem down to the point where one may carry in his head an appreciation of the nature of each of the surviving patterns. As a final activity within Step 3, symbolic descriptions of patterns are strung together tentatively in sequence, each such train of patterns to serve as the outline of a fleshed out scenario.

4. *Step 4* calls for the writing of the scenarios outlined in the prior step of analysis. Consideration of course was given to sequential consistency in making the outlines for such scenarios, but the act of telling a plausible tale turns out to be a finer means of discrimination than the earlier workings with symbolic, shorthand designations of alternative patterns. Modification of the earlier symbolic outlines usually seems needed to some extent, and feelings as to the relative plausibility of the several scenarios are quickened.

The product from Step 4 feeds directly into Step 1, to start another cycle of analysis. The set of scenarios produced forms a basis for a greatly refined appreciation of the options available; that improved appreciation is used as a basis for modifying the original taxonomy so as to make it more serviceable. A new and more exhausting round of manipulations and morphological expansion of apparent alternatives is accomplished; and the scenarios from the first cycle are retouched or (as often happens at this stage) in some instances entirely replaced by others.

If the second cycle exposes any very noticeable differences when compared with the first, and if time and resources permit, a third and still more careful cycle is advisable. If, however, the taxonomy seems nicely fitted to the scenarios finally produced, and if the general appreciation of the future options for the field in question seems to have changed little as a result of the second cycle, the *anomalies* have been *relaxed* and the job is done.

COMPARABILITY OF PATTERNS: The form of taxonomy called for

in Step 2 of the FAR method is distinctive, and that mode of categorization of information promises to be useful in the symbolic designation of alternative whole patterns even where futures projections are not to be undertaken. It was developed to facilitate rapid comparisons between alternative field patterns. It is holistic, being addressed to distinctions between alternative whole states or conditions rather than (as in nearly all established scientific taxonomies) the precise designation of particular parts of such wholes. A holistic taxonomy of this sort might be used to compare libraries, where the more normal one would be used to file and then recover particular books.

Two sorts of constructs are used, Sectors and Factors. The former are categories of description, relevant to the field in question and secondarily, to the concerns of the agency for whose use the taxonomy is to be constructed. Factors, in contrast, describe alternative states that might characterize the Sector to which they pertain.

Sectors are chosen with the criterion of relevance of skeletal significance primarily in mind. It is as though one were asked to describe a life pattern—an ecological field—to an intelligent but not specifically informed person and to give as good an impression as possible of the structure and character of the infinitely diverse whole while talking only about a selected half dozen or so of its aspects. In developing a symbology with which to describe different life patterns that might plausibly emerge within the United States at some time during the next three decades, twelve different Sectors were considered and used in various combinations; in the third (and last) cycle of FAR analysis, the seven shaded Sectors shown in Figure 23-1 were used. The remaining five, incidentally, can be used to good advantage for *fine tuning* a field description expressed just in terms of the primary seven.

We are not concerned here with the question whether or not these seven (or the extended list of twelve) Sectors are the best that might be chosen; they have served well, and the proof lies in utility, but the author and his associates already feel that others (such as Recreation) might well have been included. The important points are two: first, the foregoing exemplify the *kinds* of topics that may be selected as Sectors for a sweeping sociopolitical

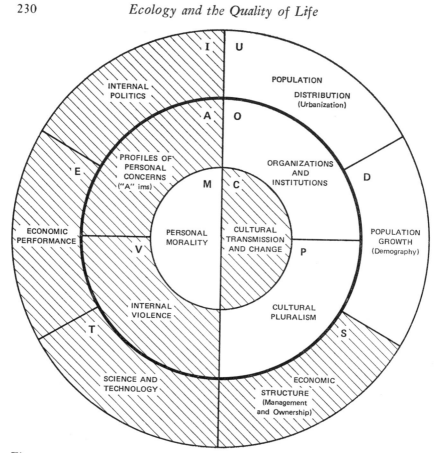

Figure 23-1 Aspects of U.S. Society for Generating Alternative Future Histories

field; second, there can be no expectation of attaining full coverage of most fields with a list of topics limited to six or seven entries, and the problem is to do as well as possible within that constraint.

Factors are quite different in character. They are not subdivisions of Sectors (as would be the case in most parts-oriented taxonomies). Instead, each Factor calls out a condition or state that might be taken on by the entire Sector to which it pertains. Furthermore, if the whole taxonomy is to meet its objective of offering a way of symbolically describing any plausible overall condition for the field under consideration, the list of Factors within a given Sector must cover all of the plausible options within that Sector—must offer filing space for description of any plausible condition there.

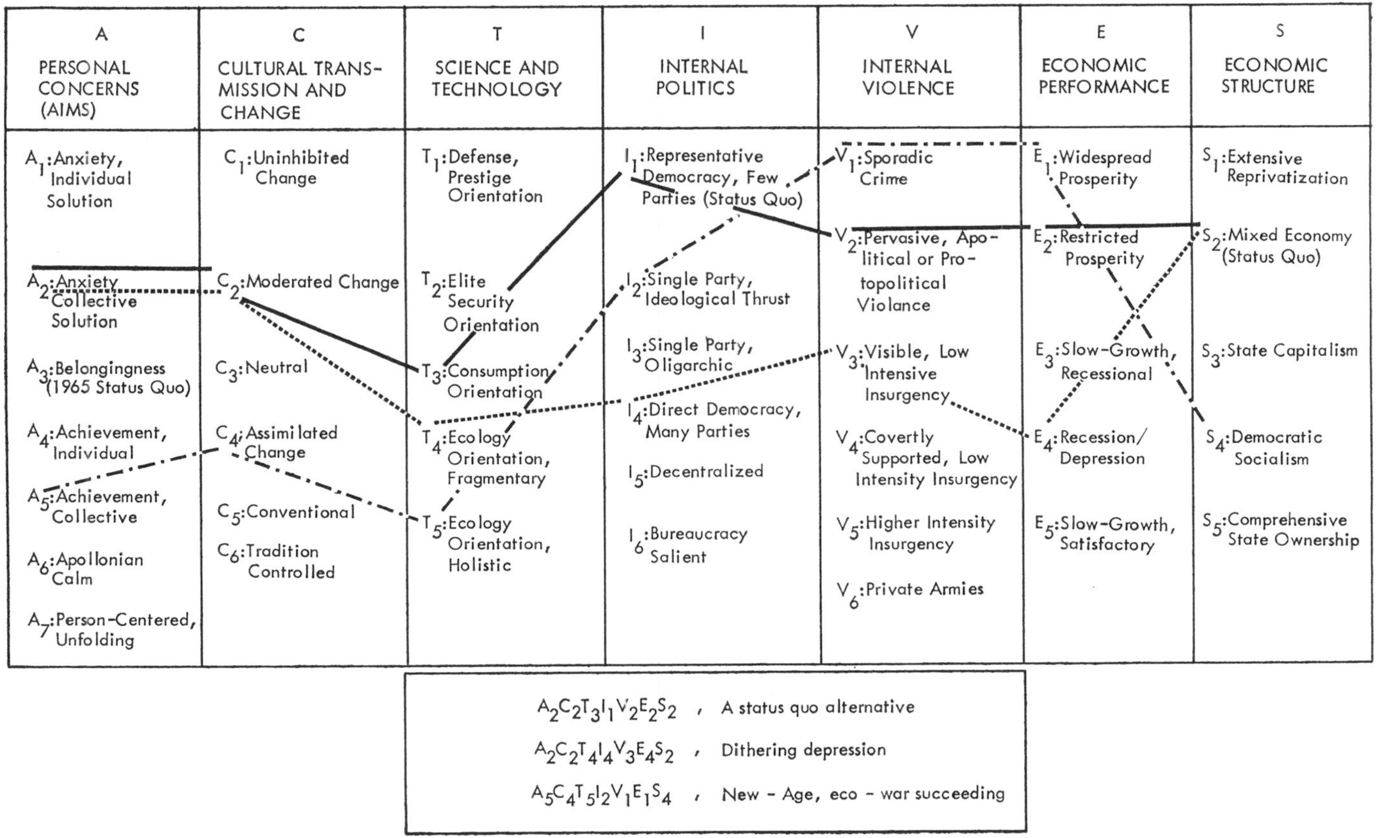

A Sector/Factor Array for Use in Projecting Alternative U.S. Futures

A PERSONAL CONCERNS (AIMS)	C CULTURAL TRANSMISSION AND CHANGE	T SCIENCE AND TECHNOLOGY	I INTERNAL POLITICS	V INTERNAL VIOLENCE	E ECONOMIC PERFORMANCE	S ECONOMIC STRUCTURE
A_1:Anxiety, Individual Solution	C_1:Uninhibited Change	T_1:Defense, Prestige Orientation	I_1:Representative Democracy, Few Parties (Status Quo)	V_1:Sporadic Crime	E_1:Widespread Prosperity	S_1:Extensive Reprivatization
A_2:Anxiety, Collective Solution	C_2:Moderated Change	T_2:Elite Security Orientation	I_2:Single Party, Ideological Thrust	V_2:Pervasive, Apolitical or Pro-topolitical Violence	E_2:Restricted Prosperity	S_2:Mixed Economy (Status Quo)
A_3:Belongingness (1965 Status Quo)	C_3:Neutral	T_3:Consumption Orientation	I_3:Single Party, Oligarchic	V_3:Visible, Low Intensive Insurgency	E_3:Slow-Growth, Recessional	S_3:State Capitalism
A_4:Achievement, Individual	C_4:Assimilated Change	T_4:Ecology Orientation, Fragmentary	I_4:Direct Democracy, Many Parties	V_4:Covertly Supported, Low Intensity Insurgency	E_4:Recession/ Depression	S_4:Democratic Socialism
A_5:Achievement, Collective	C_5:Conventional	T_5:Ecology Orientation, Holistic	I_5:Decentralized	V_5:Higher Intensity Insurgency	E_5:Slow-Growth, Satisfactory	S_5:Comprehensive State Ownership
A_6:Apollonian Calm	C_6:Tradition Controlled		I_6:Bureaucracy Salient	V_6:Private Armies		
A_7:Person-Centered, Unfolding						

$A_2 C_2 T_3 I_1 V_2' E_2 S_2$, A status quo alternative

$A_2 C_2 T_4 I_4 V_3 E_4 S_2$, Dithering depression

$A_5 C_4 T_5 I_2 V_1 E_1 S_4$, New – Age, eco – war succeeding

Figure 23-2 A Sector/Factor Array for Use in Projecting Alternative U.S. Futures

If the Factors within the "Violence" Sector, as indicated in Figure 23-2, do not offer a place within which to put any condition of violence that is admitted to be plausible for America during the next thirty years, they should be redefined and/or the list extended.

These constructs are used to describe the overall field conditions by selecting one Factor from each Sector, as is indicated graphically in Figure 23-2 by the jagged lines linking particular Factors together. Each such condition can be described succinctly by a single *word* composed of seven letters to designate each of the seven Sectors with a subscript for each letter to show which Factor was selected to typify that Sector. Any such configuration represents a potentially plausible field condition, since each of the Factors was chosen to cover a plausible range of circumstances within its Sector, and the large number of alternatives that can be distinctly represented in such ways indicates the fineness with which this approach permits a field to be characterized. An array of six Sectors each with six Factors would, for instance, permit the designation of about 46,000 distinct alternative field conditions. The particular array shown in Figure 23-2 offers 189,000 alternatives. It proves, luckily, that only a small portion of such whole configurations prove even tolerably plausible, as combinations of Factors are considered together. The 189,000 cases from Figure 23-2, for instance, filtered down to fewer than 100 full configurations to be used in composing the CUSP scenarios.

Experience with such schemes of categorization matches with psychological theory in indicating that seven Sectors with about seven Factors in each Sector is as large an array as can be used without sacrificing the ease of comparison that is the prime objective. Indeed, moving beyond a six by six array amplifies the difficulties encountered while using such a system, although on occasion such difficulties seem worth accepting in order to permit richer description. This cut-off seems to exist because so many people prove to be able very readily to carry six related bits of information in whatever part of the brain corresponds to the rapid-access file of a computer. Seven bits can be almost as quickly recalled by most of us with some effort, and eight slows the process dramatically.

The Sectors that might be most appropriate for skeletal description of any particular kind of field (e.g. a major nation of alternatively, a strip of coast land or an urban complex) seems likely to be much the same. If some sort of policy formulation other than that in the field of education had been the object of concern during the projection of the CUSP scenarios, a different set of primary Sectors might well have been chosen from the dozen shown in Figure 23-1, and others might well have been added to the extended list. After having made such projections for several major nations or world regions, however, one would expect the master list of Sectors to undergo little further change for that class of fields.

Factors seem almost sure to be more variable from one application to another. The spread of plausible, alternative conditions of violence within the USSR during the next few decades promises, for instance, to be quite different from that in the U.S.A., and their descriptions in terms such as to evoke experiential, commonsense evaluation of combinations of Factors (e.g. A Violence Factor and one typifying the structure of the economy) would be even more distinctive.

For the present, in any case, a new Sector/Factor array should be considered for each ecological field and perhaps for each distinctive policy focus relating to it.

A SET OF SCENARIOS: Finally, it always is necessary to select an illustrative few scenarios from those that appear reasonably plausible as descriptive of things to come within a given whole field, the third of the methodological criteria listed earlier. In the FAR cycle of analysis, this selection is done in Steps 1 and 4. Nothing can prevent such selection from being judgemental and therefore subjective in the long run. Nevertheless, a morphological approach such as that underlying the FAR method offers a large number of explicitly described alternative scenario outlines, and selection from within such a set calls for deliberate rejections of the alternatives not chosen for elaboration. At least, this partially defends us from that common failing of subjective inquiry in which one hides his assumptions from himself and rejects that which he does not like to consider without ever seriously looking at it.

Summary

It has been argued here that:
1. Man produces most of the disturbances of life patterns on earth and also directs the more powerful corrective forces tending to contain such disturbances. He therefore must be thought of as one

of the many interactive components *within* most major ecological fields; that seems almost certainly to be the case where quality of (human) life is at issue.

2. Our comprehensions of the *laws* of human preference and their realization through politics are obviously very poor, and our understanding of secondary impacts from our efforts to shape the environment of which we are a part is only slightly better. Our efforts toward manipulation of the environment, therefore, seem destined to produce adverse surprises in the future somewhat as they have in the past, making any steady approach to environmental equilibrium extremely unlikely during coming decades. Our mistakes will call for corrections, which will in turn breed further mistakes.

3. This prospect for continued, unpredictable change is enhanced by the way in which many world problems now seem to merge together within a macroproblem, thus expanding the scope of the ecological fields to be treated as unitary wholes, and lessening the chance they will be appreciated by those (such as voters and designated decision makers) who must take action concerning them. Breadth of appreciation of the wholeness of fields and contempt for simplistic *solutions* will moderate but not erase this prospect.

4. The characteristic *answer* from ecologists concerning the likely effects of this or that contemplated quality-of-life policy therefore should not be a described end point (since such are unlikely even to be approached closely in this era), but rather a difference between scenarios of change with and without policy intervention in question. The continuing uncertainty introduced by our salience within the ecological fields of concern makes it inappropriate that prospective impacts be estimated in relation to just on *undisturbed* scenario, since there is no way of judging which is the most likely such line of future evolution. A *set* of illustrative, comparably plausible, alternative scenarios for each field is needed.

5. Three desiderata stand out when one considers the nature of the projections needed for quality-of-life policy formulation. Each scenario should be internally consistent, so as to form a unitary whole at any time and through time; all conditions described for the field in question along any one of the set of scenarios pertaining to its future should be designated in ways such as to facilitate comparison among them; and the set of scenarios finally offered to decision makers as working materials whereby their appreciations of future options may be broadened and refined should be fairly illustrative of the spread of plausible future variability.

6. The Field Anomaly Relaxation method described above seems to meet all three of these criteria; the author has been able to find no other approach that does so well.

[CHAPTER TWENTY-FOUR]

PLANNING AMID FORCES FOR INSTITUTIONAL CHANGE*

Willis W. Harman

IN THE WORK of this Center† we have attempted to construct a comprehensive set of *alternative future histories* for this nation from now until the year 2000.[140] (This was accomplished by devising an adequately rich coded description of the state of society and then systematically examining which sequences of these states are feasible for the next thirty years.) The results of this analysis indicate that the vast majority of the *future histories* so constructed are clearly to be avoided if possible. The reasons vary widely—from authoritarian governments to economic collapse, from ecological catastrophe to exhaustion from continuous warfare. The very small percentage of desirable *paths to the future*—desirable in the sense of leading toward the national goals implicit in the nation's founding documents—appear to require *a drastic and prompt shift in the operative values of the society, and a corresponding change in its institutions.*

*A presentation at the symposium "Planning in the Seventies," co-sponsored by the Washington Chapter of the American Society for Public Administration and the National Bureau of Standards on May 3-4, 1971. An earlier version of the talk was presented at the Jersey City State College Conference on Human Ecology, April 23, 1971.

†Center for the Study of Social Policy, Stanford Research Institute.

It will be our purpose here to explore concisely (a) the reasons for considering such a far-reaching cultural and institutional metamorphosis to be plausible and perhaps even likely (though uncomfortable), (b) the nature of the change, and (c) some of the most important implications for our social institutions.

Let us first be explicit as regards the magniture and pervasiveness of the transformation being posited. This is thoroughgoing systematic change, to a degree comparable at least with such historic transitions as the Fall of Rome, the Reformation, and the Industrial Revolution, involving changes in basic cultural premises, the root image of man-in-society, fundamental value postulates, and all aspects of social roles and institutions.

Lewis Mumford notes that there have probably been not more than a half-dozen profound transformations of Western society since primitive man. Each of these "has rested on a new metaphysical and ideological base; or rather, upon deeper stirrings and intuitions whose rationalized expression takes the forms of a new picture of the cosmos and the nature of man."[143] I want clearly to distinguish what we are hypothesizing from other changes which are revolutionary in a social or political sense but do not involve transformation of the basic, implicit, unchallenged, taken-as-given metaphysic. We might apply to it, by analogy, the Greek word for religious conversion, *metanoia*: "a fundamental transformation of mind."[144]

This is by no means the first suggestion you have heard that we may be at a historic watershed, so I shall make the arguments to that point quite concise. I want to dwell particularly on some aspects of the fundamental nature of the transition (which, with the general speedup of events, may take place in the space of a decade or two rather than the century of religious warfare that accompanied the Reformation), and on what this means for our social institutions.

Bear in mind, I am not saying that *metanoia* must inexorably take place; rather, that it appears *necessary for a desirable future* that some cultural movement toward its accomplishment is evident and that our social and political choices over the next few years may be fateful, in that by fostering or repressing the forces for *metanoia* they can drastically affect the future of the human experiment.

I *Necessity of Paradigm Change*

It will be helpful to introduce another term. In his seminal study of the structure of scientific revolutions, T. S. Kuhn[145] uses the term *dominant paradigm* to refer to *the basic way of perceiving, thinking, and doing, associated with a particular vision of reality,* largely embodied in unquestioned, tacit understanding transmitted primarily through exemplars. Thus applying this concept to the whole society, a paradigm is more than an ideology or a world view, and less than a total culture. Kuhn documents the sequence of phenomena that tend to accompany the breakdown of influence of an old paradigm and its replacement by a new one. Growing awareness of problems which appear to be intrinsic to, and unresolvable within, the old paradigm is one such sign.

In historical retrospect we can see that a paradigm, which began its climb to dominance several centuries ago, has since influenced all aspects of Western society. This industrial-state paradigm, sharply differing from the dominant paradigm of the Middle Ages, is characterized by:

Development and application of scientific method.
Wedding of scientific and technological advance.
Industrialization through division of labor.
Progress defined as technological and economic growth.
Man seeking control over nature; positivistic theory of knowledge.
Acquisitive materialism, work ethic, economic-man image.

Born out of this paradigm are the fabulous products of modern industrial organization and modern technology. The beginnings of breakdown of the paradigm are dramatically shown in the fact that its successes underlie all the serious social problems of our day. Table XIII illustrates this. The left hand column lists the achievements of industrial society; the right hand column shows the corresponding problems to which these have led. These problems are ultimately unsolvable in the present paradigm precisely because their origins are in the success of that paradigm.

This breakdown of the industrial-state paradigm is at least fivefold:

1. *It fails to promote further accomplishment of one of the most fundamental functions of a society, namely to provide each individual with an opportunity to contribute to the society and to be affirmed by it in return.* This involves much more than a failure to achieve

TABLE XIII

SUMMARY DISPLAY OF THE WAYS IN WHICH MAJOR
CONTEMPORARY SOCIETAL PROBLEMS ARE CONSEQUENCES
OF THE SUCCESSES OF THE INDUSTRIAL-STATE PARADIGM[146]

Successes of the technological era	*Resulting problems of being too successful*
Prolonging the life span	Overpopulation; problems of the aged
Weapons for national defense	Hazard of mass destruction through nuclear and biological weapons
Machine replacement of manual and routine labor	Exacerbated unemployment
Advances in communication and transportation	Urbanization; *shrinking world;* vulnerability of a complex society to break down (natural or deliberate)
Efficiency	Dehumanization of the world of work
Growth in the power of systematized knowledge	Threats to privacy and freedoms (e.g. surveillance of technology, *bioengineering*); *knowledge barrier* to underclass
Affluence	Increased per capita environmental impact, pollution, energy shortage
Satisfaction of basic needs; ascendance up the *need-level hierarchy*	Worldwide revolutions of *rising expectations,* rebellion against *nonmeaningful work;* unrest among affluent students
Expanded power of human choice	Management breakdown as regards control of consequences of technological applications
Expanded wealth of developed nations	Intrinsically increasing gap between have and have-not nations
Development of prepotent high-technology	Apparent economic necessity of continuous *war* to use up the output of the *megamachine.*

reasonably full employment with an adequate income-maintenance provision. The problem is that of an ever-increasing segment of the society who are defined as *not needed,* because in whatever work they feel fitted to do they have been replaced by a machine or could be. (The number clearly would be far greater had we not had a war-stimulated economy for over thirty years.) The psychological consequences of having nothing to offer that the society values are not dealt with by keeping these persons as pets on some sort of income-maintenance arrangement. Ironically, the humane aim of relieving people, through technology, of burdensome and routine labor, results in the end with their being deprived of the privilege of performing educative, mind-forming, self-rewarding, appreciated work.

2. *It fails to foster more equitable distribution of power, wealth, and justice.* There is a fundamental power instability intrinsic to any conceivable society: The having of physical, political, economic, or knowledge power is conducive to gaining more; the lack of such

power makes for vulnerability to further loss. (Them as has, gets.) Every stable society has had to devise some way of counteracting the ultimate disruptiveness of this instability, including some form of legitimized coercion. (This was accomplished in the traditional society by a caste structure with traditional and legal rights associated with each caste level. Some small societies have had egalitarian communist structures and ethics. In every case some limiting mechanism ultimately counteracted the tendency of power to accumulate indefinitely.)

In the modern industrial democracy this accumulative tendency has been held in check by a tradition of equality of opportunity and of mobility through socioeconomic classes, backed up by a variety of regulating measures—anti-trust laws, fair trade agreements, graduated income tax, checks and balances in government, collective bargaining arrangements, regulatory commissions, and so on. These mechanisms are proving inadequate to move toward a more equitable distribution of power and wealth, partly because of the growth of a network of giant corporations with such enormous economic power that they are relatively immune to normal processes of community control, but more fundamentally because the basic paradigm contains within it no rationale for redistribution. That rationale has always been provided by an altruistic ethic based in transcendental values which were external to the basic paradigm of the industrial era. That ethic was seriously eroded during the twentieth century by the rise of positivistic, materialistic science. With the decline of *American civil religion*[147] comes a decline in the efficacy of those social-regulation mechanisms which require it for their smooth functioning.

3. *It fails to foster socially responsible management of the development and application of technology.* We listed earlier the societal problems resulting from the *Faustian powers* of technology. These have been the direct result of the unspoken policy that whenever technology could make a profit for an individual or a corporation, or could contribute to a nation's ability to carry on warfare, that technology would be developed and applied. The values and policies that have thus far governed industrialization and technological development clearly will not suffice to insure that these ever more potent powers will be used for the overall benefit of humanity. Our past practice has been to allow arms races, pollution, environmental degradation, ecological imbalance, or denuding of the land to proceed until the situation obviously became intolerable and then to attempt some corrective action. Some sort of transnational control over scientific and technological innovations is essential,[148] clearly involving some new institutional forms. But if these are to work, they have to be backed up with a changed ethic which gives the general good a more commanding position.

This failure, and also the failure to achieve more equitable distribution of wealth, relate directly to what Heilbroner[149] terms "a central weakness of the market system—its inability to formulate public needs above those of the marketplace." It does appear that some more socialist forms of the industrial state can distribute wealth and regulate technological impact more successfully than the forms in which more dependence is placed on the market system. The costs of this gain are a centralist tendency, and risks of bureaucratic stultification and authoritarian inflexibility. As Heilbroner puts it, "The central problem which is likely to confront the societies of tomorrow is nothing less than the creation of *a new relationship between the economic aspect of existence and human life in its totality.*"

4. *It fails to provide goals which will enlist the deepest loyalties and commitments of the nation's citizens.* The implicit goals of expanding economic growth and affluence are not adequate. Having contributed to the solution of most of the how-to-do-it questions we can imagine, the paradigm fails to shed light on the question of what is worth doing. Again it is important to note that those goals which have, in the past, enlisted the nation's deepest loyalties and commitments, are part of the *American civil religion* which grows out of a competing paradigm (Judeo-Christian tradition, Western political tradition) whose force has declined as the industrial-state paradigm gained in dominance. (The Declaration of Independence asserts, "We hold these truths to be self-evident," and to the deductions from those truths concludes, "we mutually pledge . . . our Lives, our Fortunes, and our Sacred Honor." Science had pronounced by early in this century that such action was either conditioned or neurotic behavior.)

5. *It fails to develop and maintain the habitability of the planet.* To the contrary, the ethic of man *controlling* and exploiting nature leads ineluctably to greater and greater disruptions of previous ecological balances, spoliation of the environment, and squandering of life-sustaining resources.

These failures are *intrinsic*, built into the paradigm itself, and awaiting only the unfolding of consequences until they become critical. Population pressure, itself a consequence of the technology-aided prolonging of life span, alters the timetable, making problems crucial earlier than they might be if population were reduced. But population limiting alone will not resolve the problems. (This fact is immediately apparent if one imagines population to remain constant but affluence and consumption levels throughout the world to be raised to those presently enjoyed by the American upper middle class.)

II *An Emerging "New Age" Paradigm*

Victor Ferkiss,[100] analyzing the unavoidable problems to which the technological ethic leads, concludes that the required "new guiding philosophy" must contain three basic and essential elements. First is what he terms a "new naturalism," which affirms that man is absolutely a part of a nature, a universe, that is always in the process of becoming. The second element, a "new holism," recognizes that "no part can be defined or understood save in relation to the whole." The third, a "new immanentism," sees that the whole is "determined not from outside but from within."

Appearing as though in response to this inferred need for a new guiding philosophy is a *New Age* paradigm, dimly defined as yet but featuring a kind of ecological consciousness that satisfies Ferkiss' three conditions. It is characterized by (a) a metaphysic asserting *transcendant man* and (b) the goal of a *person-centered society*. Whether this seemingly spontaneous emergence of a new outlook is fortuitous coincidence or response to a subliminally perceived need of society is a moot but unimportant point. In either event, the coincidence of the need and the emergence of a possible answer to the need increases the likelihood that we are witnessing the beginnings of a thoroughgoing paradigm shift.

Clues to the nature of the *New Age* premises are to be found in the swelling interest in religious, metaphysical, psychic, and arcane literature and discussion groups; in the *consciousness-expanding* activities of the *human potential* movement, ranging from yoga and transcendental meditation to psychedelic drugs and efforts to develop *psychic openings*; in the juxtaposition, in underground newspapers, and other activities of *the movement* of revolutionary messages with material on religious, esoteric, and psychic topics.[150] Most significant, as an indication of the growing challenge to the prevailing positivistic premise of conventional science, is the growing scientific and popular interest in *altered states of consciousness*,[151] that is, in that realm of subjective experience in which is rooted the most fundamental beliefs and value postulates of this or any culture.[152]

The basic premises of the *New Age* paradigm are by no means new. The belief in transcendent man, with unlimited potentiality to comprehend the innermost workings of his universe, to have immediate perception of a supersensible reality and of his intimate relationship with it, has been the esoteric tradition of all the world's religions for thousands of years.[153] The goal of a person-centered society was the foundation stone of this nation. "The Declaration (of Independence) put the individual squarely at the center, as of supreme importance. It completely reversed the age-old order; it defined government as the servant of the individual, not his master."[154] It would be the becoming dominant and operative of these premises and goals which would be new—which would comprise *metanoia*.

The 1960 report of the President's Commission on National Goals stated emphatically:

> The paramount goal . . . is to guard the rights of the individual, to ensure his development, and to enlarge his opportunity . . . All of our institutions—political, social, and economic—must further enhance the dignity of the citizen, promote the maximum development of his capabilities, stimulate their responsible exercise, and widen the range and effectiveness of opportunities for individual choice . . . The first national goals to be pursued . . . should be the development of each individual to his fullest potential . . . Self-fulfillment is placed at the summit (of the order of values). All other goods are regulated to lower orders of priority . . . The central goal, therefore, should be a renewal of faith in the infinite value and the unlimited possibilities of individual development.

What was not clearly understood in 1960 and is more apparent now, is that *a fundamental incompatibility exists between these aims and the dominant paradigm of the industrial state.*

III *Some Specific Implications for Society*

Thus we have argued that: (a) the industrial era, which can be thought of as (in historical terms) a gigantic unprecedented step toward new possibilities for man, has been based in a paradigm which, however well suited to that step, seems now fundamentally inappropriate to the task of constructing a humane world on the base of those technological accomplishments; and (b) a new and suitable paradigm may be in process of replacing the old.[155]

If this (admittedly audacious and nondemonstrable) proposition turns out to be accurate, and the claimant *New Age* paradigm does become dominant, it will—as we have noted—amount to a profound and pervasive systemic change. All institutions of the society will be affected.

The meaning of the *metanoia* can be better grasped if we attempt to guess at likely changes in specific areas. We do this, not as an attempt at prediction, but in the endeavor to better understand what this change might mean for society.

SCIENCE: Science in the claimant paradigm will be clearly understood to be a *moral inquiry*. That is to say, it will deal with what is empirically found to be good for us, in much the same sense that the science of nutrition deals with what foods are wholesome for us. It will place particular emphasis on the systematic exploration of subjective experience, the ultimate source of our value postulates. In this respect it will resemble the humanities and religion; and the boundaries between these three disciplines will become less sharp, as is already presaged in the recent writings of some psychotherapists.[156]

The new psychology will incorporate, in some form, the age-old yet radical doctrine that we perceive the world and ourselves in it as we have been culturally *hypnotized* to perceive it. The typical commonsense-scientific view of reality will be considered to be a valid but partial view—a particular metaphor, so to speak. This new psychology will include some way of referring to the subjective experiencing of a unity in all things (the *divine Ground* of Aldous Huxley's *The Perennial Philosophy*), and of a *higher self* (Emerson's *Oversoul*), and will view favorably the development of a self-image congruent with this experiencing. It will allow for a much more unified view of human experiences now categorized under such diverse headings as creativity, hypnosis, mystical experience, religious insight, extrasensory perception, self discovery, and personality growth. It will tend to be evolutionary and emergent, viewing human needs and values as varying in a hierarchical way as the individual's development proceeds (as exemplified in Maslow's postulated hierarchy of needs).[157]

Applied science, particularly educational research, will look strongly in the direction of new potentialities suggested by the newly appreciated powers of belief, imagination, and suggestion. To conscious choice and subconscious choice (repression, projection, sublimation, etc.) will be added what might be termed *supraconscious choice*,[158] intuition, creative imagination, choosing *better than we know*, with as much impact upon our policies regarding education, welfare, criminal rehabilitation, and justice as the Freudian concept of *subconscious choice* had, some years earlier. Finally, the new science would become also a sort of *civil religion*, supporting the value postulates of the Founding Fathers rather than being neutral or undermining as was the old science.

INSTITUTIONS: Clearly the new metaphysic would tend to support effective institutionalization of such values as society serving the self-fulfillment of the individual, equality of justice before the law, individual fulfillment through community, human dignity and meaning, honesty and trust, self-determination for individuals and minority groups, and responsibility for humankind and the planet. However, values do not become operative simply by being deemed *good*. Let us look at some arguments that suggest these values might become operative because they work.

As the social system becomes more and more highly interdependent, the need becomes greater for accurate information to be available throughout the system. Just as the modern banking and credit system would not operate smoothly with the low trust level of a warrior culture, so highly complex task operations (such as putting a man on the moon) require a higher level of honesty, openness, and trust than suffice in advertising and merchandising. For quite practical, rather than moralistic reasons, the demanded level of honesty and openness can be expected to increase.

Similarly, as the complexity of societal operations increases, hierarchically organized bureaucratic structures tend to have communication overloads near the top and discouragements to entrepreneurship and responsibility-taking, lower down. Adaptive organic forms, with relatively autonomous subsystems, seem better adapted to complex tasks and provide more satisfying experiences to the people involved.

In general, the more significant a fraction of the whole is a subsystem, the more important it becomes that its goals be in close alignment with those of the overall system. It would be quite practical to foster (through changes in corporation, tax, and anti-trust laws, credit policies, special subsidies, etc.) the development of profit-making corporations whose *operative* goals include active response to social problems (as of those of nonprofit corporations already do) and fostering the educational growth and development of all persons involved (as the goals of universities already do). In fact, if something like this does not take place the amount of government regulation required for pollution control, fair business and employment practice, resource conservation, etc. can only increase without limit.

In short, the institutionalization of the values of the *person-centered society* would appear to be not only morally desirable, but *good business* for the nation.

ECONOMIC SYSTEM: The portion of the industrial-state paradigm underlying the present operation of the economic system involves such concepts as man as infinite consumer of goods and services (providing his appetites are properly whetted through advertising), profit maximizing and economic growth as preeminent goals, and government as master regulator of employment level, growth rate, wage and price stability, and a modicum of fair play. The new paradigm would remind us that the root meaning of *economics* is home management, and that the planet earth is man's home. Managing the earth, with its finite supplies of space and resources and its delicate ecological balance, and conserving and developing it as a suitable habitat for evolving man, is a far different task than that for which the present economic system was set up.

Furthermore, an economic theory is inevitably based upon a theory of social psychology. If man is not *economic man* in a self-regulating free market, nor an infinite consumer with manipulable motivations, but something quite different, then we need a radical correction to economic theory.

So some changes will take place in our economic institutions and practices of which we can see only the general directions. One clear need is a network of citizen-participation policy and planning centers at local, regional, and national levels, linked together with a common understanding of the alternatives that lie before the society and some unifying agreement as to the futures to be desired and those to be avoided.

EDUCATION: If the society does indeed undergo *metanoia*, one of the most significant ways in which the transformation will be manifested will be in the premise that education is the paramount function of society. Robert Hutchins[159] describes "the learning society" as one that will have transformed:

its values in such a way that learning, fulfillment, becoming human, had become its aims *and all its institutions were directed to this end.* This is what the Athenians did . . . They made their society one designed to bring all its members to the fullest development of their highest powers . . . Education was not a segregated activity, conducted for certain hours, in certain places, at a certain time of life. It was the aim of the society . . . The Athenian was educated by the culture, by Paidea. And the central task of Paidea was the search for the Divine Center.[160]

The individual will have several careers during his lifetime. This is not because they are forced upon him by job obsolescence in a technological-industrial megamachine madly careening out of control and ever faster. Rather, it will be because it is in this way that one best realizes one's own potentialities and maximizes one's own fulfillment. But this will require institutional changes to accommodate to more or less continuous education throughout life, with particularly intense learning activity during periods of career change.

The precise way in which this will be resolved cannot be foreseen, of course. Perhaps a multiplicity of institutional forms will be required, including new kinds of collaborative arrangements between educational institutions and industrial and commercial organizations. The emergence of new types of profit-making corporations with diversified goals, as suggested above, might help to legitimate the growth-promoting and educational activities which seem impracticable under present laws affecting corporations.

It is along these lines that the society would approach the *unneeded people* problem which was earlier identified as one of the key ways in which the breakdown of the industrial-state paradigm is becoming manifest. The *recycling* of those persons engaged in career change will take the stigma off the recycling of those which the modern industrial state shunts out of the productive mainstream, usually irretrievably—those labeled *technologically disemployed, unemployable, dropout, poor, delinquent, criminal, deviant,* and *mentally ill.* Appropriate emotional support and educational opportunity will be the assumed responsibility of widely distributed public, private, and voluntary organizations, rather than the charge of a huge welfare bureaucracy which dispenses *income maintenance* but not human concern.

IV *The Relevance to Present Decision-Making*

The intent of this paper is neither alarmist nor utopian, but practical. All policy decisions are guided by some interpretation of the past and some vision of the future—or of alternative futures. We have examined an interpretation of recent indications of social ferment (as associated with paradigm change) and a vision of one alternative future (institutional changes associated with the new paradigm become dominant), both in a most abbreviated form.

A competing view would see neither necessity for, nor evidence suggesting, such a basic paradigmatic change. In this view the future would be approximated by a smooth continuation of past trends.[161]

Two observations are crucial: (a) at this point in history each of these two alternative views can be made plausible, and each is held by many reasonable people and (b) the rational national policies which would be derived from the two views differ greatly; some policies which seem sensible in one view appear harmful in the other.

Thus at the least, it would seem prudent to test policy decisions both against the eventuality that the view presented here may prove accurate, and also against the opposite eventuality, that it may simply turn out to be wrong and our current travails will be interpreted in some other way.

Under the assumption that the paradigm-shift interpretation is more or less correct (that is, that the shift becomes possible and desirable, but by no means automatic), it follows that the main challenge to society is to bring about the transition without shaking itself apart in the process. Every major policy decision tends either to foster the change or to impede it. Actions which attempt to force it too fast can be socially disruptive; actions which attempt to hold it back can make the transition more difficult and perhaps bloody. For example, there can be little doubt that maintenance of strong economic and legal-enforcement systems through the transition period is essential; yet these systems too must be flexible to change. Seldom in history has such delicacy of balance been required to achieve a major social transformation rapidly and yet not rupture the social fabric.

[CHAPTER TWENTY-FIVE]

ENDS, MEANS, AND THE
QUALITY OF LIFE

PETER KIVY

> The Walrus and the Carpenter
> Were walking close at hand:
> They wept like anything to see
> Such quantities of sand:
> "If this were only cleared away,"
> They said, "it would be grand!"
>
> Tweedledee*

WE ARE CONTINUALLY told by environmentalists, ecologists, conservationists, city planners, and many other kinds of well-meaning *futurists*, all on the side of the angels, that our prospects are very bleak indeed unless some far-reaching *plan* is adopted for the improvement of the *quality of life*. We are told that we do not plan enough for the future and that in consequence of this the quality of life is on the decline. But what is *the quality of life*? And can it be improved by *planning*? These are the questions I want to raise here. I want to argue, as the Devil's Advocate, that there is at least *some* reason to doubt that we can all agree, on rational grounds, as to what a *quality* life is; and I want to argue, again as the *Advocatus Diaboli*, that there is at least *some* reason to doubt that a *planned* future will mean an improvement in the quality of life, *not* because plans sometimes go wrong, but for the more curious reason that *any*

*Carroll Lewis: *Through the Looking Glass*. New York, Modern Library, p. 184, 1936.

248

planned future may be viewed by some as, *ipso facto*, a life of unacceptable quality.

What do we mean by *the quality of life* when we say that the
quality of life is on the decline, or that we must raise the quality
of life?

No doubt, the key to the meanings of such statements is to be
found in another, even more familiar one, to the effect that "It's
quality, not quantity that counts." So, for example: (a) a small
diamond of a certain *quality* will be preferred to a large diamond
of a lower *quality* because "It's *quality*, not quantity that counts";
and (b) Achilles preferred a short and glorious life on the plains of
Troy to a long dreary one on the farm because (of course) in life,
as well as in diamonds, "It's *quality*, not quantity that counts."

But, it might be suggested, such a distinction is only a provisional
one: for, surely, the quality of one diamond is higher than the
quality of another in virtue of its possessing *something* in greater
quantity; and so quality, at least in principle, can always be reduced
to quantity. And this must apply to a life as well as a diamond. A
life of twenty years may be of higher quality than a life of sixty,
but only because there is more of *something* in the short life than in
the long one, not more years, but more *something*. What is that
something? Find *that*, one would think, and you find out how to
raise the quality of life, just as you raise the quality of a frankfurter
by adding more meat.

Perhaps we can go to the hedonist for the answer to the question
of what constitutes the quality of life. Pleasure, let us say, and the
absence of pain is the secret ingredient, pleasure and pain being
here construed in the widest possible sense, making (say) the satisfaction of solving an equation a *pleasure* and the dissatisfaction of
failing to solve it a *pain*. We now have a ready answer to the question, "What makes a life of twenty years' duration higher in quality
than a life of sixty?" It is: the quantity of pleasure, calculated by
adding *units* of pleasure and subtracting from them *units* of pain.
So we can say that life A is higher in quality than life B if any one of
the following five possibilities obtain: (a) there is an excess of
pleasure over pain in both A and B, but the excess in A is greater
than the excess in B; (b) there is an excess of pleasure over pain in A
and an equal amount of pleasure and pain in B; (c) there is an excess

of pleasure over pain in A and an excess of pain over pleasure in B; (d) there is an equal amount of pleasure and pain in A and an excess of pain over pleasure in B; (e) there is an excess of pain over pleasure in both A and B, but the excess is less in A.[162] We shall say, for short, although it is not quite accurate, that all five of the above are instances in which there is more *pleasure* in A than in B.

But notice that the rather simple-minded hedonism we have adopted can only give us the answer to the question, "What makes *a* life higher in quality than another, or than some others?" It cannot answer the question, "What makes *life*, life in general, life on this planet, higher or lower than it was (say) in the eighteenth century?" Or, "What will make life (say) in the year two thousand of a higher or lower quality than our own?" And, of course, if we do not know *what* makes life in general higher or lower in quality, we cannot know what steps to take to raise it, or what steps to take to avoid lowering it.

It is at this point that the hedonist may become a utilitarian; and I believe most futurists, most actual and would-be arrangers and engineers of things to come, are, at heart, consciously or unconsciously utilitarians of one kind or another. The shortest step from simple hedonism of the kind outlined above to utilitarianism would be to say that the quality of life consists in pleasure, and that the quality of life at time t is higher than the quality of life at time $t + 1$ if the total units of pleasure minus the total units of pain is greater at time t than the total units of pleasure minus the total units of pain at time $t + 1$. And this, of course, would involve taking into consideration the pleasure and pain of every sentient being, which is why utilitarianism is described as urging *the greatest happiness for the greatest number*, happiness being construed as presence of pleasure and absence of pain. (Of course, the same five possibilities listed above will apply in comparing the pleasure and/or pain at time t with the pleasure and/or pain at time $t + 1$ as in comparing the lives of A and B. And we will use the same shorthand here, referring to any of the five possibilities as instances in which there is more *pleasure* at time t than at time $t + 1$.)

Now only a moment's reflection will reveal that this answer is unsatisfactory. We do not mean by the quality of life merely the sum of pleasure minus pain. Who, for example, would say that the quality of life in a community of satisfied pigs is higher than the quality of life in a community of men and women who were as wise as Socrates and as gentle as Jesus. Yet a community of one million pigs, by sheer force of numbers, might very well produce a larger sum of pleasure than a community of ten wise and gentle men and women.

To meet such counter-examples, John Stuart Mill, perhaps the most well-known of all utilitarians, insisted that it is not only the quantity of pleasure that the utilitarian must take into account, but the *quality* of pleasure as well. "It is quite compatible with the principle of utility," he wrote, "to recognize the fact that some kinds of pleasure are more desirable and more valuable than others. It would be absurd that, while in estimating all other things quality is considered as well as quantity, the estimation of pleasure should be supposed to depend on quantity alone."[163]

But if we follow Mill here, we will be letting a fox get into the hen house. We started, remember, by asking what might be meant by *the quality of life*. And on the assumption that the quality of life is something like the quality of a diamond, or a frankfurter, we decided that perhaps what is meant by the quality of life at time t being greater than at time $t + 1$ is that there is a greater quantity of something at time t than at time $t + 1$. That something, we suggested, might be pleasure. Yet there seem to be cases in which we would want to say: "There is more pleasure at time t than at time $t + 1$, but the quality of life is higher at time $t + 1$." Hence we cannot mean by *quality of life* simply *quantity of pleasure*. It is now suggested that if we acknowledge that there are various grades —that is qualities—of pleasure, we can save our hypothesis: we may still say that quality of life is a function of quantity of pleasure, as long as we are sure to add the proviso that it is a complex function— a function both of quantity *and* quality of pleasure. But what have we really gained? We have tried to define what we mean by *quality* in terms solely of *quantity*. And we have clearly failed: for the term *quality* appears in our definiens. We have not reduced *quality* to *quantity*, which was the point of our strategy. *Quality of pleasure* is no less obscure than *quality of life*. We are left again with the imponderable *quality*.

Mill suggested that we explicate *quality of pleasure* in the following way: one pleasure is higher in quality than another if most or all of those who have experienced both prefer the one to the other. But it is clear, I think, that when we pass judgments on the quality of pleasure (or the quality of life) we are not making judgments we think can be supported by taking polls or surveys. That the whole world should prefer the pleasures of pigs to the pleasures of Socrates is irrelevant to the question of whether Socrates' pleasures, or the pigs', are of higher quality; or, for that matter, whether the quality of life of a community of pigs is higher than the quality of life of a community of saints. As C. D. Broad concludes, in a related context, "to me this kind of answer seems utterly irrelevant to this kind of question."[165]

There is, however, a more promising form of utilitarianism than Mill's, which seems better able to cope with our counter-example. Mill, as we have seen, is a hedonistic utilitarian, identifying happiness with pleasure. ("By happiness is intended pleasure and the absence of pain; by unhappiness, pain and the privation of pleasure.")[166] But what is becoming clear, through our analysis, is that pleasure, and the absence of pain, although major contributors to happiness, are not its whole substance. A certain amount of pleasure may, indeed, be a necessary condition for happiness, and the presence of pain, beyond a certain point, a sufficient condition for unhappiness. But if the excess of pleasure over pain in community A is greater than the excess of pleasure over pain in community B, this is not a sufficient condition for there being more *happiness* in A; and if the excess of pain over pleasure in community C is greater than the excess of pain over pleasure in community D, this is not a sufficient condition for there being more *unhappiness* in C. Perhaps, then, we should take *happiness* and *unhappiness*, rather than pleasure and pain, as our basic measure of the quality of life. Can we not say that the quality of life at time t is greater than at time $t + 1$ if the quantity of *happiness* at time t is greater than at time $t + 1$; and, further, that the sum of pleasure minus pain at time $t + 1$ might be greater than at time t, and yet the quantity of *happiness* be greater at time t? We can then dispatch our counter-example quite handily; for although the quantity of pleasure minus pain might be greater in a community of one million satisfied pigs than in a community of ten dissatisfied men and women as wise as Socrates and as gentle as Jesus, the quantity of *happiness* is greater in the community of men and women than in the community of pigs—and hence the quality of life is higher in the community of men and women than in the community of pigs.

I believe this is indeed the correct move to make. But it by no means gives us the kind of answer to our original question that we were looking for when we posed it. For our concept of happiness has now become so broad and far-ranging that it is no clearer or more specific than our concept of *quality of life*. Far from being an explication of *quality of life*, *happiness* seems to be rather a synonym, with nothing gained in the way of simplicity. To say that a community of ten dissatisfied saints contains more happiness than a community of one million satisfied pigs is to say nothing more nor less than that the quality of life in the community of saints is higher than in the community of pigs; or, to use a third synonym, a community of ten dissatisfied saints is leading an *intrinsically better* life than a community of one million satisfied pigs. As a recent, and very sophisticated utilitarian, J. J. C. Smart, has put the case, "to call a person *happy* is to say more than that he is contented for most of the time, or even that he frequently enjoys himself and is rarely discontented or in pain. It is, I think, in part to express a favourable attitude to the idea of such a form of contentment and enjoyment."[166] And it is just such an evaluative moment that gives the phrase *quality of life* its distinctive use. To pass a judgment on the quality of life, among other things, is to express some ultimate moral commitment to it; or, contrariwise, to express some deep moral aversion to it. It is not to make an ethically neutral statement like "Such-and-such a number of people are in favor of (or against) it"— which is just why Mill's analysis of *quality of pleasure* fails to capture the sense of that phrase.

It is all too often unreflectively assumed by well-intentioned social and environmental reformers of many persuasions that we all really know exactly what we are talking about when we talk about *the quality of life*. Of course we do know how to use the phrase; but this is far from showing that we are in substantial agreement about what the quality of life is. What we must realize is that when two parties agree that "The quality of life should be raised," or that (what amounts to the same thing) "The amount of happiness in the world should be increased," they may still be in absolute and utter disagreement about *What is to be done*, because their ends in view—what they think of as the happy life or the *quality life*—are vastly different, the difference being in ethical attitude, ultimate ethical commitment.

There have been a number of highly influential philosophical movements in Britain and America which have held the view that disagreements about ultimate ethical commitments—of which disagreements about happiness or the quality of life are paradigm cases —are, in principle, irreconcilable by scientific methods, or rational procedures of any kind. Twenty years ago this was a very firmly entrenched view. Today there are other currents stirring in Anglo-American philosophy which have weakened the position somewhat. Nevertheless, such ethical *skepticism* is not easy to meet. And any social planner who is not aware of this deep and difficult philosophical issue is not, in my opinion, prepared for his work, any more than is the ethical philosopher who is ignorant of the pressing moral and social issues of his time.

My first challenge, then, to the planners of *my* Brave New World, is this: Do not assume that because I agree with your goal of raising the quality of life, I agree with you about *anything* except the most trivial of maxims, namely, that we should make the world *better*. But Hitler too shared *this* maxim with us . . . . I challenge you, therefore, to make clear to me what *your* concept of the *quality life*—the *happy* life—is. And I challenge you then, if our ultimate ethical commitments are different, to justify yours to me. Be aware, too, that there *may*, in the final analysis, be *no* rational means of your bringing me to your view, or my bringing you to mine.

The second question I want to raise concerns the end in view and the means of bringing it into being. I do not, however, intend to raise the familiar question of ends justifying means, but a more annoying and perhaps paradoxical one which can best be introduced with the following (rather farfetched) example.

Suppose I were fond of visiting a quaint old medieval city with crooked streets, unexpected vistas, hospitable little inns, nestled on a hillside overlooking the sea, with an impressive collection of houses dating from the eleventh century. Suppose, further, that I one day discover, never mind how, that it is not a quaint *old* city at all but a recent creation of Walt Disney Productions, so meticulously executed that even after being apprised of its real origin, I cannot detect any signs of it in the city itself. There is no detail of the city that I see now which I did not see before my disillusionment. Yet I no longer enjoy my visits to the city the way I used to. For my *knowledge* of its origin has changed my experience and poisoned it. My experience of the city depends, after all, not only upon the observable details of the city which, by hypothesis, are indistinguishable from what they would be if the city were really of genuine medieval origin. It depends as well upon my state of mind while I am observing. And my state of mind while observing a city I take to have evolved gradually from the eleventh century is quite different than my state of mind while observing the very same city with the knowledge that it came into being in 1965 in the space of three hectic months. My knowledge of how the city came into being makes my experience of it a different one than it was before. So, in describing the state of affairs in which the city figures, you must not only include a detailed description of the city, but a description of the states of mind of those experiencing it; and my state of mind is a function, in part, of what I know about the city's origin.

Consider, now, an analogous case. A social planner, whom I will call S, has an end in view, a certain state of affairs which I will call state of affairs E. He believes that the quality of life in E will be higher than it presently is. He also finds that those for whom he is planning share his view that the quality of life in E will be higher than it is now. In short, S and his constituency share a favorable ethical attitude toward E. So S sits down at his drawing board and devises the means of effectuating E. And (his luck still holding) he convinces everyone that his plan P, will indeed bring E into being.

But at this point a rather perplexing problem arises. For one of the individuals who up to this point has gone along with S now balks on the following grounds: "I share your approval of E. But I do not share your approval of E if we can have E only as the result of a *plan.* Nor am I objecting to your particular plan, P. It will not answer my objection if you bring forth an alternate plan to effectuate E. What I object to is E *plus* the knowledge I will have that E is not a spontaneous state of affairs but an *arranged, planned, engi-*

neered state of affairs. Plan me no plans!' "

Perhaps such an individual will not be taken seriously; perhaps he will be put down as an eccentric or a troublemaker. But his objection remains to be answered. What does the social planner say to someone who rejects *any* future in which we know that our future was the product of *social engineering?* What does the arranger of futures answer to the Underground Man who says: "I approve of *E*—but never *E* if what must accompany it is knowledge that *E* was the result of *any P?*"

I can think of one rather bizarre answer—but no more bizarre perhaps than the Underground Man's objection. We will tell the Underground Man this: we will give him a drug, or brainwash him, or whatever, and obliterate completely his knowledge that *E* is the result of any *P*. We will, at the appropriate time, implant in him the (false) belief that *E* is a *spontaneous* result.

But that will never satisfy the Underground Man. For he will doubtless disapprove—as I certainly do—of a community in which artificially induced ignorance is a ubiquitous state of affairs. It is more obviously odious than the state of affairs it is supposed to improve. Nor will it do to reply that *after* one has been so tampered with he will not disapprove of the state of affairs because he will not know that it is a state of affairs in which his ignorance has been assured and his belief artificially produced. I disapprove *here and now* of the quality of life in *E*, where I will, at that future time, be ignorant of what produced *E* and will, at that future time, *not* disapprove of the quality of life in *E*. It is my disapproval *here and now* that *S* must deal with; and he cannot deal with it by assuring me that in the future state of affairs of which I *here and now* disapprove I will not disapprove. Because "for *A* to call *B happy*, *A* must be contented at the prospect of *B* being in his present state of mind and at the prospect of *A*, himself, should the opportunity arise, enjoying that sort of state of mind."[166] And for me to call a future state of affairs higher in quality of life than the present one in which I find myself, I must approve of the states of minds of the people living in that future time, and I must approve of the prospect of myself being in such a state of mind. This approval our Underground Man will never give. He disapproves here and now of the quality of life in *E*, if we all know in *E* that *E* was not produced spontaneously, but according to plan; and he disapproves here and now of the quality of life in E if we believe (falsely) that E was not produced according to plan, but came about spontaneously.

So my second challenge to the planners of *my* Brave New World is this: Be prepared for the Underground Man who may share your approval of your end in view, *simpliciter*, but not of your end in view as the result of *any* self-conscious social planning.

Perhaps you will think such a paradoxical objection to *plans for the future* is merely a quibble for the sake of quibbling, and remote from the actual opinions and feelings of men and women. But I am not so sure. For it seems to me that some of what is being said by *rebellious youth* is something very like this sort of thing. It is not just our end in view that is being rejected, or our particular means of achieving it, but our end in view *as* the result of plan and blueprint. And so we cannot reply petulantly, "All you do is criticise— you never offer a plan of your own," for it completely misses the point. You cannot please someone who does not like dogs because he does not like pets by offering him a cat or a canary instead.

[CHAPTER TWENTY-SIX]

SUMMARY
IS THERE A POINT
OF NO RETURN?

Sylvan J. Kaplan

WE HAVE SEEN diversity of thought in the preceding chapters. Is it possible to draw conclusions? Have we crossed any Rubicons? Is there a point of no return which constitutes a challenge which we can not ignore?

Regarding the Issues, Factors, and Questions

Paul Henshaw, in Chapter Two, makes a definition for "Quality of Life." He suggests that perhaps this abstraction is a function of three factors: our feelings of safety and sense of security to survive, our reasonable state of good health, and the many things in this world which permit our self-expression as individuals. Dr. Henshaw suggests too, in his opening remarks, that we might measure life's quality in terms of quantifiable elements such as food and acceptable amounts of worldly possessions. But, says this author, *"in the last analysis, it can be said that quality of life equates to flexibility of options, freedom of responsible action, and to level of interpersonal relations."*

The ISSUES, FACTORS and QUESTIONS chapter went far deeper than that extremely challenging definition. It advanced the position that the human race has an ability "to comprehend, understand, and control the forces of nature." The human being is now the "conscience for evolution"—this species has emerged as the decision-maker for the planet. Through the evolution of this being's growth and change, the human animal has deciphered means for organizing its fellow creatures into social groups, developed means for governance, established modalities and techniques for rendering a reward and punishment system for what it considers right and wrong. People have established coin of the realm for barter and trade, and have set limits regarding the meaning of work and play. Through wisdom this species developed, rules and laws have been devised, and requirements set for all to live by. Dr. Henshaw then goes on to add, that having done all this, the human species has somehow or other failed to manifest insight into what it has done; lacking is a self-connecting *servo-mechanism* which tells man where he is failing, failing at least to maintain a steady state form. The consequence is that the *quality of life* is threatened. This *quality of life* may deteriorate by war, by ecological collapse, by economic collapse, or by anarchy wherein the individual rebels against the existing social order.

To forestall this deterioration, Dr. Henshaw searches for options and the probability of constructive action with marked shifts on the part of humanity, (a) from a growth economy to a balanced economy, (b) from imbalance to equilibrium of resource production and use, and (c) to a modification of existing societal structures which could lead to a redistribution of wealth.

Can the human being do what Paul Henshaw asks? Can humankind behave rationally? Dr. Henshaw credits the human animal with having the rational capability to do this, but admits that such a line of thinking may be *Henshavian* visionary and over-idealistic dreaming. The author does assert, however, that the human race is at a stage in its history when new concepts are required and that the scientist, among others, must rise to this requirement. Paul Henshaw never asserts that human beings can do what is required to bring about the basic shifts he describes. But he does ask humanity to do so.

Will human beings try to become more rational and meet their challenges? Dr. Henshaw hopes so, and so do we all. Will humanity comprehend the issues, factors, and questions sufficiently to act with precision and unity? Again, **Dr.** Henshaw hopes so, and so do all of us. But there are grave doubts that our species is able to. Why? Ronald Munson has said it well in Chapter Three. It seems, as Dr. Munson would put it, that we have to tell ourselves what we do not want in order to consider better what is acceptable to us. We distrust planning, for planning behavior might destroy our freedoms. Dr. Munson, upon alerting his reader to the fear evoked by the social planner, goes on to add that planning, which can be an aid to the very realization of the democratic state, often is seen as a threatening mechanism to individual freedoms.

Thus a dichotomy is implied by Dr. Munson, confirming my own doubts regarding the human capacity: planning—using rational means to problem-solve, the human being's great gift, is also his and her gravest threat. Human beings frighten themselves and attack their own reason by the emotion they evoke by planning or thinking ahead. The issues, factors, and questions are somewhat distressing. We are in trouble as a species; we know enough to overcome our problems; but in exercising our capability to so overcome we initiate a fear which attenuates our reason. This in turn reduces our capacity to behave as reasonable animals and suppors the plausibility that we will behave unreasonably. Will we? In the jargon of the psychiatrist and psychologist, humanity is in a double bind. The reasonable actions of the human race evoke in the species unreasonable counter actions.

Regarding the Givens

The section on the givens should alert us to the fact that the clock ticks on to the stroke of midnight. Robert Cook and Sheldon Segal (Chapters Four and Five, respectively) emphasize how humankind might prevail—with time. Mr. Cook has, for more than half a century, asked the world to take heed of the dilemma it faces, and his timely chapter in this book is a testimony to his awareness of the issues of the seventies when he wrote Chapter Four for *The Nation* magazine in the sixties!

Dr. Segal, a foremost authority on contraception, describes the progress of the human race and lauds the efforts being made to slow the human metastasis, but he sees that the growth in numbers will continue and that time will run out for humanity. Segal concludes, "if we do not make voluntary systems work now, our future chances of retaining this right, this human dignity, may be slim indeed."

Have we the organic and inorganic resources to prevail? Hubert Risser (Chapter Six) says, "progress will require new attitudes . . . The quantities demanded will depend on the number of people and the amounts required to satisfy their wants . . ." Donald Kline (Chapter Seven), in speaking to the needs of humanity says, "the green revolution, with or without nuclear centers, may aid the *plow* in the race with the *stork*. But a potential disaster may at any time negate the gains won and more." Earl Cook (Chapter Eight) starts: "Man cannot continue to expand his numbers indefinitely. At some point in the future, his global birth rate and death rate must come into balance . . . ." While this author gives an optimistic picture regarding the availability of energy for the human race for many years to come, he concludes in the end of his erudite chapter, "if the species is to continue with any large fraction of its members living at a culturally comfortable level, a continual rise in economic cost of power may be good . . . for only cost will cause man to budget his resources, to limit his appetite, and perhaps even to share those resources, short of ecological disaster."(!)

The Attitudes: Answers?

This leads me to speak of attitudes. The issues seem clear. This humankind has the ability to control its destiny if it can control its affective or emotional nature. It has a reasonable supply of both organic and inorganic materials to keep it viable for some time to come, even while fighting with desperation to bring birth and death rates into a dynamic equilibrium. But can it and will it? What does humanity do with its diversity of views? And are these views diverse? Do the contributing authors differ so greatly in this book?

Captain Gilven Slonin (Chapter Nine) offers the ocean as a resource and a pleasuring ground, as an educational institution, and a means for self-expression. Both ministers of religion, Reverends Gold (Chapter Ten) and Archibald (Chapter Eleven) independently recognize that change and the contemporary scene ask the best of the human being, to accept relativism rather than absolutism.

Both churchmen stress the concept of giving expression to individuality rather than to that of saving souls. Both ministers stress
human togetherness and human investment in persons rather than in
things. Reverend Archibald calls attention to the responsibility the
church has accepted for guarding the richness of the earth itself.
This would seem a departure from the ever present stereotype of
the church's traditional concentration upon the saving of man's
soul. Adaptability, flexibility, and reason seem to be stressed in both
the chapters on the future of religion under discussion. Variation,
diversity, and relevance in the face of change, seem to be common
bywords for both clergymen.

Dr. Thomas Green (Chapter Twelve) asks for new looks at
work and play and these views are not at all incompatible with
those of the ministers. Dr. Green stresses that new attitudes must
be developed in order that we understand work and play. Do
not *use* time, he asks of us. Time is not something to be used; leisure is not something to *work* at. The truly human experience is
to enjoy—leisure is the ideal. "The problem of leisure is really trying to figure out how one can reach the point where one does not
find it necessary to *use* time . . . Leisure," says Dr. Green, "is a
state of character." There will always be work—work weeks will
not diminish—but this work need not be labor. If we think in terms
of the *character* of leisure, work will become an expression of the
individual, not of the days he or she labors.

The playgrounds for humanity are addressed by Lee Talbot,
Marya Mannes, Barry Bruce-Briggs, and Charles Williams (Chapters
Thirteen through Sixteen). The first author stresses that man's expanding numbers and resource utilization make it imperative that
preserves be insured on the planet. Dr. Talbot is concerned that
park areas be saved more as museums, gene pools, and laboratories in order that humanity will insure its future in terms of food,
diversity of species, and preserves against destructive change. While
Lee Talbot acknowledges the need for the park as a recreation
ground, he asks for it also in behalf of a continuation of knowledge,
attainable only through the existence of the contents of such preserves.

Marya Mannes speaks of her obsession to save the pleasuring
ground, the wildernesses, so that humanity will maintain a *revelation*

area. Ms. Mannes asks that man be forced to respect nature or be restrained from exploiting it. For those who cannot respect nature she suggests alternatives by way of other enjoyments for them. And in every man-made habitat she asks for untampered lands where all ages of humanity might fraternize. Ms. Mannes, then, opts with Revs. Gold and Archibald for human togetherness and the preservation of the spirit, and with the ministers of religion and the ecologist Lee Talbot in their demands for the preservation of nature.

Mr. Bruce-Briggs (Chapter Fifteen) calls our attention to the conflict in thinking one might fall into if one believes that an environmentalist and a conservationist are necessarily brothers of one mind. "The historical conservationist," Bruce-Briggs points out, "made a clean separation between man and nature." *Ecosystems people* are, however, a new breed of conservationists. This type of conservationist may introduce national decisions, trade-offs, and cost-benefit analyses into the issue of what of nature it is appropriate to conserve. Suddenly the question becomes one of how much we are to pay for nature. In one conclusion Bruce-Briggs can foresee man in harmony with nature; in another situation this author sees man in complete domination over nature. This rational and analytic examination of the attitudes of man are extrapolated even further by Charles Williams (Chapter Sixteen). Mr. Williams asks that man's image of nature be divided and scrutinized into four categories:

1. Nature, as a threat to survival which must be overcome.
2. Nature, as a material resource to be exploited.
3. Nature, as a system to which man must adapt.
4. Nature, as a source of enjoyment.

When one so examines nature under these terms, it becomes clear to Mr. Williams that we must change "not only our concepts of nature and our relationship with nature, but also the systems we have structured by which we intervene in natural processes." This requires that we decide more conclusively than we have to date exactly what we think the nature of man to be. "We can decide that we are only animal; . . . fully behavioristic, deterministic creatures, (or we may conclude man is something more than an animal) that man has a spiritual, metaphysical quality . . ." But if we do, this author goes on to say, we will need a new spiritualism, a new economics involving a new medium of exchange, and a new technology. Finally, Mr. Williams implies, if we had those new concepts of man we would need *a new institutional adaptability*. It is clear, says author Williams, that those institutions we now have are not viewing man nor nature quite in the context of the philosophy being called for. Mr. Williams says, "if we could dare to imagine it, I suspect we could create it."

Raymond Nelson (Chapter Seventeen) doubts that it is possible to get man to imagine what Charles Williams hopes for. Mr. Nelson is aware of the problem. He feels that to reach the human race is to appeal to its emotions. But he concedes that to operate in this manner is to cause unpredictable responses in the human subject. He sees man as an *inebriate* who becomes irascible when handed something he does not want or when something is taken from that which he does want. Mr. Nelson seems to conclude, "There just is not enough to go around. It would be difficult to find enough of the necessary items for existence for an appreciable length of time if all of us were sober, impossible if we remain drunk." Raymond Nelson adds, "Only when man *wants* to (give up anything), will he."

Dr. Paul Wilcox, a student of behavior, deals with this irrational portion of the mind in Chapter Eighteen. His is a more optimistic argument in part than those of the preceding authors. He concedes that the human animal has unconscious drives to kill, to take, and to distort reality. But Dr. Wilcox feels that there is an inherent mechanism in the organism of the human being, which he calls the Intrinsic Spontaneous Self-Organizing Tendency (ISSOT), which has the capacity to find better ways to solve life's dilemmas. This hypothesis is particularly reassuring if ultimately it can be proven a fact, for such an idea suggests that it is the nature of the human animal to regroup its response systems for *health*, that is, for more adaptive and appropriate means than self destruction. Moreover, while author Wilcox does not explicitly state it, the implications can be found in the ISSOT concept that it is not necessarily so that the human being must rely on reason for its salvation, a commodity that has generated the afore-mentioned *double bind*. Dr. Wilcox feels that if the ISSOT can be released on the human race to function at its best level, there is nothing in this ISSOT which is incompatible with good social order. Paul Wilcox actually is arguing that there is no real limit to one's inventive consciousness. "The problem," says the author, "is to modulate the forces within us so that they are expressed in controlled power patterns." In short, if the unconscious forces of the psyche can be properly managed (and Paul Wilcox suggests that this is possible) the human race can control its destiny. Since this emminent psychiatrist is arguing that the emotional system falls within what he calls the Intrinsic Spontaneous Self-Organizing Tendency (ISSOT), he is postulating a more hopeful resolution to the human race's problem. His postulate undoubtedly will be controversial and one which many of his colleagues might not be willing to accept. I, for one, feel that the task is enormous but the possibility for group *psychopenetration,* as Dr. Wilcox calls the effective entry into the inner reaches of the psyche, makes hopeful, with the ISSOT concept, a solution to the evolution of humanity to an acceptable quality of life.

George Miller (Chapter Nineteen) indicates the necessity of the human race to deal with its aggressive nature. By implication, author Miller makes author Wilcox's hypothetical ISSOT the more attractive to contemplate. Admiral Miller does not ignore the questions posed by the other authors, but introduces his chapter with a recognition of the population growth and its corresponding consumption of energy and the resources of nature which this growing human race depletes. From this point on in his discussion, Admiral Miller deals with the more relevant issue to him and to those who are concerned with human survival by means of prevention of armed conflict through military and naval strategy. Premising his arguments upon the concept that the human animal will fight if it is free to do so and is able to win, the admiral addresses national security. His entire paper is a commentary on how the human intellect must devote itself to this prevention of conflict through armed preparedness. The admiral calls attention to the historical evidence that "the primary motive for initiating a surprise attack is high confidence on the part of the attacker that he will thereby gain a decisive military advantage." The author feels that there are aggressors in the world and that there is only one course which can securely halt the aggressive tendencies on the part of those aggressors, viz., to "make it physically *impossible* for them to achieve decisive military advantage through attack." The principles enunciated in Chapter Nineteen represent strong convictions that quality of life is deeply associated with what Paul Henshaw has defined as a feeling of safety and the need for a sense of security to survive. Admiral Miller does not entertain the risks of accepting that the unconscious killing drive, acknowledged by psychiatrist Wilcox to exist, will not be placed in action. Nor is he willing to await the resolution of this aggressive tendency without taking strong precautionary measures to halt its activation. The fact that this view prevails in great strength across the globe makes it essential that the readers of this book be alerted to the awareness that drastic solutions to world problems may include deterrent stratagems as well as nonforce employing mechanisms.

Elise Boulding (Chapter Twenty) attempts to give added perspective to the diversity of attitudes already expressed. Dr. Boulding asks that we stop thinking of the world's problems only from our own viewpoint. Let us recognize, she argues, that there are many other ways to describe the macroproblems of this planet than those seen by Western eyes. Moreover, there are many examples of how qualities of life have been measured over the past centuries and we would do well to examine other measures of life's quality rather than to assume our Western measuring rods are best. Dr. Boulding argues that it is likely that we are somewhat dubious of our competence to assess the world situation—we are not certain at all that we have the competence to problem-solve the social issues of our time. With these admonitions and cautions the author concludes, "there is much reason for optimism . . . if we can be faithful to our planetary commitment and examine the whole range of human resources available to modern man, great possibilities are opened up. Although we have more problems than we thought we did, we do not need to remain trapped by our global ethnocentrism, our specialized set of data banks, or our brash rhetoric of pseudocompetence." Dr. Boulding would have human beings bring a broader repetoire of ideas to the matter of dealing on a larger scale with human relationships, an idea not at all unacceptable to every contributor to this compendium.

Robert Matthews (Chapter Twenty-One) makes a plea for humankind to take note of the lessons of history for addressing the future. While planning for short range goals, Mr. Matthews presumes that people deal with the *means* for effecting change; long-range planning deals with the *ends* and involves *guiding* or even *determining* the future. What is even more significantly stated by this author is the fact that "as long-range planning achieves greater efficiency, the independent datum disappears . . . feedback to the planners is reduced and these persons are left with a serious control and monitoring problem . . . Feedback becomes uninformative. This problem increases with the effectiveness of the long-range planning." In light of this phenomenon—i.e., the more ends—oriented, the more effective the long-range planner might become—Mr. Matthews suggests that he who would look at the future must look "backward from desired goals to see how *ends* might be achieved." To achieve what Robert Matthews asks of the long-range planner, author Matthews argues that the planner must understand the development of man. The history of man's efforts reveal his planning endeavors. Coupling that knowledge and good judgment, Mr. Matthews feels that a planner could notice developments and trends which unify long periods of history. These developments can then be tied to planning. From this tie, the planner will perceive "*other* lined possibilities . . . (and will be able to better perceive) a rich but complex, interweaving of social institutions, beliefs, habits, values, activities, and the like."

Harland Westermann (Chapter Twenty-Two) scathingly asks that human beings plan with greater sanity and employ more reasonable governance. He asks them to try a concept of *range management* which, it is noted, works well enough for other animals! Dean Westermann argues that society has hemmed itself in by the *golden* and not so golden ghettos (golden with reference to *new towns;* ghettos, with reference to inner city slums). Author Westermann stresses that society has certainly not utilized its know-how to develop city-states which are more manageable and less destructive to the individual. He suggests that redistribution of population might well reconstitute the quality of life.

Russell Rhyne (Chapter Twenty-Three) gives an example of a methodology for planning ahead. Dr. Rhyne, in particular, describes a system which asserts the great uncertainty of long-range planning and the means he and his collaborators have arrived at for reducing this uncertainty through the development of options and alternative future scenarios which may be viewed as sufficiently plausible to build upon as goals for life styles.

Willis Harman (Chapter Twenty-Four) stresses that humankind is in one of the few transitional periods of its brief history, and needed for the transition is a "metanoia, or a fundamental transformation of mind." While Dr. Harman does not say this metanoia must occur, he feels that its occurrence is essential for a desirable future and an acceptable quality of life. In documenting his ideas, this author shows that the way of thinking present in this *industrial-state* world seems to militate against the opportunity for the individual "to contribute to the society and to be affirmed by it in return." Dr. Harman sees that the industrial-state *fails* to foster equitable distribution of power, wealth, and justice; to provide socially responsible management of the development and application of technology; to provide goals which enlist the loyalties and commitments of the nation's citizens; and to develop and maintain the habitability of the planet. In short, Willis Harman's comments tend to imply that Paul Henshaw's definitions for an acceptable quality of life cannot be achieved without a transformation in the minds of men and women; the present way will not attain such a quality.

To deal with this insufficiency, Harman borrows from Victor Ferkiss who would ask that man be viewed, (a) as a part of a universe which is always in the process of becoming, (b) that all the universe, including man, be defined in relation to the whole, and finally (c) that the "whole is determined not from outside but from within." These concepts would represent a new–age philosophy—a philosophy of process wherein the unlimited possibilities for human development are given primary emphasis.

As described by Willis Harman and Victor Ferkiss, can this be done? Peter Kivy gives the problem added complexity (Chapter Twenty-Five). This philosopher offers that the meaning of *quality of life* has various forms of relative values to various individuals. Dr. Kivy asserts, "do not assume because I agree with your goal of raising the quality of life, I agree with you about *anything* except the most trivial of maxims, namely, that we should make the world *better*. I challenge you," this author goes on to say, "if our ultimate ethical commitments are different, to justify yours to me. Be aware, too, that there *may* in the final analysis be *no* rational means of your bringing me to your view, in my bringing you to mine."

My elaboration to this point is the result of the idea of twenty-five minds speaking. Have they spoken together? The assertions seem to take on some common characteristics and many differences. Most noteworthy among the similarities and differences is the call for *reason* by so many, and its denial as a viable mechanism for the resolution of the human condition by so many others. It is my growing conviction that the human being cannot be a reasoning animal for the greater part of its every day. Man is far more frequently a feeling, emoting, willing, and probably a conditioned animal first and foremost. When he encounters an obstacle which causes him to exercise reason impassively, he can do so, provided he has no inflammatory reactions to the obstacle. And the absence of such inflammation is rare indeed. In my psychological practice of more than a quarter century, I have found little clinical evidence to support the thesis that the human being reasons of its own natural volition in order to problem-solve, and much to support the idea that this animal is driven to do so principally by feeling. I have often seen the human animal pushed from an inner force or inherent drive while far less often have I seen it magnetized into action by an outward goal.

If this be the Wilcox Intrinsic Spontaneous Self-Organizing Tendency (ISSOT) which causes the driving force, or if this is the Adlerian need for status and power, or a Freudian requirement to reduce anxiety, I can not tell. I know only that it appears to me that the nature of the beast, that is, the human being is principally quasi-rational—not irrational, but also not rational. This being feels and it acts. It then feels its actions and acts again—*ad infinitum*. If this augers for or even supports the metanoia, or the new philosophy and enhancement of life's quality, it seems to me, is not really the point. There is before all human beings a prevailing need to be themselves *and* to *accept one another*. Since this acceptance is conditioned by the quasi-nature of man's reasonableness, one can understand the guarded views of each person who has spoken, taking exception to one another in this text.

The human animal has its psychic territory, and it defends that territory with the passions of a jungle animal. Its ideas are some of the nourishment it is defending; but so too are its emotional investments in its individuality. More than anything else, the human being does not wish to relinquish that. These are my experiences and conclusions as a psychologist. I have watched my fellow human beings try to give way to a common cause, to share intimacy, to accept belongingness. I have yet to see that those efforts persist over lengthy periods of time.

It is in this incapacity that I see the point of no return, not in the analysis of the world macroproblem, not in offers for its resolutions, but in the contradictory tendencies in how we interact for a societal resolution. The more fundamental question is not whether we have passed a point of no return, but rather, can humankind adapt its duality of reason and emotion to the hands of the clock.

"La Coeur a ses raisons que la raison ne connait pas." La Rouchefoucauld.[168]

"Humankind is an irrational mixture of the rational and the irrational." Matthew Dumont.[169]

REFERENCES

1. D.H. Meadows, D.L. Meadows, J. Randers, and W.W. Behreus, III, *The Limits to Growth*. Boston, Universe Books, Inc., 1972.
2. G. Hardin, The tragedy of the commons. *Science, 162*:1243-1248, 1968.
3. S.J. Kaplan, et al., *Reach*, U.S. National Park Service Document, April 1971.
4. A. Toffler, *Future Shock*. New York, Random House, Inc., 1970.
5. M. Hubbert, *Resources and Man*. San Francisco, Freeman, Cooper and Co., 1969.
6. K. Ehricke, *Extraterrestrial Imperative*. New York, Doubleday and Co., Inc., in press.
7. Plato, *The Republic of Plato*. Trans. with notes by Allen Bloom. New York: Basic Books, Inc., 1968.
8. F. Bacon, New Atlantis. In *Selected Writings of Francis Bacon*, ed. Hugh G. Dick. New York: Random House, Inc., 1955.
9. T. More, *Utopia*. Trans. and ed. H.V.S. Ogden. New York, Apple-ton-Century-Crofts, Inc., 1949.
10. B.F. Skinner, *Walden Two*. New York, Macmillan Co., 1948.
11. J. Swift, *Gulliver's Travels*. Robert A. Greenberg, ed. New York, W.W. Norton and Co., Inc., 1961.
12. E. Zamiatin, *We*. New York, E.P. Dutton and Co., Inc., 1924, p. 8.
13. Ibid., p. 8.
14. Ibid., p. 13.
15. Ibid., p. 3.
16. A. Huxley, *Brave New World*. New York, Harper and Bros., 1932.
17. H.G. Wells, Men Like Gods. In *Atlantic Edition of the Works of H.G. Wells, 28*. New York, Charles Scribner's Sons, 1927.
18. G. Orwell, *Nineteen Eighty-Four*. New York, Harcourt, Brace, 1949.
19. A. Spilhaus, Ecolibrium. *Science, 175*:714, 1972.
20. W. Lippmann. In Herbert J. Muller, ed., *The Children of Frankenstein*. Bloomington, Indiana University Press, 1970, p. 375.
21. A. Huxley, *Brave New World Revisited*. New York, Harper and Brothers, 1958, p. 26.
22. A. Spilhaus, *op. cit.*, p. 711.

23. J. Dewey, "What Is Freedom?" in *Human Nature and Conduct*. New York, Modern Library, 1930, pp. 303-314.

24. B.F. Skinner, *Beyond Freedom and Dignity*. New York, Alfred A. Knopf, Inc., 1971.

25. Van Rensselaer Potter, *Bioethics*. Englewood Cliffs, Prentice-Hall, Inc., 1971, p. 67.

26. Ibid., p. 75.

27. E. Mayr, Biological man in the year 2000. *Daedalus*, Summer, 1967, p. 832.

28. W. Paddock, and O. Paddock, *Famine 1975*. Boston, Little, Brown and Co., 1967.

29. G. Borgstrom, *The Hungry Planet*. New York, Collier Books, 1965.

30a. L. Brown, *Man, Land, and Food*. Dept. of Agriculture Report, No. 11, Washington, D.C., Nov., 1963.

30b. L. Brown, *The Social Impact of the Green Revolution*. International Conciliation, Carnegie Endowment for International Peace, No. 581, Jan., 1971.

31. N.E. Borlaug, *The Green Revolution, Peace and Humanity*. Population Reference Bureau Bulletin, No. 35, Jan., 1971.

32. A. Weinberg, *Can Technology Replace Social Engineering?* Bulletin of the Atomic Scientists, Vol. 21, No. 5, Dec., 1966.

33. United Nations Publication, *The Future Growth of the World Population*, 1958.

34. B. Watt, and A. Merrill, *The Consumption of Foods*. Dept. of Agriculture, Washington, D.C., 1963, pp. 6-67.

35. President's Advisory Committee Report, *Panel on World Food Supply*. Washington, Government Printing Office, 1968.

36. United Nations, *FAO Trade Yearbook*.

37. G.J. Harrar, "The Green Revolution as an historical phenomenon." In *The Green Revolution*. Symposium on Science and Foreign Affairs, Subcommittee on National Security Policy and Scientific Developments, House Committee on Foreign Affairs, Dec. 5, 1968.

38. United States Agency for International Development, *War on Hunger*. April, 1972, p. 18.

39. U.S. Dept. of Agriculture, Economic Research Dept. as reported in L. Brown, *The Social Impact of the Green Revolution*, No. 581. New York, Carnegie Endowment for International Peace, International Conciliation, Jan., 1972.

40. J. Lelvyeld, Green Revolution Transforming Indian Farming; But it has a long way to go. *New York Times*, May 28, 1969, p. 12.

41. D.C. Anderson, A Squabble Over the Green Revolution. *The Wall Street Journal*, Oct. 6, 1970, p. 20.

42. *The Green Revolution*. Symposium on Science and Foreign Policy. Washington, D.C., Government Printing Office, Dec. 5, 1969.

43. A.T. Mosher, Statement in symposium on the Green Revolution, Session II. *The Political, Social, Cultural, and Economic Impact of the Green Revolution.* Washington, D.C., Government Printing Office, Dec. 5, 1969.

44. *India: Ready or Not, Here They Come.* Population Reference Bureau Bulletin, Vol. 26, No. 5, Nov., 1970.

45. Taken and adapted from J.C. Moyers, and H. Kahns, "World Arid Summary." From *Reviews of Research of Arid Zone Hydrology.* Geneva, UNESCO, 1953; and P. Mays, Geography of Coastal Deserts. Arid Zone Research, Report No. 8, Geneva, UNESCO, 1966.

46. *Nuclear Energy Centers: Industrial and Agro Industrial Complexes.* Oak Ridge, Oak Ridge National Laboratory, ORNL 4290, Nov., 1968.

47. R.L. Meir, *Resource.* Conserving Urbanism in South Asia III: Two Nuclear Power Agro-Industrial Complexes. Berkeley, University of California Press, 1968.

48. *Nuclear-Powered Agro-Industrial Complex.* Bombay, Government of India, Atomic Energy Commission, Bhabha Research Center, June, 1970.

49. A. Mason, An Analysis of Nuclear Agro-Industrial Complexes. In C. Nader and A.B. Zahlan, eds., *Science and Technology in Developing Countries.* Cambridge, University Press, 1969, p. 118. Also Oak Ridge National Laboratory, ORNL 4290, Nov., 1968.

50. R. Hammond, "A Strategy Against Famine." Unpublished paper issued by Oak Ridge National Laboratory, Dec. 26, 1967.

51. R.L. Meier, *The Social Impact of A Nuplex.* Bulletin of the Atomic Scientists, March, 1969.

52. *Consideration in the Implementation of an Agro-Industrial Nuplex Project.* Policy Institute, Syracuse Univ. Research Corp., May, 1969.

53. Teenage genius discovers formula which can save mankind from starvation. *Midnight, 17:*No. 44, May 17, 1971.

54. L. Mumford, *Technico and Civilization.* New York, Harcourt, Brace and World, 1934.

55. L. White, Jr., *Medieval Technology and Social Change.* Oxford, Clarendon Press, 1962.

56. P.C. Putnam, *Energy in the Future.* New York, Van Nostrand Reinhold Co., 1953.

57. M.K. Hubbert, Energy Resources. In *Resources and Man.* San Francisco, W.H. Freeman, 1969.

58. *Pocket Data Book,* U.S. Bureau of the Census. Washington, D.C., 1969.

59. L.P. Gaucher, Energy sources of the future for the United States. *Solar Energy, 9:*119-126, 1965.

60. M.K. Hubbert, Energy Resources for Power Production. Paper pre-

sented in symposium on *Environmental Aspects of Nuclear Power Stations*, Intl. Atomic Energy Agency, UN Headquarters, New York, Aug., 1970, pp. 10-14.

61. L.J. Cohan, and J.H. Fernandes, Heat, value of refuse. *Mechanical Engineering, 19*:47-51, 1897.

62. H.H. Landsberg, and S.H. Schur, *Energy in the United States.* New York, Random House, Inc., 1968.

63. D.E. Glaser, Satellite solar power station. *Solar Energy, 12*:353-361, 1969.

64. F. Daniels, *Direct Use of the Sun's Energy.* New Haven, Yale University Press, 1964.

65. H. Brown, *The Challenge of Man's Future.* New York, Viking Press, Inc., 1965.

66. J. McHale, World energy resources of the future. *Futures, 1*:1-13, 1968.

67. A.M. Weinberg, and R.P. Hammond, Limits to the use of energy. *American Scientist, 58*:412-418, 1970.

68. E. Teller, Energy from oil and from the nucleus. *Journal Petroleum Technology, 17*:505-508, 1965.

69. F.L. Parker, Radioactive wastes from fusion reactors. *Science, 159*:83-84, 1968.

70. G.A. Mills, H.R. Johnson, and H. Perry, Fuels management in an environmental age. *Environmental Science and Technology, 5*:30-38, 1971.

71. H. Brown, Technological Denudation. In W.L. Thomas, Jr., ed., *Man's Role in Changing the Face of the Earth.* Chicago, University of Chicago Press, 1956.

72. A.M. Weinberg, Raw materials unlimited. *Texas Quarterly, 11*:90-102, 1968.

73. R.P. Hammond, Low cost energy: a new dimension. *Science Journal, 5*:34-44, 1969.

74. B.L. Spinrad, The Role of Nuclear Power in Meeting World Energy Needs. Paper presented in symposium on *Environmental Aspects of Nuclear Power Stations*. Intl. Atomic Energy Agency, United Nations Headquarters, New York, Aug., 1970, pp. 10-14.

75. P.E. Cloud, Jr., Realities of mineral distribution. *Texas Quarterly, 11*: 90-122, 1968.

76. J. Kahn, and A.J. Wiener, *The Year 2000.* Toronto, The Macmillan Co., 1969.

77. A.M. Lindbergh, *Gift From the Sea.* New York, Vintage, 1955, p. 100.

78. L.H. Day, and A.T. Day, *Too Many Americans.* Boston, Houghton Mifflin Co., 1964, p. 1.

79. R. Buckminster Fuller, "Wealth and the Ocean," Keynote Address. Symposium, Washington, D.C., Feb., 1970.

80. G. Nelson, Stop Killing the Oceans. *Reader's Digest*, Feb., 1971. (Condensed from *National Wildlife*, Aug.-Sept., 1970.)

81. W. Friedman, *The Future of the Oceans*. New York, George Braziller, Inc., 1971, p. 21.

82. E. Shannon. In Introduction of The Honorable John Warner of the Navy for *Humanities of the Sea* course, University of Virginia, Fairfax, Va., Jan. 19, 1972.

83. H.M. Kallen, *Toward an Introduction to a Philosophy of the Seas*. Charlottesville, University of Virginia Press, 1972.

84. W. Wordsworth, Lines Composed a Few Miles Above Tintern Abbey. In *Bartlett's Familiar Quotations*, 13th centennial ed. Boston, Little, Brown and Co., 1955, p. 404.

85. Address by Dr. George Borgstrom, Nashville, Tennessee, Sept. 9, 1971.

86. *Population Crisis Resolution*, adopted by the General Conference of the United Methodist Church at St. Louis, Missouri, April 25, 1970.

87. Address by Maurice F. Strong, Secretary-General of the United Nations Conference on the Human Environment, Stockholm, Sweden, June, 1972.

88. N. Faramelli, *Technethics*. New York, Friendship Press, 1971, p. 154.

89. *Congressional Record*, Vol. 118, No. 29, Feb., 1972.

90. *Bulletin of the Coalition on National Priorities and Military Policy*, Aug. 2, 1971.

91. H. Cox, Future of Christianity and the church. *The Futurist*, 4:No. 4, Aug., 1970.

92. Ibid.

93. Ibid.

94. A.T. Robinson, *Honest to God*. Philadelphia, Westminster Press, 1963.

95. J. Fletcher, *Situation Ethics, the New Morality*. Philadelphia, Westminster Press, 1966.

96. A.L. Weber, and T. Rice, *Jesus Christ Superstar*. A rock opera, New York, Decca Records, a division of MCA, Inc., 1970.

97. Theodore J. Gordon, Address before the Conference on Religion and the Future, November 20-23, 1969, King of Prussia, Pa. As reported in *The Futurist*, 4:No. 4, Aug., 1970.

98. F. Edgarton, translator and interpreter of, *Bhagavad-Gita*. Cambridge, Harvard University Press, 1946.

99. M. Mannes, *They*. New York, Doubleday and Co., Inc., 1968.

100. V.C. Ferkiss, *Technological Man: The Myth and the Reality*. New York, George Braziller, Inc., 1969.

101. P.H. Wilcox, Psychopenetration: I. Questions, Revised. Unpublished manuscript, Wilcox Clinic, Traverse City, Mich., Jan. 11, 1950.

102. P.H. Wilcox, Psychopenetration. *Diseases of Nervous System*, 12:35-38, 1951.

103. P.H. Wilcox, *Unconscious Superstitions.* Unpublished manuscript, Wilcox Clinic, Traverse City, Mich., Dec. 18, 1957.

104. P.H. Wilcox, *Psychic Organization, Operational Diagram.* Unpublished Diagram, Wilcox Clinic, Traverse City, Mich., Dec. 18, 1957.

105. P.H. Wilcox, Unconscious confabulation drive and religious beliefs. *Human Potential, 1*:36-39, 1967.

106. P.H. Wilcox, *Man's Grand Delusion.* Unpublished manuscript, Wilcox Clinic, Traverse City, Mich., 1961.

107. P.H. Wilcox, *Superstition Test.* Unpublished manuscript, Wilcox Clinic, Traverse City, Mich., 1963.

108. P.H. Wilcox, *Inactivation of Intelligency by Superstitions.* Unpublished manuscript, Wilcox Clinic, Traverse City, Mich., 1961.

109. P.H. Wilcox, *Violence Unlimited—How Can We Harness It?* Unpublished manuscript, Wilcox Clinic, Traverse City, Mich., 1964.

110. P.H. Wilcox, and I. Robb, *Psychopenetration Technique for Counteracting Unconscious Superstitions in Children Supplement I.* Unpublished manuscript, Wilcox Clinic, Traverse City, Mich., 1965.

111. P.H. Wilcox, and I. Robb, *Psychopenetration Technique for Counteracting Unconscious Superstitions in Children Supplement I.* Unpublished manuscript, Wilcox Clinic, Traverse City, Mich., 1970.

112. T. Sorenson, *Kennedy.* New York, Harper and Row Publishers, Inc., 1965.

113. President's Report to Congress, *U.S. Foreign Policy for 1970's, Building for Peace.* Feb. 25, 1971.

114. President's Message to Congress, Oct. 23, 1968, culminating in Merchant Marine Act of 1970, Public Law 91-469.

115. Outward Bound Program, U.S. Office of Economic Opportunities, Washington, D.C.

116. L.A. Orleans, and R.P. Suttneir, The Mao ethic and environmental quality. *Science, 170*:8963, 1970.

117. S. Narayan, *Relevance of Ghandian Economics.* Ahmedabab, India, Navajiva Publishing House, 1970.

118. B. Russett, et al., *World Handbook of Social and Political Indicators.* New Haven, Yale University Press, 1964.

119. I. Adelman, and C.T. Morris, *Society, Politics and Economic Development: A Quantitative Approach.* Baltimore, The Johns Hopkins Press, 1967.

120. A.W. Sametz, Production of Goods and Services. In Sheldon and Moore, eds., *Indicators of Social Change: Concepts and Measurements.* New York, Russell Sage Foundation, 1968, pp. 77-96.

121. S. Kuznets, *Economic Change.* New York, W.W. Norton and Co., Inc., 1963; and (a) *Income and Wealth.* Cambridge, England, Bowes and Bowes, 1951.

122. N. Buster, and W. Scott, Levels of Living and Economic Growth:

A Comparative Study of Six Countries 1950-1965. In *A Report on an Institute Study*. Geneva, UNRISD, 1969.

123. E. Boulding, and T. Mukerjee, an unpublished memo on *National Welfare Profiles*. Institute of Behavioral Science, University of Colorado, 1970.

124. M. Prawdin, *The Mongol Empire: Its Rise and Legacy*. New York, The Free Press, 1940, 1967.

125. P. Aries, *Centuries of Childhood*, Vols. 1 and 2. New York, Alfred A. Knopf, Inc., 1962.

126. C.B. Darlington, *Evolution of Man and Society*. New York, Simon and Schuster, Inc., 1969.

127. M. Bloch, *Feudal Society*. Chicago, University of Chicago Press, 1961.

128. R. Warren, Sociology of knowledge and the problem of the inner cities. *Social Science Quarterly*, Dec., 1971, pp. 469-491.

129. E. Boulding, *Integration and Competence in Family Community: An Exploratory Study*. A paper presented at the Annual Meeting, American Sociological Association, Washington, D.C., Aug. 31-Sept. 3, 1970.

130. E. Boulding, *Conditions of Fertility Decline in Traditional and Industrializing Societies*. Unpublished manuscript, University of Michigan, 1966.

131. For example, the Bayler and Schaefer study, Correlations of Maternal and Child Behaviors with Development of Mental Abilities: Data from the Berkeley Growth Study. (No. 97), *Monographs of the Society for Research in Child Development*, XXIX, 29:p. 6, 1964.

132. E. Boulding, and P.B. Trainer, Quality of Life, U.S.A.: Costs and Benefits of Urbanization and Industrialization, 1900-1970. In *Proceedings of Institute of Environmental Sciences*, Second Annual Session, "Environmental Awareness," San Diego, California, April, 1971.

133. M.E. Montaigne, *The Complete Essays*. Trans. by Donald Frame. Stanford, Calif., Stanford University Press, 1958, III. 13, p. 819.

134. L. Goldmann, *Sciences Humanines et Philosophie*. Paris, Presses Universitaires, de France, 1952.

135. K. Popper, *Open Society and Its Enemies I-II*. London, Routledge, Kegan, Paul, 1945.

136. Aristotle, *Nicomachean Ethics* 1095[a]. Trans. by W.D. Ross, in Richard McKeon, ed., *The Basic Works of Aristotle*. New York, Random House, Inc., 1941.

137. See the interview with Gombrich, *Diacritics, I* 47-51, Dec., 1971. Vol. 1 (1971), pp. 47-55.

138. A. Peccei, *The Chasm Ahead*. New York, Macmillan Co., 1969.
(a) See also several papers by Willis Harman, Educational Policy Research Center, Stanford Research Institute, Menlo Park, California.

139. Douglas Aircraft Co., and Johnson Research Assoc., *Projected World Patterns*, Volumes I and II.
140. *Contingent U.S. Patterns, 1970 to 2000 A.D.*, Rhyne, Johnson, and Hanks, Patterns and Systems, International; *Research Memorandum* 69-3 (San Carlos, Calif., 1969). (Note: originally issued under Patterns and Systems, International's previous name, Johnson Research Association).
141. R. Rhyne, Projection Whole—Body Future Patterns. *The Field Anomaly Relaxation (FAR) Method.* EPRC 6747-10, Stanford Research Institute, Menlo Park, Calif., 1971.
142. K. Lewin, *Field Theory and Social Sciences.* Dorwin Cartwright, ed. New York, Harper and Row Publishers, Inc., 1964.
(a) Various reports of the Educational Policy Research Center, Stanford Research Institute, including: *Alternative Futures and Educational Policy*, Research Memorandum 6747-6, Feb., 1970. *Alternative Futures: Contexts in Which Social Indicators Must Work*, Research Note 6747-11, Feb., 1970.
143. L. Mumford, *The Transformations of Man.* New York, Harper and Brothers, 1956, p. 231.
144. J. Pearce, *The Crack in the Cosmic Egg.* New York, Julian Press, Inc., 1971.
145. T.S. Kuhn, *The Structure of Scientific Revolutions.* Chicago, University of Chicago Press, 1962.
(a) Further discussion of the psychological threat involved in paradigm change may be found in:
M. Polanyi, *Personal Knowledge.* Chicago, University of Chicago Press, 1958.
A. Maslow, *The Psychology of Science.* New York, Harper-Row Publishers, Inc., 1966.
F. Matson, *The Broken Image.* New York, George Braziller, Inc., 1964.
M. Rokeach, *The Open and Closed Mind.* New York, Basic Books, Inc., 1960.
(b) These remarks are based on the more extensive analysis of contemporary revolutionary forces as found in:
N. McEachron, *A Contemporary Framework for Social Change.* EPRC RN-12, June, 1971.
146. L. Mumford, *The Pentagon of Power.* New York, Harcourt, Brace, Jovanovich, 1970.
147. R.N. Bellah, et al., Commentary on civil religion in America. *Daedalus*, Winter 1967, pp. 1-21. Also H.G. Gabriel, *The Course of American Democratic Thought.* New York, Ronald Press Company, 1956.
148. H. Wheeler, Bringing science under law. *The Center Magazine*, 2:56-67, 1969.

149. R.L. Heilbroner, *The Making of Economic Society.* Englewood Cliffs, Prentice Hall, Inc., 1970.

150. See for example, J. Needleman, *The New Religions.* Garden City, Doubleday and Co., Inc., 1970. Also see T. Roszak, *The Making of a Counter-Culture.* Garden City, Doubleday and Co., Inc., 1969.

151. C. Tart, *Altered States of Consciousness.* New York, John Wiley & Sons, Inc., 1969.
    (a) also a discussion of the significance of new experimental tools for the study of physical and physiological correlates of inner states may be found in:
    W. Harman, The New Copernican Revolution. *Journal Humanistic Psych.,* 9:27-134, 1969.

152. This is not an entirely new concern of scientists, as is evidenced by such works as William James' *Varieties of Religious Experience.* New York, Macmillan Company, 1971; *Richard Buck's Cosmic Consciousness.* New York, Citadel Press (NYC), 1970; and Pitirim Sorokin's *The Ways of Power and Love.* Chicago, Henry Regnery Company, 1967.

153. A. Huxley, *The Perennial Philosophy.* New York, Harper Brothers, 1945.

154. *Goals for Americans.* Presented by the president's Goal Commission. Englewood Cliffs, Prentice Hall, Inc., 1960, p. 1, 3, 53, 57.

155. J.R. Platt, *The Step to Man.* New York, John Wiley & Sons, Inc., 1966.

156. To mention a few: Carl Jung, Erich Fromm, Rollo May, Ira Progoff, Carl Rodgers, Roberto Assagioli, J.F.T. Bugental.

157. A. Maslow, *Towards a Psychology of Being.* New York, Van Nostrand, 1962. See also, Elizabeth Drews, *Policy Implications of Hierarchy of Values.* Research Memorandum 6747-8 of the Educational Policy Research Center, Stanford Research Institute, Menlo Park, Calif.

158. P. Sorokin, *The Ways of Power and Love.* Chicago, Henry Regnery Company, 1967.

159. R. Hutchins, The Learning Society. New York, Praeger Publishers, 1968.

160. W. Jaeger, *Paidea: The Ideals of Greek Culture.* Basil Blackwell, Oxford Press, 1945.

161. H. Kahn, and A. Wiener, *The Year 2000: A Framework for Speculation.* New York, Macmillan Company, 1967.
    (a) The majority of future forecasts do not assume a paradigm change, one which appears to have an alarmingly high probability is:
    B. Gross, Friendly Fascism: a model for America. *Social Policy,* Nov.-Dec., 1970, pp. 44-52.

162. G.E. Moore, *Ethics.* London, Oxford University Press, 1958, p. 18.

163. J.S. Mill, *Utilitarianism*. New York, The Library of Liberal Arts Press, 1957, p. 12.
164. C.D. Broad, Five Steps of Ethical Theory. Totowa, Littlefield, Adams & Co., 1965, p. 115.
165. J.S. Mill, *op. cit.* p. 10.
166. J.J.C. Smart, *An Outline of a System of Utilitarian Ethics*. London, Cambridge University Press, 1961, pp. 13-14.
167. Ibid., p. 14.
168. La Rouchefoucauld, *The Maxims of La Rouchefoucauld*. Paris, Libraire Classique Larousse, 1948.
169. M.P. Dumont, Unpublished statement by the author of *The Absurd Healer*. New York, Science House, 1968.

NAME INDEX

SUBJECT INDEX

H

Happiness, conditions of, 10
Harvard Divinity School, 128
"Haves," 14, 85
"Have-nots," 14, 85, 170
Hedonism, 250
History of hostility, 42
    of waste, 42
    maritime, 114
Holistic, 22, 23, 220, 224, 229
Holistic perception of world state, 209
    attitudes, 209
    beliefs, 209
    habits, 209
    interweaving, 209
    social institutions, 209
    values, 209
Homiletical skills, 128
Homo sapiens, 11
Honest to God, 133
House of Man, 48
Human
    ecologist, 226
    ecology, 210
    environment, 210
    issue, 219
    reproduction, 51
    settlement, 215
    wants, 107
Human Activities, 148
    artificial lakes, 148
    changes, 148
    cultivation 148
    transportation, 148
    urbanization, 148
Human Character, 19
    animality, 22, 23
    beastial, 19
    considerate, 19
    compassionate, 19
    distrust, 20
    doubt, 20
    rationality, 22, 23
Human Environment, features of
    arrogance, 14
    complexity, 14
    control, 14
    economics, 14
    foreign policy, 14
    governance, 14
    management, 14
    restraints, 14
    warfare, 14
Human Race, 5
    animal, 6
    attitude, 14
    capability, 6
    experimentation, 8
    future of, 5
    values, 47
Humanness, 127
Human Experiences
    creativity, 243
    extrasensory perception, 243
    hypnosis, 243
    mystical experience, 243
    personality growth, 243
    self-discovery, 243
    religious insight, 243
Humankind, 195
Human Relationships, increasing
    scale of, 201
Human Spirit, 127
Hunger Gap, 67
Hydrocarbons
    fluid, 97
    solid, 97
Hypocrisy, 19

I

ICBM's, 186
Information, 11, 12, 23, 73
    acquisition, 11
    DNA, 11
    genetic, 11, 12
    storage, 11
India, 46, 50
Indirect effects of human activities, 148
    grazing, 148
    lumbering, 148
    pollutants, 148
    use of pesticides, 148
Indonesia, 50
Individuality, 29, 33
    destruction of, 32
    loss of, 30
    restriction on, 32
Industry, consumption, 163